Praise for

The Knowledge Gap

"There's a huge gulf between what teachers believe about how to teach reading and what scientists have found—which is why so many students have continued to struggle despite their teachers' often heroic efforts. The key to success, it turns out, is exactly the thing teachers have been taught to scorn most: knowledge. It's far more important than the supposedly transferable comprehension 'skills' they're trained to focus on. This critical volume, in which Natalie Wexler deftly lays out the case for knowledge, should begin tipping the scales back toward what best serves students of every age and background."

—Doug Lemov, author of *Teach Like a Champion 2.0: 62 Techniques that Put Students on the Path to College*; coauthor of *Reading Reconsidered: A Practical Guide to Rigorous Literacy Instruction*

"Using concrete and compelling examples, Natalie Wexler reveals that most American classrooms follow a misguided approach to teaching reading that is especially damaging to students from low-income families. But she also shows that when educators rely on materials backed by research, they can go a long way toward producing the educated citizens we need. For anyone concerned about educational equity and excellence, *The Knowledge Gap* provides a way to think about both the problem and solutions."

—Karin Chenoweth, author of *Schools that Succeed: How Educators Marshal the Power of Systems for Improvement*; creator of the *ExtraOrdinary Districts* podcast

"Natalie Wexler is a powerfully engaging writer, and *The Knowledge Gap* is a timely and sobering investigation of what is broken in the nation's education system. Artfully weaving together portraits of teachers and students with scientific findings on the learning process, Wexler thoughtfully explores the power of knowledge—and makes a strong case for how and why the nation should harness it to improve outcomes for all students."

—Ulrich Boser, author of *Learn Better: Mastering the Skills for Success in Life, Business, and School, or, How to Become an Expert in Just about Anything*

"As a teacher and the leader of a state school system, I have seen the debilitating impact on a child of an education devoid of historical, cultural, and scientific knowledge—and the human potential unleashed when that knowledge is allowed to develop. Natalie Wexler is not the first to boldly raise this issue, but *The Knowledge Gap* may be the clearest and most cogent telling of a story not told often enough. As an industry, education is often ignorant of its own past and of how the present came to be. Masterfully capturing a complex tale, Wexler shows us that something is wrong, explains how it happened, and reminds us that it doesn't have to be that way."

—John White, Louisiana State Superintendent of Education

"Using real world examples, Natalie Wexler convincingly affirms the primary responsibility of elementary schools to empower the most disadvantaged students with knowledge of the words and worlds that a society assumes is necessary for human flourishing. She makes a compelling case that depriving students of this core knowledge in the name of teaching 'skills and strategies' or embracing the latest educational fads only exacerbates their disadvantage. *The Knowledge Gap* is a must read for educators genuinely interested in achieving better outcomes for kids."

—Ian Rowe, Chief Executive Officer, Public Prep Network

The
KNOWLEDGE
GAP

The Hidden Cause of America's Broken Education System—and How to Fix It

Natalie Wexler

AVERY

an imprint of Penguin Random House LLC

New York

AVERY

An imprint of Penguin Random House LLC
penguinrandomhouse.com

First trade paperback edition 2020

Most Avery books are available at special quantity discounts for bulk purchase for
sales promotions, premiums, fund-raising, and educational needs. Special books
or book excerpts also can be created to fit specific needs. For details,
write SpecialMarkets@penguinrandomhouse.com.

LIBRARY OF CONGRESS CATALOGING-IN-PUBLICATION DATA
Names: Wexler, Natalie, auhtor.
Title: The knowledge gap : the hidden cause of America's broken education
system—and how to fix it / Natalie Wexler.
Description: New York : Avery, 2019. | Includes bibliographical references and index.
Identifiers: LCCN 2018058484| ISBN 9780735213555 (hardback) |
ISBN 9780735213579 (ebook)
Subjects: LCSH: Language arts (Elementary)—United States. | Education,
Elementary—Curricula—United States. | Educational change—United States. |
Children with social disabilities—Education (Elementary)—United States. |
Poor children—Education (Elementary)—United States. | BISAC:
EDUCATION / Educational Policy & Reform / General. |
FAMILY & RELATIONSHIPS / Education. | EDUCATION / Curricula.
Classification: LCC LB1576 .W4848 2019 | DDC 372.6—dc23
LC record available at https://lccn.loc.gov/2018058484

ISBN: 9780735213562 (paperback)

Printed in the United States of America
1 3 5 7 9 10 8 6 4 2

Text on pages 53–54 from The Kids' Site of Canadian Settlement / Inuit © Government
of Canada. Reproduced with the permission of Library and Archives Canada (2018).

In memory of my mother, Henrietta Wexler,

who as a parent, grandparent, aunt, and teacher

delighted in nurturing children's curiosity

about the world

CONTENTS

PART ONE

The Way We Teach Now:
All You Need Is Skills

PART TWO

How We Got Here:
The History Behind the Content-Free Curriculum

PART THREE

How We Can Change:
Creating and Delivering Content-Focused Curriculum

NOTE: While I have generally used people's real names, I have changed students' names to protect their privacy. I have also used pseudonyms for two teachers, "Gaby Arredondo" and "Abby Bauer," and for the schools where they teach.

THE KNOWLEDGE GAP

PART ONE

The Way
We Teach Now

All You Need Is Skills

CHAPTER 1

The Water They've Been Swimming In

O N A SUNNY NOVEMBER morning in 2016, Gaby Arredondo is trying to initiate twenty first-graders into the mysteries of reading.

Today's particular mystery is captions. Ms. Arredondo recently gave a test that asked her students to identify a caption, and—even though she had spent fifteen minutes teaching the concept—many chose the title of the passage instead. Maybe they were confused because the captions she had taught as examples were all at the top of the page, like a title, whereas the caption on the test appeared *under* the picture. Her goal today is to show her students that what makes something a caption isn't where it appears on the page or what it looks like but what it does: it's a label that describes a picture.

"What is a *caption*?" Ms. Arredondo begins brightly to the first group of five students gathered before her at a semicircular table. As she speaks, she writes *caption* on a whiteboard next to her chair. No one answers. Ms. Arredondo writes a second word: *label*.

"It's a label," volunteers one girl.

"What *kind* of a label?" Ms. Arredondo prods.

A boy chimes in: "It's a label that describes things."

"What kinds of things? Does it tell us the author or the title?"

"It tells us the author and the title," the boy repeats dutifully.

"No," Ms. Arredondo says. "It tells us about the *picture*."

She shows them a photo from a book called *Mothers*, which has the words *daughters*, *mother*, and *son* superimposed in the appropriate spots. "So, what is a caption?"

"Words?" a girl named Nevaeh ventures.

The Washington, D.C., charter school where Ms. Arredondo teaches, Star Academy, has a good reputation and has benefited from both philanthropic and government funding. Located in a high-poverty African American community, the school has a staff that includes a full-time occupational therapist, two speech-and-language therapists, and two school psychologists—critical resources, considering that 17 percent of the students need special education services and all families are poor enough to qualify for free or reduced school meals.

And Ms. Arredondo, in her second year of teaching, is a highly valued faculty member. She graduated from Princeton University, the first in her working-class family to go to college—an achievement that was possible, she feels, only because she managed to get into a selective public high school. She became a teacher in hopes of helping other kids transform their circumstances through education.

During the months I've been observing Ms. Arredondo's class, I've seen that she's skilled at classroom management techniques, firm when she needs to be but also warm enough to establish bonds with her students. She's hardworking, dedicated, and patient with these often rambunctious kids.

But after Nevaeh suggests that *caption* just means *words*, Ms. Arredondo's patience seems to be fraying. She starts pointing to the text on the page opposite the photo, asking, "Is *this* a caption? . . . Is *this* a caption? . . . Is *this* a caption?" The kids repeatedly answer, "No."

"It's not just any *word*," she says. "The words describe *what*? I'm a little upset right now, because I've said it."

"A label?" one of the kids offers again.

"What does the caption *tell* us?" Ms. Arredondo says more softly.

"About the pictures," a girl says at last.

"The *pictures*," Ms. Arredondo echoes.

The kids in the next group keep trying to pull the discussion away from the abstract nature of a caption and toward the concrete. One of the nonfiction books that Ms. Arredondo is holding up is about sharks, with vivid photos that pique the children's curiosity—especially one showing a shark that has half-swallowed what the caption at the side simply identifies as a "sea animal."

"Oooh!" the students cry out. "What's he eating? Oh my God! Is it a fish?"

"If you were going to write a caption on this page, what would you write?" Ms. Arredondo asks. The students don't answer.

Next, she shows them a picture of a planet that the students decide is the moon. They point to the title, the subheading—anything but the caption. Finally, she points to the caption herself and reads it aloud: "Now you can take a trip to Mars without ever leaving Earth."

"Right there!" she exclaims. "That's our caption. This *isn't* the moon! It's Mars! So we have to read the caption so we know what the picture is about!"

The kids aren't buying it. "It's the moon," one student declares.

"I thought Mars was *red*," a girl says skeptically. The photo is in black and white.

Ms. Arredondo doesn't respond. It's time to move on to the culminating activity she has planned: students will write their *own* captions. She shows them a funny photo of a group of goats perched on the branches of a tree, like absurd four-legged birds. I find myself wondering why goats would be up in a tree, but the students don't ask, and Ms. Arredondo doesn't volunteer an explanation. The point of this lesson isn't to learn about tree-climbing goats—or sharks or planets. It's to learn about captions.

Ms. Arredondo goes off to check on the students who are working independently elsewhere in the classroom while the kids at the table write a variety of captions on Post-it notes, some legible and some not. One boy colors with markers. Another student writes *riog*. Two boys who are sitting next to each other both write *goll*. When I ask one of them what his caption says, he tells me it says *giggles*.

But when Ms. Arredondo comes back, the boy says the word is supposed to be *goat*. When another student objects that he hasn't spelled the word right, Ms. Arredondo answers calmly, "That's okay. That's how he spells *goat*." Her response reflects prevailing views on the best way to handle spelling errors in the early-elementary grades: she doesn't want to get sidetracked into a spelling lesson, and she doesn't want her students to lose confidence about writing down their ideas.

Ms. Arredondo sticks one of the Post-its with the word *goll* under the photograph of the tree-climbing goats, saying, "That tells us more about this picture."

WHILE MS. ARREDONDO'S APPROACH might seem peculiar, it's the way she and virtually all other elementary teachers in the United States have been trained. If she's having a hard time engaging her students, it's not because she's a bad teacher. In many ways, she does an excellent job.

The theory that has shaped the American approach to elementary education goes like this: Reading—a term used to encompass not just matching letters to sounds but also comprehension—is a set of skills that can be taught completely disconnected from content. It doesn't really matter *what* students are reading. Teach them to identify captions in a simple text—or find the main idea, or make inferences, or any one of a number of other skills—and eventually they'll be able to grasp the meaning of any text put in front of them.

And, the argument goes, through the third grade, children need to spend their time "learning to read" before they can progress to "reading to learn." Social studies and science can wait; history is too abstract for their young minds and *should* wait. In the early years, the focus must be on the reading skills that will equip students to acquire knowledge about the world—later.

It's not surprising, then, that reading has long dominated the elementary curriculum. As far back as 1977, early-elementary teachers were spending more than twice as much time on reading as on science and social studies combined. Even in the upper-elementary grades, when students have presumably already acquired basic reading skills, teachers spent twice as much time on reading as on either science or social studies alone.

That focus only intensified after Congress passed the No Child Left Behind legislation in 2001. NCLB required annual reading and math tests in grades three through eight and once in high school—and threatened significant consequences if schools failed to get 100 percent of their students to proficiency by 2014, a goal that was widely recognized as impossible to meet. As a result, the amount of time schools spent on reading and math grew, while time spent on other subjects—particularly social studies—correspondingly decreased.

By 2012, early-elementary teachers reported spending an average of only sixteen minutes a day on social studies and nineteen on science—figures that, because they are self-reported, may well be overestimates. The elementary "literacy block," largely focused on reading, now consumes anywhere from ninety minutes to three hours each day. And teachers have shaped their reading instruction in ways they believe will prepare their students to do well on standardized tests, which aim to assess comprehension skills. The rest of the day is devoted mostly to math.

The schedule may allot half an hour or forty-five minutes to social studies or science a few times a week, usually at the end of the day, when students are tired: a simple science experiment or a read-aloud about George Washington or Abraham Lincoln before Presidents' Day. (Struggling readers are unlikely to get even that, because they're often pulled from social studies and science to get extra help.) In any event—and especially when the same teacher is responsible for teaching all subjects, as is usually the case—often that time ends up also being spent on reading or math.

The state-mandated tests each spring represent only a small fraction of the time consumed by related activities. Up to a quarter of the school year is spent preparing for tests, taking practice tests, and taking "benchmark" tests designed to predict performance at the end of the year.

Opposition to testing began brewing soon after the passage of No Child Left Behind, but it reached a fever pitch after most states adopted the Common Core starting in 2010. The new tests created to align with those academic standards were longer and significantly tougher. Across the country, especially in affluent suburban districts, many parents joined an "opt-out" movement. Even then-Secretary of Education Arne Duncan, whom many blamed for the orgy of testing, acknowledged that the situation had gotten out of hand. In 2015, Congress replaced NCLB with the Every Student Succeeds Act, which attaches fewer consequences to low scores. States are still required to give annual reading and math exams and report the results, however, and there is little evidence they're reducing either the amount of testing or the importance placed on it.

To be sure, there are compelling arguments in favor of testing. No Child Left Behind required that schools report scores for various subgroups— including minority and low-income students—which brought to light serious and long-hidden inequities. And reading tests are seen as the only way to hold schools accountable for giving children the skills they'll need to learn history, science, and other subjects later on. Students who aren't reading on grade level by third grade are four times less likely to graduate from high school. If the child is poor, the odds are even worse.

Still, an overwhelming majority of teachers deplore the emphasis on testing and the consequent narrowing of the curriculum. Many would prefer to spend more time on social studies and science, and they know their students would as well. As Ms. Arredondo observed, "They love learning about things they don't know anything about."

But she feels that the time spent on reading is necessary. Teaching the concept of captions, she told me, was an important first step in helping her students understand the difference between fiction, which generally doesn't have captions, and nonfiction. Captions also provide information in a more manageable format than lengthy paragraphs, which struggling readers like her students may find overwhelming.

Like Ms. Arredondo, most teachers don't question the idea of trying to teach reading comprehension as a set of discrete skills. It's simply the water they've been swimming in, so universal and taken for granted they don't even notice it. It's not about test scores; it's just the way to teach kids to read. And if kids don't seem to be getting it, the solution is to double down, through middle school, if necessary.

But there's a conundrum at the heart of these efforts: despite many hours of practice and an enormous expenditure of resources, American students' reading abilities have shown little improvement over more than twenty years, with about two-thirds of students consistently scoring below the "proficient" level. Most fourth-graders aren't actually ready to progress from "learning to read" to "reading to learn." Writing scores are even worse: about three-quarters of eighth- and twelfth-graders score below proficient. International tests have shown that our literacy levels are falling, for both children and adults.

"We seem to be declining as other systems improve," a federal official who oversees the administration of international tests has observed. "There is a lot to be concerned about."

THE STAGNATION IN reading scores isn't the only distressing feature of the education landscape: many American students lack basic knowledge about the world. On the most recent nationwide test of eighth-graders, only 18 percent scored proficient or above in US history, as did only 23 percent in civics and 27 percent in geography—the lowest scores on national tests in any core subject areas.

Even students at well-regarded colleges can display a weak grasp of history and government. In 2014, students chosen at random on the campus of Texas Tech University were unable to answer questions such as who won the Civil War ("The South?"), who the vice president is ("I have no idea"), and what country we gained our independence from ("Um . . . France?"). One survey of American adults found that only a quarter of respondents could name all three branches of government, and more than a third couldn't name any of the rights guaranteed under the First Amendment. Another found that more than half of Americans didn't know that the first ten amendments to the Constitution are called the Bill of Rights, a third didn't know who delivered the Gettysburg Address, and about 40 percent didn't know how many senators are elected from each state.

In the wake of Donald Trump's election in 2016, some commentators began connecting the dismal state of American politics to deficiencies in our education system. Researchers who evaluated students' ability to distinguish between reliable and unreliable online sources of information were "shocked" by the poor results, terming the situation a "threat to democracy." The solution, some said, was to beef up civics education, and high schools around the country have been attempting to do just that.

To be sure, education is essential if democracy is going to function. But a high school civics course may be too little and too late. An understanding of civics fundamentally depends on an understanding of history. It's hard to grasp how the system operates if you have no idea where it came from and no context in which to place it. And students who have had little or no exposure to history in elementary and middle school struggle to absorb and retain historical concepts when they encounter them for the first time in high school. Adults who lack basic knowledge about American government likely took a civics course in high school; the information just didn't stick.

And yet, it is believed, devoting more time to history would rob students of their best chance of learning to read—clearly a vital prerequisite for becoming a well-informed and responsible citizen. Besides, educators argue, young children are neither interested in history nor able to grasp its abstractions.

ACROSS TOWN from Ms. Arredondo's classroom, in a neighborhood where the median home price nears a million dollars, Abby Bauer is leading the two-hour literacy block for her twenty-four first-graders at Reeves Elementary. The demographics at Reeves are vastly different from those at Star Academy; the proportion of economically disadvantaged kids is under 19 percent. But the pedagogical approach is much the same.

"What skill are we working on this week?" Ms. Bauer asks her students, who sit cross-legged on the rug. A few raise their hands. "Every hand should be up," she coaxes.

More hands come into view, and one student provides the answer: summarizing. Ms. Bauer asks what that means. "The main idea," offers one boy. "Finding the main idea" is actually considered a separate skill, and perhaps that's why Ms. Bauer rephrases the boy's answer, leading the class in a choral recitation of the definition listed on a chart behind her and using hand gestures designed to help them remember it: "Summarizing is *key ideas.*"

And why, she asks, is it important to know how to summarize? "So you're a better reader," supplies one girl. "It helps you remember the story better," says another. A boy chimes in: "It helps us better *understand* the story."

Ms. Bauer opens *Peanut Butter & Cupcake!*, a whimsical picture book about an anthropomorphic slice of white bread—slathered generously with peanut butter—who roams his neighborhood, searching for someone to play with. He gets turned down by Hamburger, Cupcake, Egg, and a few others, until he ultimately finds the perfect playmate: Jelly.

After introducing the first couple of characters who reject Peanut Butter's invitation to play, Ms. Bauer asks the kids how they think Peanut Butter is feeling. This provides an opportunity for one girl to bring in last week's skill, making inferences.

"I *infer* he's feeling sad," she says.

When she finishes the book, Ms. Bauer prompts her students to answer the five summarizing questions displayed behind her: who are the main characters, what do they want, what is the problem, how do they solve it, and what happens at the end. The children's answers are all spot-on.

Then they break into small groups for more skills practice, rotating through different "centers" around the room. At one, they get little blank books that prompt them to summarize *Peanut Butter & Cupcake!*, through words and drawings: "Somebody . . . First . . . Next . . . Then . . . Finally . . ." At another, they fill out phonics worksheets. Some retrieve plastic baggies of books at their individual reading levels. "Remember to practice summarizing!" Ms. Bauer reminds them.

There's shockingly little data on what goes on inside most American classrooms. Very few states even track what textbooks and other materials are being used. Still, it's safe to say that if you walk into the vast majority of early-elementary classrooms in the United States, you will find much the same routine: a ten-to-fifteen-minute "mini-lesson" on a comprehension skill, followed by "center time," during which most students are supposed to work independently on the skill or on an aspect of phonics.

Teachers who use one of the reading textbooks called basal readers—as do 50 percent or more, including Ms. Arredondo—teach whatever skill the book identifies for that week and generally use the reading selections to introduce it. Teachers who don't use a basal reader, like Ms. Bauer, ground their instruction in commercially available children's books, choosing texts for their suitability in demonstrating whatever skill they're focusing on.

At Ms. Bauer's school, the teachers have collectively created a sequence of skills to be taught. But elsewhere, teachers are often left to their own devices. They may try to assess their students' particular needs, or look to the reading assessments administered every few weeks to see what skill will be tested next. Either way, they're often saddled with figuring out *what* to teach as well as *how* to teach it—a burden that can be oppressive, especially for teachers with little experience.

During the mini-lesson, the teacher will often not only explain a comprehension skill but model it with a "think aloud." If she's demonstrating finding the main idea, for example, she might read aloud from a book and pause every once in a while, saying things like, "Hmm, I'm noticing that this particular phrase keeps coming up, so I'm thinking that's the main idea of this text." She might not read at all. One popular method of introducing "comparing and contrasting" is to bring two students to the front of the classroom and have others note the differences in what they're wearing.

How teachers allocate time in the literacy block varies, but the lion's share is generally reserved for center time. (Ms. Bauer devotes just under an hour to that, versus forty minutes for writing and thirty minutes for phonics.) Each group of students spends roughly twenty minutes at each center—until their turn for guided reading with the teacher, which is considered the heart of reading instruction.

Teachers periodically measure students' reading levels, often using an A-to-Z scale keyed to the number of mistakes made while reading passages classified at different levels of difficulty. Each student in a guided reading group has tested at a similar level and has a copy of the same "just right" book: hard enough to be challenging but not so hard as to be frustrating. The teacher moves from one student to the next, listening to them read and helping them practice their phonics and comprehension skills. The idea is that dividing students into small groups enables teachers to give all children individualized attention. But, since most elementary classrooms have only one teacher, the system assumes that the children who are not engaged in guided reading—the majority of the class at any given time—will be able to work independently and quietly for extended periods. Whether or not that holds true depends a lot on the personalities of the students and the degree to which they have absorbed classroom management routines—which depends partly on the skill of the individual teacher and partly on the culture of the school as a whole. In fact, the benefits students derive from the small-group format of guided reading are generally canceled out by the lack of learning in the rest of the classroom.

Ms. Bauer, with several years of experience under her belt, has perfected the balance of warmth and authority educators strive for. Drawings tacked on the wall above her desk are evidence of the fact that some of her students believe, with the fervor typical of six-year-olds, that she's the best teacher in the world. Unlike Ms. Arredondo, she's working in a school with few significant discipline problems, and for the most part, her students apply themselves diligently at their centers. But as in any first-grade classroom, some wander off task—like the two girls engrossed in a quiet conversation that has nothing to do with the book that is spread out before them, untouched.

The two groups who take turns meeting with Ms. Bauer for guided reading today are working on books that, like *Peanut Butter & Cupcake!*, contain simple stories with vivid illustrations. She avoids having them read nonfiction until the end of the year, at which point they engage in group research projects on different animals. In this respect, Ms. Bauer's classroom is unusual. While a steady diet of fiction used to be de rigueur in early-elementary classrooms, that changed with the Common Core. In an effort to build elementary students' knowledge of the world, the standards specify that 50 percent of their reading should be nonfiction.

Still, the fundamental approach hasn't changed: nonfiction texts are seen as another delivery mechanism for skills. Hence Ms. Arredondo's focus on captions, one of the "text features"—along with tables of contents, glossaries, subtitles, and text boxes—that are common to nonfiction. The assumption is that if students read about random subjects—birds one day, clouds the next, bridges the day after that—and practice identifying certain structures and features, they'll become expert readers of nonfiction.

First-graders at Reeves do get some science instruction, but any exposure to social studies comes only through the portion of the literacy block devoted to writing—for example, bits of information about figures in black history during Black History Month. Like Ms. Arredondo, Ms. Bauer wishes she could spend more time on social studies, because she's found the kids "like that kind of stuff." But, despite the fact that Reeves has some of the highest test scores in the city, she feels "a lot of pressure" to focus on reading, writing, and math.

The topic for today's writing-cum-social-studies lesson is "American symbols," and the symbol of the day is the flag. The lesson includes not only the American flag but also the Kenyan flag—a relic of a brief period when the school's curriculum embraced the study of Kenya. That focus has fallen by the wayside, but the flag remains.

The point is to teach students about symbols—and have them write a couple of sentences giving examples of the symbols in each flag—rather than anything specific about America or Kenya. "What's a symbol?" Ms. Bauer begins. It's a concept students have discussed before.

"It's something that tells you something but not with words, with a picture," says one girl. Prompted by Ms. Bauer, other kids offer examples: a clover for good luck, a peace sign, emojis. After checking to make sure they understand the word *represent*, Ms. Bauer leads the class in reciting a definition, with accompanying hand gestures: "Symbols represent ideas." She holds up a small American flag and asks the children if they see any symbols. They come up with a couple: fifty stars for the fifty states (although an initial estimate puts the number of stars at thirty) and thirteen stripes for the thirteen colonies. Ms. Bauer then reads *A Flag for All*, the story of three kids who go around their neighborhood asking adults what the flag means to them. One says "freedom," another "independence," and a third says "hope."

Ms. Bauer asks the children to recount the different answers. They get *freedom* and *hope*, but forget the word *independence*, so she supplies it. "When we were first becoming a country," she explains, "we had to get our independence, to make our own country." Then she sums up the main idea of the story: "The flag means different things to different people."

Now it's time to turn to the Kenyan flag. Ms. Bauer doesn't have a book about that, but she reads from a piece of paper: black stands for the Kenyan people, red for the blood that was shed during their fight for independence, and so on. The design in the center, she explains, is a shield that symbolizes the Maasai tribe and their protection of the ideas the flag represents.

Afterward, none of the children can remember that the shield represents the Maasai—perhaps because this is the first time they've ever heard the word, and they have no information about the Maasai. Nor have they learned anything about Kenyan history, or even anything about the events that led to the creation of the American flag: the colonial era, the American Revolution, or what Ms. Bauer means when she says, "We had to get our independence."

One boy asks who made the flags, which could provide an opportunity to talk about some of the history behind them. But that's not part of the lesson plan. Getting ready to move on, Ms. Bauer says she doesn't know who made the Kenyan flag, but the first American flag was made by Betsy Ross—also not a topic the class has covered.

SOCIAL STUDIES, a discipline invented in the early twentieth century, is supposed to be a combination of civics, economics, geography, and history. Traditionally, though, lessons in the early grades have centered on children's lives, their families, and their communities. As a result, many educators simply haven't seen social studies as particularly important.

Often, the subject gets subsumed into the literacy block, where—as in Ms. Bauer's classroom—it's treated primarily as a medium for developing skills. If there's any content presented about the larger world, it's vague and ahistorical: principles of good citizenship, customs in various countries, stories of social activism from different time periods. History makes a cameo appearance within broad themes like "Families Now and Long Ago, Near and Far." Historical figures are presented out of order and context: George Washington in kindergarten, Eleanor Roosevelt in first grade, Abraham Lincoln in second, Thomas Jefferson in third.

When I've asked educators why this is the case, I've found their answers rest on two basic assumptions. One is that young children are primarily interested in subjects that relate to their own lives. The other is that history is "developmentally inappropriate" for the early grades. Relying on the work of the influential twentieth-century psychologist Jean Piaget, education schools have long trained teachers to believe that historical concepts are simply too abstract for children below third or fourth grade to grasp. That also goes for any aspects of science that can't be communicated through simple, hands-on experiments.

These assumptions are widespread—and not just in public schools. At an independent school in a major East Coast city, where tuition exceeds $35,000 a year, I encountered the same attitude. Test prep isn't an issue, since private schools aren't required to give standardized tests. The administration sets broad themes for each grade level—"patterns" in kindergarten, "relationships" in first grade, "structures" in second, "change" in third—to allow for interdisciplinary projects.

These projects can be ambitious and engaging. First-graders spend weeks learning about urban planning, visiting a nearby city to help with their research and ultimately creating a sprawling model town. At the same time, the vagueness of the themes gives individual teachers a lot of leeway on the specifics. As in the vast majority of public schools, what students learn at one grade level may or may not lay the groundwork for the next. And one thing students *won't* learn about, before third grade, is history. That subject, I was told by school administrators, isn't developmentally appropriate.

AMERICANS IN GENERAL are deeply concerned about the state of education. One national survey found that 72 percent of respondents identified education as a top priority for the president and Congress, just one point lower than the percentage who chose terrorism.

Still, most public school parents are highly satisfied with the schools their own children attend. If the school is devoting time to reading and math and neglecting other subjects, they may feel they can compensate by reading books at home and taking their kids on enriching excursions.

"What I care about is being able to walk to school," said one mother of a third-grader who lives in a gentrifying D.C. neighborhood where schools are under pressure to raise test scores.

At the same time, many parents are concerned about the amount of time spent on testing and test prep, as the opt-out movement has made clear. At least a few also feel there's an inordinate focus on comprehension skills. Joe Weedon, a middle-class D.C. parent whose children attend schools where scores are relatively low, says the only homework his fifth-grade son has brought home for two years has been on reading skills. At his daughter's middle school, all students were given more reading instruction than the schedule called for, whether they needed it or not.

Parents at schools where test scores are high can experience similar frustrations. A woman I'll call Catherine Burch—a former parent at Reeves Elementary, where Ms. Bauer teaches—says her children would bring home packets centered on skills like "finding the main idea," to be practiced on texts that imparted random bits of information. The reading passage for Martin Luther King Day, for example, focused on King's sister's memories of how the two siblings used to play together. Burch did her best to fill the gaps, but her son was so bored in class that he often got into trouble for not paying attention.

Burch tried to convince the principal at Reeves to adopt a curriculum called Core Knowledge, which introduced historical and scientific topics before third grade. But she was told it would be developmentally inappropriate. One fifth-grade teacher, Burch says, even got into trouble for spending too much time on the Constitution and the Bill of Rights and not enough time on reading. Burch's children have now moved on to their neighborhood middle and high schools, where, she says, many students "struggle to contextualize" in history classes, even those for advanced students. She suspects their lack of exposure to coherent historical content at the elementary level is to blame.

Other parents who have tried to bring more substance into the school day have also encountered resistance. One parent I know tried to get her children's private school to adopt the Core Knowledge curriculum. But, despite the fact that her position on the school's board gave her a direct line of communication to administrators, she was unable to make any headway.

For the most part, however, parent activism has focused on getting rid of or reducing testing rather than on what the curriculum should look like if testing disappeared. Many parents I've spoken with are unaware of the prevailing view that teaching history and non-hands-on science is developmentally inappropriate—as I was when my own children were in elementary school. Like me, they've seen their kids become fascinated by those topics through books they read at home and family outings to museums and places like Williamsburg. It's never occurred to them that the topics are inappropriate, and they may not even notice that the school curriculum fails to include them.

And sometimes it's not the school but the parents who resist change. In the 1990s, before the era of high-stakes testing, my own neighborhood elementary school was teaching the standard "me and my community" social studies curriculum. A parent suggested adopting the information-packed Core Knowledge approach instead. The teachers were interested, but other parents dismissed the idea, saying kids didn't need or want that. One, suspecting a conservative political agenda, called the prospect "scary."

At Reeves, Burch says, parents didn't actively oppose a more substantive curriculum, but few openly shared her frustration. Most either bought into the school's argument that more history and science would be developmentally inappropriate or simply weren't aware there was anything to complain about. At the school where her children were previously enrolled, which drew from a lower-income community, parents were more on her wavelength. And, generally speaking, African Americans, Latinos, and Native Americans—groups that are disproportionately represented at the lower end of the socioeconomic scale—are far less likely to have positive feelings about their neighborhood schools than whites or Asian Americans.

In 2017, one such parent protested at a D.C. public hearing that the principal at her children's school had cut everything but reading and math. Choking back tears, Andrea Tucker argued that children like hers were being passed from grade to grade without learning what they needed to succeed. Why wasn't the D.C. Public Schools system requiring all teachers to spend forty-five minutes a day on either social studies or science, as its official curriculum prescribed? Many parents at the school, which serves a largely low-income African American community, were "in an uproar." But top education officials had ignored their complaints—despite the fact that the school system's chancellor's children were enrolled at the school.

"This primarily affects minority children," Tucker said at the hearing. "Are our children any different from other children? Are they not deserving of the same education?"

ALL AMERICAN ELEMENTARY SCHOOLS, regardless of student demographics, prioritize reading and math over other subjects. And—as at Reeves—the universal approach to reading is to focus on comprehension skills. Even teachers in one of the most affluent counties in the nation often frame lesson objectives in terms that are generic and vague: "Examine text features of informational texts . . . Ask and answer questions about text . . . Students use structure and key words from texts to identify the text type." In one fourth-grade classroom, the two questions of the day were "How can readers describe concepts using a cause-and-effect relationship?" and "How does understanding the text structure of a nonfiction text help in understanding it?"

But, like Tucker, many observers believe that schools serving low-income students take a narrower, more skills-focused approach. There's evidence to back them up: a 2007 study found that about half of all children in schools serving students who were middle class or above were subjected to repetitive instruction in basic skills, but in schools serving low-income children, the proportion soared to 91 percent. One thing is clear: when schools are under pressure to raise test scores, administrators and teachers maximize the time spent on reading and math.

And yet, those efforts have been no more effective with students at the lowest end of the score spectrum than with the student population as a whole. Test scores for low-income and minority students are consistently far below those of their more affluent, largely white peers—a phenomenon usually referred to as the *achievement gap*, although some prefer *opportunity gap*. The most accurate and neutral term would be *test-score gap*. Whatever it's called, it's significant. On nationwide reading tests, about 80 percent of low-income fourth- and eighth-graders score below the proficient level, compared to about 50 percent of their higher-income peers. On writing tests for eighth-graders, the percentages below proficient are about 90 and 65, respectively, with 32 percent of low-income students scoring below the basic level. When it comes to US history, only 5 percent of students whose parents lack a high school diploma score at or above proficient. For children of college graduates, the figure is 27 percent.

Despite billions of dollars and massive efforts on the part of thousands of highly dedicated and intelligent people over the past twenty-five years, the size of the gap between the wealthiest and the poorest students hasn't changed. Our mediocre standing on international literacy rankings is largely a reflection of how low our lowest scores are.

The gap goes beyond test scores. While high school students in Catherine Burch's affluent D.C. neighborhood may "struggle to contextualize" in their Advanced Placement history classes, their counterparts in high-poverty schools on the other side of the city face even greater obstacles. Teachers at those schools have told me they've had students at all levels of ability, including the highest, but some of their stories were deeply disturbing.

Their high school students often lack a sense of chronology, they said. Students may confuse the Civil War and the civil rights movement. They may think Frederick Douglass and Martin Luther King Jr. were contemporaries. In a world history class studying the segregation faced by black soldiers returning to the United States after World War I, some students were under the impression that slavery still existed in 1918. In a course on the United States after the Civil War, the teacher couldn't assume that students knew what happened *before* that war, even though they had already taken a class that covered it. "You have to start with: there was a War of Independence," she said, "and this is who we won our independence from."

Others told me their students don't understand the difference between a country and a continent, or between a city and a state. One kid in an SAT prep class—one of the better students, according to his teacher, who cited the fact that "he could place the United States on a world map"—was surprised by the term *South America* when he saw it on a map, apparently for the first time: How could it be called *America* if it wasn't *in* America?

Another high school teacher said she's even had a few students who don't know the name of the country they live in. "They think Washington, D.C., is their country," she said.

Urban school systems have been faced with the impossible task of turning ninth-graders who arrive with gaps like these into "college- and career-ready" graduates in four years—and threatened with consequences under federal law if graduation rates dip below 67 percent. For a while, the threats appeared to be working: in 2016, the national graduation rate reached an all-time high of more than 84 percent. But within months, it became clear that some urban school systems have turned to subterfuges. These include having students pass courses by taking far less rigorous online versions and changing attendance records. In Washington, D.C.—a city that many reformers have pointed to as a model, and where the graduation rate rose twenty points in six years—an investigation revealed that a full third of the 2017 graduates hadn't met requirements.

These problems don't end at high school. Studies suggest that students with low test scores are less likely to pursue higher education, obtain and keep jobs, provide for their families, exercise their civic rights and responsibilities, and lead fulfilling lives. Education is supposed to enable everyone to do those things. It represents our best hope for breaking the cycle of multigenerational poverty. Really, it's our *only* hope.

And it's not working. Socioeconomic inequality in the United States is on the rise. Many students proudly enroll in college—the surest route to success—only to discover they're so ill-prepared they need to take remedial reading and math. The vast majority of lower-income students never manage to get that coveted degree.

WE'D ALL LIKE to give children more social studies and science, even if only of the ahistorical and hands-on varieties, but it seems impossible to reconcile that desire with the need to teach them to read—and boost their test scores. We'd all like to produce high school graduates with a solid grasp of history—and the familiarity with civics that could develop from it—but it's not clear how to lay the foundation for that learning if, as educators believe, elementary students aren't equipped to absorb historical concepts. And we'd all like education to act as a true engine of social mobility, but no one has been able to figure out how to make that happen.

But what if it's possible to provide all students, including the neediest, with the kind of education that enables them to enjoy learning, understand

and retain what they read, become responsible citizens—and even increase test scores? What if it turns out that the best way to boost reading comprehension is not to focus on comprehension skills at all but to teach kids, as early as possible, the history and science we've been putting off until it's too late?

A handful of schools across the country have been experimenting with that approach—which, in the context of American education, represents a radical break with the status quo—with sometimes astonishing results.

CHAPTER 2

A Problem Hiding
in Plain Sight

ADRIENNE WILLIAMS IS about to read a book on mummies to her first-graders. But first, she asks them what they already know about the subject—or what they think they know.

"They chase you!" says one.

"They don't exist."

"They walk like they're crazy!"

"They're wrapped in paper."

"They kidnap you."

"You all have a lot of ideas about mummies," Ms. Williams says calmly. After taking some questions ("Are they real?" "What do they do?"), she puts the book into a projector so the kids can follow along.

"Eww!" they chorus delightedly, as the screen reveals a photograph of a mummy with its hands pressed to its cheeks, its teeth fixed in a ghoulish smile.

The children are rapt as Ms. Williams reads about how mummies are dead bodies that have been preserved, sometimes for thousands of years, and the things that scientists can tell about them: that one ancient man used hair gel, that another's last meal was vegetable soup.

Along the way she casually points out the "text features" that, in a typical elementary classroom, would be the focus of instruction: the table of contents ("So if I want to make a mummy, what page do I go to? . . . Yes, page 18, 'How to Make a Mummy'"), and a text box that contains a definition of bacteria ("You already know about bacteria after studying germs," she reminds them). There's a picture of a sarcophagus. "We're going to learn that word," she says.

Ms. Williams teaches at the Brightwood campus of the Center City charter network in D.C., which—like Star Academy, the charter school where Ms. Arredondo teaches—serves a low-income population on a first-come, first-served basis. While some of the network's six campuses predominantly enroll children of native-born African American parents, Brightwood has a high proportion of kids from non-English-speaking families, mostly Hispanic or Ethiopian. Many students are still learning English themselves.

When Ms. Williams started at Center City, the network used the standard skills-focused approach, and she could see that her students weren't particularly engaged. "It was just an isolated set of skills," she says. "There was no bigger context."

At the same time, her colleagues were struggling to adapt to the new demands of the Common Core. In 2013, Center City got a new leader, Russ Williams, who heard teacher after teacher ask for more guidance. Williams (no relation to Adrienne Williams) decided that they were asking for a curriculum.

Many believe the Common Core *is* a curriculum, but it's just a list of skills students are supposed to acquire at each grade level—for example, connecting claims about a text's meaning to evidence in the text. The literacy standards don't specify particular texts to be read, aside from a few at the high school level, and they don't provide teachers with guidance on how to ensure students gain the skills. The word *curriculum* has a range of meanings, from vague to quite detailed, and, like the Common Core, literacy curricula generally put skills in the foreground—but they usually do more than just list them. They might provide a lesson plan for how to teach each skill, along with reading passages to use to demonstrate it.

Russ Williams's concept was radically different. Instead of focusing on comprehension skills, as teachers were used to doing, he thought they should focus on content—and the skills would follow. When the new curriculum was unveiled, many Center City teachers were in shock. Not only was it vastly different from what they were used to, some felt it infringed on their freedom to teach whatever and however they wanted.

Teachers in kindergarten through second grade were confronted with Core Knowledge Language Arts—more or less the same curriculum that parents like Catherine Burch had tried unsuccessfully to get their children's schools to adopt. The schedule preserved some time for guided and independent reading, but the bulk of instruction would involve the teacher reading aloud to the entire class from information-packed texts and leading discussions focused on their content.

Even more surprising were the subjects the curriculum would cover—twelve each year, with students spending a couple of weeks on each. Kindergarteners would learn about the five senses, Native Americans, and life in colonial times. First-graders would study the human body, astronomy, and the American Revolution. Second-graders would study the ancient Greeks, insects, and the War of 1812.

Other content-focused curricula have since become available that are less drastically different from what teachers are used to. But at the time, Core Knowledge was pretty much the only option. Teachers felt it would be too demanding and abstract; even Adrienne Williams was apprehensive. But soon, she and her colleagues realized how much their students were able to absorb and how much they enjoyed learning actual *stuff*. Within a few years, test scores began to rise significantly as well.

For today's lesson, Ms. Williams was supposed to read aloud a story about ancient Mesopotamia. But over the two years she's been teaching Core Knowledge, she's become comfortable enough to put her own spin on the material, making it more interactive and engaging. Her first-graders arrived to find two curving lines of blue construction paper taped to the classroom floor—the Tigris and Euphrates Rivers. After "paddling" down the rivers, they came to sit in front of a wall-size poster of Babylon and, with their eyes closed, listened as Ms. Williams described what they were "seeing": the city's stone palaces and hanging gardens. Along the way, she introduced words like *fertile* and concepts like the importance of water to the development of civilization.

The words *soil* and *crops* and the notion that plants and animals need water were already familiar to these students from kindergarten, when they studied plants and farms. Next year, when they study ancient Asian and Greek civilizations, the kids will meet them again. Even during their first year using the curriculum, teachers were struck by how many connections children were able to make between the concepts they were learning and how proud they were of their new knowledge. The school began adding books that went deeper into certain topics— like mummies.

After ten minutes of reading aloud, Ms. Williams asks for questions. Hands fly up.

"Can they tell how the mummy died?"

"Was the soup still in the mummy's stomach?"

One boy asks thoughtfully: "So how do the mummies run?"

"Okay, let's think about this," Ms. Williams says. "Do the mummies move? No. So do they run?"

The boy shakes his head.

"What you see on TV," Ms. Williams continues, "about people who come back to life—that's made up. That's fiction. We're studying about what really happened."

Then it's time to stop, much to the disappointment of the kids who still have their hands in the air, their questions unanswered.

Ms. Williams smiles and makes a promise: "You're going to find out."

THERE ARE, to be sure, many differences between Ms. Williams's first-grade classroom on the one hand and Ms. Arredondo's and Ms. Bauer's on the other. No two classrooms, and no two teachers, are identical. But all three are considered effective and well-trained teachers.

Ms. Williams is naturally gifted, but the fact that her lesson was so much meatier and more engaging than the others' is largely a matter of luck: she happened to be using a curriculum that emphasized building knowledge. It turns out that children not only can handle learning about things that are remote from their own experience, they often love it.

The widespread belief among educators that history and non-hands-on science are inappropriate for young children isn't just at odds with what many parents sense intuitively. It's also not supported by the evidence. A few educational approaches, like the century-old Montessori movement, have long been introducing children to these subjects with great success. At one elementary school I visited in Nevada, where teachers had been using Core Knowledge for several years, students were engaging in thoughtful discussions of a kind their teachers had never seen before, drawing on knowledge they'd acquired in earlier grades.

A fourth-grade teacher named Kitty Gillette told me her students even requested permission to research and write reports at home that went into further depth on topics they'd learned about in previous years, like ancient Mesopotamia and Greek myths, and present them to their classmates.

Although educators rely on the work of psychologist Jean Piaget in arguing that history and similar "abstractions" are developmentally inappropriate, it's far from clear that he intended to bar teachers from introducing children to these topics. In any event, his theories have been largely superseded by more recent research. Children's development doesn't proceed in a series of fixed, discrete stages, but depends on the child, the task, and even the day. And young children are more capable of abstract thinking than Piaget believed. As another iconic twentieth-century educational psychologist, Jerome Bruner, argued, "any subject can be taught effectively in some intellectually honest form to any child at any stage of development."

The fact is, history is a series of stories. And kids love stories. The same is true for science topics that don't lend themselves to hands-on activities. It's ironic that truly abstract concepts like captions and symbols are considered appropriate for six-year-olds, but informational tales about history, science, and the arts are not.

But it's not just that students can understand and *enjoy* the stuff we've been withholding from them. It turns out that it's also *good* for them; if young children are introduced to history and science in concrete and understandable ways, chances are they'll be far better equipped to reengage with them with more nuance later on. At the same time, teaching disconnected comprehension skills boosts neither comprehension nor reading scores. It's just empty calories. In effect, kids are clamoring for broccoli and spinach while adults insist on a steady diet of donuts.

IN 1987, two researchers in Wisconsin, Donna Recht and Lauren Leslie, constructed a miniature baseball field and installed it in an empty classroom in a junior high school. They peopled it with four-inch wooden baseball players arranged to simulate the beginning of a game. Then they brought in sixty-four seventh- and eighth-grade students who had been tested both for their general reading ability and their knowledge of baseball.

The goal was to determine to what extent a child's ability to understand a text depended on her prior knowledge of the topic. Recht and Leslie chose baseball because they figured lots of kids in junior high school who weren't great readers nevertheless knew a fair amount about the subject. Each student was asked to read a text describing half an inning of a fictional baseball game and move the wooden figures around the board to reenact the action described.

Churniak swings and hits a slow bouncing ball toward the shortstop, the passage began. *Haley comes in, fields it, and throws to first, but too late. Churniak is on first with a single, Johnson stayed on third. The next batter is Whitcomb, the Cougars' left-fielder.*

It turned out that prior knowledge of baseball made a huge difference in students' ability to understand the text—more of a difference than their supposed reading level. The kids who knew little about baseball, including the "good" readers, all did poorly. And among those who knew a lot about baseball, the "good" readers and the "bad" readers all did well. In fact, the bad readers who knew a lot about baseball outperformed the good readers who didn't.

In another study, researchers read preschoolers from mixed socioeconomic backgrounds a book about birds, a subject they had determined the higher-income kids already knew more about. When they tested comprehension, the wealthier children did significantly better. But then they read a story about a subject neither group knew anything about: made-up animals called *wugs*. When prior knowledge was equalized, comprehension was essentially the same. In other words, the gap in comprehension wasn't a gap in skills. It was a gap in knowledge.

The implication is clear: abstract "reading ability" is largely a mirage constructed by reading tests. A student's ability to comprehend a text will vary depending on his familiarity with the subject; no degree of "skill" will help if he lacks the knowledge to understand it. While instruction in the early grades has focused on "learning to read" rather than "reading to learn," educators have overlooked the fact that part of "learning to read" is acquiring knowledge.

Research has established that one aspect of reading does need to be taught and practiced as a set of skills, much like math: decoding, the part that involves matching sounds to letters. The problem is that the other aspect of reading—comprehension—is also being taught that way. While there's plenty of evidence that *some* instruction in *some* comprehension strategies can be helpful for *some* children, there's no reason to believe it can turn struggling readers into accomplished ones.

That's particularly true when it comes to nonfiction, which generally assumes more specialized background knowledge. To acquire the knowledge and vocabulary that will help them understand nonfiction, children need to do more than read a single book on a topic before skipping to another one while practicing how to identify text features or determine text structure. They need to stick with a topic for days or weeks, encountering the same vocabulary and concepts repeatedly so they will stick. Knowing how to identify a caption in a book about sea mammals is unlikely to help them understand a book about the solar system or the Civil War.

It's not so much that particular bits of information are vital in and of themselves—although some certainly are. It's more that people need to have enough facts in their heads to have what one commentator has called "a knowledge party"—a bunch of accumulated associations that will enable them to absorb, retain, and analyze new information. Education certainly shouldn't *end* with facts. But if it doesn't begin there, many students will never acquire the knowledge and analytical abilities they need to thrive both in school and in life.

Children of wealthier and more educated parents may not be gaining much knowledge of the world at school, but they typically acquire more of it *outside* school than their disadvantaged peers. And that often boosts their performance on tests. In countries that have a national curriculum, standardized tests can focus on the content required at each grade level. But in the United States, where schools are all teaching different things, test designers try to assess general reading ability by presenting students with passages on a range of subjects and asking multiple-choice questions. Many of these questions mirror the American approach to literacy instruction: What's the main idea? What's the author's purpose? What inferences can you make?

Test designers also attempt to compensate for the inevitable variation in students' background knowledge. Students living in the West might happen to know more about the Rocky Mountains, while those in the South might know more about hurricanes. So the tests might include one passage on each topic. But kids with less overall knowledge and vocabulary are always at a disadvantage. While the tests purport to measure skills, it's impossible for students to demonstrate those skills if they haven't understood the text in the first place.

The bottom line is that the test-score gap is, at its heart, a knowledge gap. The theory behind skills-focused instruction is that if students read enough, diligently practicing their skills, they will gradually advance from one level to the next, and their test scores will improve. But there's little evidence to support that theory. Often, difficulties begin to emerge in fourth grade, when children are confronted with nonfiction and texts that use more sophisticated vocabulary. At high-poverty schools, it's not unusual to find eleventh- and twelfth-graders reading at fifth- or sixth-grade levels. In many cases, they continue to be assigned texts at their individual levels rather than at the levels expected for their grade—the levels that most of their more affluent peers have reached.

"Leveled texts," one reading expert has observed, "lead to leveled lives."

IT'S NOT THAT educators are unaware of the importance of knowledge and vocabulary. One frequently taught reading comprehension strategy is "activating prior knowledge." If the story is about a trip on an airplane, for example, the teacher might ask kids if they've ever taken one. And if a text assumes knowledge many students don't have, he might quickly supply it. But that kind of on-the-spot injection of information is unlikely to stick without reinforcement.

Teachers are more likely to be aware of the need to build students' vocabulary rather than their knowledge; those gaps are more obvious, and more research has been done on the importance of vocabulary to comprehension. To be sure, it's important to focus on words that are used frequently in academic writing but are unlikely to be acquired through spoken language—words like *merchant*, *fortunate*, and *benevolent*. But it's impossible to equip children with all the vocabulary they need by teaching it to them directly. During the first several years of schooling, children add eight words a day to their vocabularies, on average; the only way to expand vocabulary that quickly is to expand knowledge. A single word is often just the tip of an iceberg of concepts and meanings, inseparable from the knowledge in which it is embedded. If you understand the word *oar*, for example, you're probably also familiar with the concepts of rowboats and paddling.

But building knowledge is trickier than teaching vocabulary. Teachers sometimes overestimate what children already know: I watched a class of second-graders struggle for half an hour through a text about slavery before their teacher realized they didn't understand the word *slavery*. Kindergarteners in one low-income community had an average score in the fifth percentile on a vocabulary test, which reflected their inability to identify pictures showing the meanings of words like *penguin, sewing,* or *parachute,* and educators have told me of students who don't know simple words like *behind* and *bead.*

At the same time, teachers can *underestimate* students' capabilities. In addition to limiting children to books at their supposed levels, they may explain an entire text in simple language before reading it aloud, thus depriving students of the chance to wrest meaning from complex language themselves.

"I believe what everybody believes," said one fifth-grade teacher at a high-poverty school in Nevada. "I don't mean to believe it, but it gets into you—this idea that certain learners are less capable of engaging with certain content. And I think that we've been making a lot of mistakes based in compassion for our students . . . We make this great effort to smooth the road for them."

After experimenting with a text she was sure would be too challenging for her students—and being surprised by how well they did—she came to realize that she'd been doing them a disservice. "Unless they learn to navigate the bumps," she said, "we're not teaching them to be thinkers or readers."

THERE ARE MULTIPLE REASONS that children from less-educated families arrive at school with less knowledge and vocabulary than their peers from highly educated ones—many having to do with wealth and income, which are highly correlated with levels of education. Children who live in poverty are far more likely to suffer the consequences of traumatic events that can interfere with their ability to learn. Wealthier parents are better able to invest in their children to compensate for the inadequate education they may be getting at school. That can mean anything from buying more books to paying for tutoring or extracurricular activities. For some, it can mean opting out of public education altogether and enrolling their children in private school.

In recent years, the difference between what lower- and higher-income parents spend on their children has increased dramatically. In

1972, the wealthiest Americans were spending five times as much per child as the lowest-income families. By 2007, parents at all economic levels were spending more on their children, but the highest-income families were spending *nine* times as much. As "human capital"—skills and education—has become increasingly vital to success, families in the top 20 percent have invested more heavily in ensuring their children can compete. It's become increasingly difficult for the bottom 80 percent to keep up.

Poor and working-class families are also more likely to practice "natural growth" parenting, according to sociologist Annette Lareau, allowing their children lots of unstructured time and tending to give directions rather than soliciting opinions. Middle-class and affluent families, on the other hand, generally practice "concerted cultivation": driving their kids to soccer practice and band recitals, engaging in family debates at dinnertime, and encouraging independent thinking. Each parenting style has its advantages, but the concerted cultivation kids are better equipped to do well in school.

And then there's language. Children whose parents read to them frequently become familiar with the sophisticated vocabulary and syntax that appears in written rather than spoken language. Talking is important too. One much-publicized study published in the 1990s estimated that by the time they reach age four, high-income children have had thirty million more words addressed to them by parents or caregivers than have low-income children. Recent research has called that estimate into question and focused instead on the number of "conversational turns," or back-and-forth verbal interactions, between parents and children; the more conversational turns, the better a child's language skills. And—although the ubiquity of cell phones and other screens has interfered with conversational turns across the spectrum—on average, higher-income families engage in more of them.

Less-educated parents are also less likely to use complex vocabulary in conversation, and teachers may not be exposing students to it either. One study found that children living in high-poverty neighborhoods get "a double dose of disadvantage" as compared to their higher-income peers: the language they hear is less sophisticated both at home and at school. While these children "may have unique linguistic strengths that serve them well in their immediate settings," they were less likely to have the language skills that would enable them to do well academically.

Whatever the causes, it's clear that children with certain risk factors begin school with skills that may be almost a year behind those of their peers. And the gap only widens over time. The more knowledge a child starts with, the more likely she is to acquire yet more knowledge. She'll read more and understand and retain information better, because knowledge, like Velcro, sticks best to other related knowledge.

This phenomenon of snowballing knowledge accumulation by kids who start out with more—while those who start out with less acquire less—has been dubbed "the Matthew effect." That's a reference to a line in the Gospel according to Matthew—"For unto every one that hath shall be given, and he shall have abundance: but from him that hath not shall be taken away even that which he hath": or, "the rich get richer and the poor get poorer." And the longer the Matthew effect is allowed to continue, the harder it is to reverse. That's why it's crucial to envelop students from less-educated families in a knowledge-building environment as early as possible.

Rather than being restricted to the simple material they can read on their own, young children need to *listen* to their teachers read more complex books aloud and engage in discussions about what they've heard—and, depending on their age, write about it. Even many middle-schoolers can take in far more sophisticated content, and the vocabulary that goes with it, through listening and speaking than through their own reading. If teachers organize their read-alouds by topic instead of the skill-of-the-week, children have the chance to hear the same concepts and vocabulary repeatedly. Once they have a general familiarity with a topic, they can read more difficult text about it independently.

IT'S HARD TO understand why a problem as fundamental and pervasive as the lack of content in elementary school—and, in some cases, middle school as well—has gone unnoticed for so long. But high school teachers who see crippling gaps in knowledge may not be able to discern the root of the problem. In 2012, when I volunteered to tutor some students at a high-poverty public high school in Washington, D.C., I quickly discovered they didn't know the meanings of words like *admirable* and *percent* and had only a vague understanding of government institutions like the Supreme Court—even though it was just a mile and a half away. I came to care about these kids, and I worried about how they would make it to and through college—as they all told me they planned to do—when it was clear they had trouble making sense of the texts they were supposed to read in tenth grade.

"What," I asked a teacher, "have they been *doing* for the last ten years?"

"We ask ourselves that question all the time," he responded wearily.

At the same time, elementary teachers may not foresee the knowledge gaps that become painfully apparent down the line. Because elementary-level texts don't assume much knowledge, it may *look* like the skills-focused approach is working. Even those who have studied the K-through-12 system as a whole have failed to notice that what seems like success in elementary school is only planting the seeds of failure in high school. In the years I spent involved in the education reform movement, attending panel discussions and touring model classrooms, I never heard anyone mention skills-focused elementary instruction as a problem—or even that it *was* skills-focused.

In fact, education reformers have generally seen elementary school as the bright spot in the system. High school is where things seem to fall apart: stubbornly low test scores, disengaged and disruptive students, discouraged—and, it is assumed, ineffective—teachers. The graduation rate scandal in D.C. has led to state and federal investigations, the removal of various administrators, and anguished soul-searching on the part of reformers across the country. As of this writing, however, no one has blamed an approach to reading instruction that leaves so many students unprepared to tackle high-school-level work. What the vast majority of educators, reformers, commentators, and government officials still haven't realized is that elementary school is where the real problem has been hiding, in plain sight.

FOR MANY YEARS, it was assumed that schools couldn't do much to correct the inequities children brought with them into the classroom. That belief has its roots in a famous report that sociologist James Coleman and his colleagues released in 1966, *Equality of Educational Opportunity*—better known as the Coleman Report—which tabulated data on more than three thousand schools and six hundred thousand students across the country. Far more important than what schools could accomplish, according to the report, were "the inequalities imposed on children by their home, neighborhood, and peer environment."

The education reform movement rejected that conclusion. Beginning in the 1990s, reformers—especially those who founded and funded so-called "no excuses" charter schools—have refused to accept, as they say, that a child's zip code must determine her destiny. But while many of these schools have had success at the elementary and middle school levels, it's been far more difficult to get their students through high school and college. Reformers have found this puzzling and discouraging—after all, the ultimate goal is not to produce fourth-graders, or even eighth-graders, who can ace a standardized test.

Critics of education reform have used this lack of progress to hark back to the Coleman Report: it's poverty, stupid. But they haven't taken into account the findings of cognitive science on the crucial role of knowledge, nor have they addressed the failure of elementary schools to build that knowledge. And they haven't explained how it's possible to break the cycle of poverty without improving education for children from less-educated families. Some reformers are turning away from schools and toward parents in an effort to change how they interact with their preschoolers. But changing the behavior of parents, especially those who are stressed and tired, is difficult. And if parents themselves have received an inadequate education, there's a limit to how much they can impart to their children. Ultimately, schools need to shoulder the responsibility of providing all children with the kind of knowledge more advantaged kids take for granted—if they can.

Our education system is facing unprecedented challenges. Throughout much of the twentieth century, high schools, with their academic and vocational tracks, were designed to sort students into career paths that were thought to be largely predetermined by socioeconomic circumstances and native intelligence. That view of education began to change in the 1960s, thanks to the War on Poverty and the civil rights movement. But even then it was possible to get a decent-paying, secure job with only a high school diploma. That's no longer the case. The economy is demanding workers with sophisticated skills and knowledge, and schools are expected to ensure that even kids from the least-educated families have a fighting chance to acquire a college degree.

At the same time, a substantial minority of American students are low-income. And because of socioeconomic segregation, many schools have student bodies drawn almost entirely from poor families. Students who are still learning English, 10 percent of the school-age population, are its fastest-growing segment. Given the education system's dismal record with students who face the greatest disadvantages, the challenge of equipping them to meet the demands of modern society may seem impossible to meet.

But it's not; consider the example of France. Until 1989, all French schools were required to adhere to a detailed, content-focused national curriculum, and many children began their education as early as age two at free preschools. These schools, in combination with elementary schools that also followed a specific curriculum, served as powerful equalizers. If a child from a low-income family started preschool at age two, by age ten, she would catch up to a highly advantaged child who started at age four—and would be ahead of a middle-class child who started at age three. That's the opposite of what happens in the United States, where gaps between socioeconomic groups widen the longer students stay in school.

Then the government passed a law requiring all elementary schools to abandon the national curriculum and adopt a more American approach. Curricula were now determined locally, with each school embracing a different focus and foregrounding skills like "critical thinking" and "learning how to learn." The law left French preschools and secondary schools untouched, and French standards for teacher preparation remained at their previous high level. Thus, it inadvertently set up a large-scale experiment on the effect of a specific, content-based curriculum at the elementary level. The results were dramatic. Between 1987 and 2007, achievement levels decreased sharply. The drop was greatest among the neediest students.

As we'll see, the United States can't simply adopt the approach the French abandoned and ordain a detailed national elementary curriculum. American law prohibits that, and in any event, our country is probably too diverse for such an effort to work. But there is much we *can* do.

States or school districts—or charter networks, or even individual schools—can adopt curricula that provide students with a body of knowledge about the world, beginning at the earliest grade levels. They will also need to convince many teachers and administrators that focusing on knowledge is worthwhile; schools of education in this country and some others have long trained teachers to reject that idea as unnecessary and stultifying. Why engage in the boring exercise of memorizing facts when you can just look them up? Students will only end up regurgitating facts they don't understand. Far better to focus on skills like critical thinking—and reading comprehension.

But skipping the step of building knowledge doesn't work. The ability to think critically—like the ability to understand what you read—can't be taught directly and in the abstract. It's inextricably linked to how much knowledge you have about the situation at hand. And critical thinking is vital not only for a student's individual success but also for the future of democracy. Remember the researchers who were shocked to discover, in the wake of the 2016 election, how difficult it was for students to distinguish real from fake news? Their proposed solution was to teach them to evaluate the reliability of websites by searching for other information online, among other things. But simply ensuring students have more knowledge of the world would be even more effective.

If we want to prevent the rote memorization many teachers fear will result from a focus on knowledge, our best strategy is to explicitly teach students to write about what they're learning. To the extent that writing is included in the curriculum at all, it's taught, like reading comprehension, in isolation from content—as though it too consisted of a set of free-floating skills. And in contrast to their systematic approach to teaching comprehension, educators assume that students will figure out how to write largely on their own. For the most part, they haven't. But if teachers break down the writing process into manageable chunks, it can serve as a powerful means of pushing students to review facts they've been taught, make connections, and think about them analytically.

It's hard to find elementary schools that are combining these approaches—teaching a coherent body of information and having students transform it into knowledge by writing about it. The authors of the Common Core's literacy standards hoped to bring about both of these changes, but most schools haven't interpreted the standards to require either. Still, the prospects for a fundamental shift may be better now than ever before. A growing number of elementary schools, including Center City, are recognizing that it's not only okay to focus on building children's knowledge, it's vital to their chances of success. And that kids love it.

To SEE what different theories about literacy instruction look like in practice, I decided to follow two classrooms for a year: one using the standard skills-focused approach, and another that had switched to building knowledge.

My plan was to continue following Adrienne Williams with her next first-grade class, but by the fall of 2016, she had moved into an administrative position for the Center City network. So I decided to follow a teacher Ms. Williams helped train, Liz Masi, who would be teaching a second-grade class made up of the same kids I'd seen Ms. Williams teach. The other class was Ms. Arredondo's first grade at Star Academy.

Inevitably, there were differences. The students at Star Academy were all African American, while those at Center City's Brightwood campus were mostly the children of immigrants. First-graders, of course, are generally less mature than second-graders—and fourteen out of Ms.

Arredondo's twenty first-graders were boys, who are less likely to be ready for school than girls. The children at Star may have been living in deeper poverty; the proportion whose families received government benefits or were otherwise considered "at risk" was more than 70 percent, compared to only 40 percent at Center City. But it's hard to know for sure: some low-income immigrant families at Center City may have been undocumented and therefore unlikely to apply for government benefits.

But both schools served low-income populations, and both teachers were considered effective. The schools had similar behavior management systems in place that helped maintain order: students earned positive points for good behavior and negative for bad, with concomitant rewards and consequences.

Both teachers also worked at charter schools rather than at traditional public schools, but that was more or less accidental. The vast majority of schools in both sectors adhere to the skills-focused approach. I decided not to follow a teacher in the D.C. Public Schools system primarily because the district was in the process of adopting its own content-focused curriculum but wasn't as far along as Center City. At the time, DCPS was betwixt and between the two approaches, and I wanted a clear contrast.

And that's what I got.

AUGUST 2016

Good morning, Scholars, reads the message on the whiteboard. *Today is Tuesday, August 23, 2016. Have a great second day of school. Love, Ms. Arredondo.*

Seated on the rug are seventeen first-graders wearing khaki pants or skirts and bright goldenrod polo shirts emblazoned with the Star Academy motto: *Start early, shine bright.*

"Want to know a secret?" Ms. Arredondo asks, bringing out a beach ball with a map of the world on it. "We're going to learn all about maps and globes this year."

After using the ball in a getting-to-know-you exercise, Ms. Arredondo says it's time to "read our message."

"What's a message?" one girl asks.

Ms. Arredondo explains that it's something written down that you need to read—in this case, it's what she's written on the board. After she reads the message aloud, she has the children read it chorally. They have the most trouble with her name.

She has them sound it out: "AH-RE-*DON*-DO."

"That sounds Spanish," a boy observes.

It *is* Spanish, Ms. Arredondo tells him, going on to explain that her father is from Puerto Rico—which, she tells them, is an island, and an island is a place that has water all around it. She draws a rudimentary diagram.

"What's your *real* name?" another boy wants to know. "In English?"

Ms. Arredondo can't help but laugh, even though she's trying to maintain a strict demeanor. Yesterday, the first day of school, things got a little out of control.

Next it's time for students to vote for their favorite subject. Writing gets eight votes, science four, and math three. Reading gets zero. Social studies isn't even one of the choices. (Two students, apparently, didn't vote.) Theoretically, the children will get two thirty-five-minute periods of either social studies or science every week—three weeks on one subject, then three on the other. In practice, that will rarely happen. Although

Ms. Arredondo has promised they'll learn all about maps and globes, she'll spend far more time helping them hear the individual sounds in words and then connect those sounds to letters. It's clear they need work on that: only four students are reading at or above grade level.

Ms. Arredondo will also spend many hours teaching reading comprehension skills, relying largely on the basal reader Star Academy has adopted, *Journeys*.

ON THE OTHER SIDE OF TOWN, at Center City's Brightwood campus, twenty-eight second-graders are gathered in front of Ms. Masi for their first day of school, also in uniform: navy or plaid pants or skirts, navy or white shirts, and an optional bright red ribbon around the collar.

Just as in Ms. Arredondo's class, today's activities include getting-to-know-you exercises. Ms. Masi tells the students they will *interview* each other—a word that one student guesses means "something about the past." They come up with possible questions: Where do you live? What is your favorite color? What is your favorite food?

"I asked Subira what is her favorite land animal," a boy named Negasi reports to the class. "She said it was an African giraffe."

Ms. Masi is new to teaching second grade but not to these students. She was their kindergarten teacher two years ago—her first year at Center City. Her previous experience had been at a preschool in a relatively affluent New Jersey suburb where she herself was raised, and she soon discovered that she needed to adjust her assumptions. She realized, for example, that kindergarteners at Brightwood didn't understand the difference between weather and seasons. If she asked what season it was, they might say "sunny."

Like many teachers at Center City, Ms. Masi was dubious about Core Knowledge, which she and her kindergarteners were encountering for the first time. She wasn't sure the information-packed curriculum was developmentally appropriate, and vocabulary words like *garment* and *deciduous* seemed overly ambitious for the kids, many of whom were still learning English. But midway through the year, something clicked.

She began to see how carefully designed the curriculum was: the vocabulary students saw in the nursery rhymes unit would come back when they were learning about kings and queens, and then again when they were learning about Christopher Columbus. And she could see her students making the connections.

Now those students are poised to begin their first second-grade unit, which focuses on fairy tales like "Beauty and the Beast" and American tall tales like Paul Bunyan and Casey Jones. All but a few are reading on grade level, and their vocabularies have expanded considerably.

When it's time for students to read independently, I strike up a conversation with a boy who's reading a book about seals.

"They're very *playful*," he informs me, showing off a new word. "They can stay underwater for thirty minutes. Then they have to come back up."

"Did you read that in the book," I ask him, "or do you just know that?"

"I just know that!" he tells me proudly. "It's not here."

CHAPTER 3

Everything Was
Surprising and Novel

ONE MORNING IN MARCH 2002, Professor Daniel Willingham—a rising star in the psychology department at the University of Virginia—was standing in the Nashville convention center, looking out over the four hundred or so teachers waiting to hear him speak. And he was panicking.

It wasn't that he was afraid of public speaking: Though soft-spoken in conversation, Willingham was at ease lecturing to large groups. As a professor, he did it all the time. Nor was he unfamiliar with his topic: "Translating Cognitive Psychology Research into Classroom Practice." Cognitive science—the study of how people think and learn—was his field. Well, he *was* unfamiliar with one part of the topic: he knew nothing about classrooms outside of the university setting, or what was practiced in them.

"Please don't come," he had begged his new girlfriend—later his wife—at the last minute. She was a teacher, and he didn't want his ignorance exposed in front of her.

More fundamentally, Willingham was sure this audience would be familiar with the basic principles of cognitive psychology he planned to discuss: things like how attention works, how working memory can get overloaded, how the mind interprets written and spoken text, and how background knowledge affects the amount of information the mind takes in and retains. These were topics he'd been teaching to undergraduates for years. For a group of practicing teachers, who had been required to take developmental psychology courses as part of their training, all of this would certainly be old news.

Tamping down his anxiety, Willingham launched into his whimsical PowerPoint presentation, projecting an image of a polar bear, for example, to illustrate how difficult it can be for students to control their thoughts ("try not to think of a white bear"). Soon, however, he realized his fears had been unjustified. Having taught for years, he'd developed a feel for when he was telling an audience things they already knew. And he could sense that for these teachers, elementary cognitive science was far from old news.

"Everything I said was surprising and novel to the teachers," he recalls.

Afterward, teachers came up to tell him how interesting they had found his presentation and how they intended to put the information to use in their classrooms. Willingham was stunned: How could they not be familiar with the basic science about how we learn? And what could he do about it?

As WILLINGHAM DISCOVERED, there's a huge gulf between what scientists know about the learning process and what teachers believe. Perhaps the most crucial gulf has to do with reading instruction. Educators have generally lumped together the two basic components of reading—decoding and comprehension—and treated them as one "subject." But cognitive scientists have found that the factors leading to success in each are fundamentally different.

Decoding refers to the process of translating alphabetic symbols into words, and there's an overwhelming scientific consensus that the best way to teach decoding is to teach foundational reading skills in a systematic and explicit manner—often referred to, somewhat inaccurately, under the umbrella term *phonics.* First, children need to learn to distinguish the sounds in spoken language and in individual words, a process called *phonemic awareness.* Then they need to learn how those sounds correspond to letters (strictly speaking, that's phonics). They also need to practice to the point where they can read fluently, with the appropriate speed and intonation. If all children were taught phonics this way, as many as 95 percent would become proficient decoders. That includes most children who are diagnosed as dyslexic, along with most "garden-variety" struggling readers, many of whom are from low-income families.

As for comprehension, the most important factor in determining whether readers can understand a text is how much relevant vocabulary or background knowledge they have (think back to that 1987 baseball experiment). While a limited amount of instruction in comprehension strategies can help some students derive meaning from text, that's only possible if they have enough knowledge to make sense of the text in the first place. In other words, comprehension, unlike decoding, doesn't occur as a result of teaching students a set of skills they then practice repeatedly. It's something people achieve more or less naturally—*if* they have enough information.

That, at least, is what scientists have concluded. Educators and professors of education, on the other hand, have come to exactly the opposite conclusions. For many years, the majority of American educators shared the fundamental belief that *decoding* was the part of reading that occurs naturally, without much skills-focused instruction. In recent years, an increasing number have embraced the systematic teaching of phonics. Still, many haven't been trained how to do it well, and many others have been taught that such instruction is not only unnecessary but actually harmful.

Some educators who oppose teaching phonics have argued that it's better to surround kids with books and encourage them to guess at words they don't know. Others see the value in *some* phonics instruction but feel it's best delivered on an as-needed basis. Quite a few believe that practicing phonics will bore children and destroy their interest in reading.

On the other hand, nearly all teachers have come to see *comprehension* not as something that arises naturally with sufficient information, as cognitive scientists have concluded, but rather as a set of strategies that need to be taught explicitly. Many dedicated and well-intentioned teachers have worked their tails off trying to teach reading, but because they've been given the wrong information about how to do it, or in some cases none at all, the results have been disastrous, both for their students and for society as a whole.

It's hard to say to what extent dismal scores on standardized reading tests are attributable to problems with decoding; the results don't distinguish between that factor and comprehension, and the two are inextricably linked. Clearly, if students can't decode at all, they won't be able to extract information. Even after they've acquired some decoding skill, they need practice to ensure it becomes automatic; if they're devoting too much effort to decoding, they won't have enough brainpower left for comprehension. This interaction works in the other direction too: if students already understand a lot about a subject, they'll be able to guess at words they're unable to decode and extract information anyway. But that shouldn't obscure the fact that the two aspects of reading need to be approached in dramatically different ways—one as a set of skills that need to be taught, the other as a natural by-product of other activities.

One reason for the widespread misconception that reading comprehension can be taught as a set of skills is a report by the National Reading Panel, a blue-ribbon group of reading experts that issued its findings in 2000. The effects have been decidedly double-edged. On the positive side, the panel concluded in no uncertain terms that systematic instruction in phonemic awareness and phonics boosted children's ability to read. That finding, combined with a $4 billion federal program to incentivize high-poverty schools to adopt phonics, had a significant effect. Even many schools of education, long resistant to the idea of systematic phonics, have added courses on the subject to their curricula.

But the National Reading Panel also endorsed instruction in comprehension strategies, while failing to note that comprehension depends primarily on building knowledge. After the release of the report, the number of teacher-training programs that included courses on reading comprehension skills and strategies ballooned, rising from 15 percent in 2006 to 75 percent ten years later.

As for writing, scientists have devoted far less attention to that aspect of literacy than to reading. And teacher-training programs have basically ignored it.

Perhaps all this wouldn't have been so harmful if teacher candidates were also learning about the importance of content. But, as Daniel Willingham was shocked to discover, that's one of the many crucial things that most never encounter.

WHAT DO PROSPECTIVE teachers learn, if not the findings of cognitive science on how to teach reading, writing, and other subjects? For the most part, a lot of pedagogical theory and developmental psychology, like Lev Vygotsky's work on the importance of social interaction in cognition and Jean Piaget's theory of children's developmental stages. Little or no time is spent on practicalities like classroom management, and some graduates of teacher-training programs complain bitterly about a lack of rigor and content.

One fundamental pedagogical precept that most budding teachers do learn is that they should spend as little time as possible imparting factual information. The prevailing theory is that students must engage in constructing their own knowledge rather than memorizing facts that will only bore them and that they don't truly understand. Teachers are also taught that education should be *child-centered*, a term that generally means learning should be driven as much as possible by the interests of the individual child—with the teacher acting as a facilitator—rather than by a curriculum.

Daniel Willingham and other cognitive scientists point out that many of these theories have been long discredited. There is, for example, a wealth of evidence showing that it's far more effective to impart information to students directly rather than having them attempt to figure it out for themselves, especially when they don't already know much about a topic. Willingham has proposed that prospective educators just learn about instructional methods that have been shown to work.

At the same time, he realizes that a suggestion like that will be viewed as beyond the pale by most professors of education. Historically, education schools have been seen as inferior to other branches of academia. Their admissions standards tend to be lower, and their curricula are perceived as lacking depth and coherence. Focusing on theory—even outdated theory—is a way of boosting their academic credibility. "The more removed knowledge is from ordinary concerns and the more closely associated it is with high culture," writes one longtime education school professor, David Labaree, "the more prestige it carries with it."

Other factors have led to the divergence between the fields of science and education. Willingham has come to see the problem as a basic difference in culture and orientation: cognitive science aims merely to discover and describe the processes that govern learning and memory, while education is goal-oriented. Another cognitive scientist, Mark Seidenberg, observes that education professors not only fail to expose teacher candidates to the findings of science, they also fail to acquaint them with general principles of scientific research, leaving them vulnerable to claims that may be appealing on an intuitive level but have no evidence behind them.

Keith Stanovich, the cognitive scientist who coined the term *Matthew effect* as applied to reading, argues that part of the problem is that scientists are by nature too cautious to attract a large following. They're competing against literacy gurus who promise their methods will not only boost test scores but also empower teachers. Scientists, trained to value skepticism, fail to communicate these kinds of warm and fuzzy messages and are loath to guarantee that any particular approach will work. And, of course, the approach that works best—building students' knowledge over a period of years—takes time. Educators are often under pressure to raise scores *yesterday*.

Whatever the reasons for the disconnect, after his experience in Nashville, Daniel Willingham decided he needed to do whatever he could to communicate the findings of cognitive science directly to practicing teachers.

"I thought, I can either try and persuade people in schools of education to train teachers differently," Willingham told me, "or I can just talk to teachers and tell them stuff I found interesting. And that sounded a whole lot easier."

ON A WARM JUNE EVENING, Willingham has traveled from his home in Charlottesville to a high school classroom in Washington, D.C., to speak about the relationship between knowledge and reading comprehension. Many of the forty or fifty people in attendance are educators, but others are members of the general public.

Shortly after delivering his talk in Nashville in 2002, Willingham began writing a column for *American Educator*, a quarterly published by the American Federation of Teachers, one of the two national teachers' unions, that goes out to almost a million teachers. Called Ask the Cognitive Scientist, the column addresses a variety of questions relating to learning.

Willingham is now the leading interpreter of scientific research on learning, and particularly on the reading process, for teachers, education policy experts, and the public. The big difference between his 2002 presentation and his talks these days may be that he no longer expects his audiences to be familiar with everything he's going to say. On the other hand, thanks to his growing influence, they're actually more likely to have at least heard of some of the concepts. Despite a somewhat forbidding appearance—he has an entirely bald pate and wears glasses with thick frames—he's mild-mannered, approachable, and possessed of a wry sense of humor that is on display in one of his YouTube videos, "Teaching Content Is Teaching Reading," which has gotten more than two hundred thousand views.

Now, in the stuffy classroom, he first establishes what he's *not* going to talk about: decoding. "Let's assume," he says, "that the reader we're talking about is a fluent decoder." That's a big assumption. But he will focus on comprehension instead, beginning with the largely uncon-scious processes that determine whether and how we make meaning from what we read.

Problems generally occur, Willingham explains, because authors in-evitably leave out information. He projects a slide of a sheepish-looking young man and reads the words on the screen in an embarrassed mum-ble: "I don't think she'll go out with me again . . . spilled some coffee on her." The man could have explained that people generally don't like hav-ing coffee spilled on them, because coffee makes a mess and it's hot. He could also have explained that the woman in question probably thinks he's a bumbling idiot. Therefore, if he were to call her, she would be un-likely to accept his invitation to go out again.

"Now, we all know people who talk like this," Willingham says to knowing chuckles. The message is clear: no one enjoys conversing with someone who explains things ad nauseam.

Authors leave out information for the same reasons we all do: they don't want to bore their audiences, they assume readers have a certain amount of knowledge, and they rely on them to use it to fill in what's missing. But there's an important difference between written and spo-ken communication. In conversation, a listener can interrupt and ask the speaker what she means or make inferences based on facial expres-sions or gestures. A reader doesn't have that option.

True, readers can try to deduce meaning from context or look up unfamiliar words. One argument heard frequently in recent years is that students no longer need to learn facts because they can "just Google them." But, as Willingham points out, it's not that simple.

"Suppose I hand you a book that's written in Russian," he scoffs, "and I tell you oh, you can just look up the words you don't know. Looking stuff up is work!"

By the time you've Googled the meaning of a word, you've interrupted the flow of understanding that comprehension depends on; readers begin to find a text difficult to understand when a mere 2 percent of the vo-cabulary is unfamiliar. And you might find the wrong definition, since meaning often changes with context. In addition, retrieving information from memory—unlike retrieving it from the internet—increases the chances that you'll remember it more easily the next time you need it. (And that's not to mention the abundance of incorrect information online. "You can find any fact on the internet," Willingham has written, "even alternative ones.")

Next, Willingham projects a slide of a sunlit garden, followed by another slide that's so blurry and out-of-focus it's no more than splotches of color. Reading, he says, should be like the first slide—like looking through a window so clear we're not even aware it's there. When the reader lacks enough knowledge to make sense of the text, the experience is more like the second slide—like trying to drive while peering through a fogged-up windshield.

Try finding the main idea of the following paragraph:

Much depended on . . . the two overnight batsmen. But this duo perished either side of lunch—the latter a little unfortunate to be adjudged leg-before—and with Andrew Symonds, too, being shown the dreaded finger off an inside edge, the inevitable beckoned, bar the pyrotechnics of Michael Clarke and the ninth wicket. Clarke clinically cut and drove to 10 fours in a 134-ball 81, before he stepped out to Kumble to present an easy stumping to Mahendra Singh Dhoni.

While that task wouldn't pose a challenge to a reader who follows the game of cricket, the meaning is likely to be opaque to anyone unfamiliar with its terminology.

Or consider this paragraph from a passage that appeared on a standardized test given to third-graders in 2015:

In one of the most remote places in the world, the Canadian Arctic, a people have survived over a thousand years. They are the Inuit. For the Inuit, the Arctic is a place teeming with life. Depending on how far north they live, the Inuit find everything from caribou herds and polar bears to beluga whales. The Inuit have adapted themselves to the various regions they inhabit. At one time they were considered to be among the healthiest people in the world. This is no longer the case; the Inuit lifestyle has changed dramatically over the past decades. The arrival of southerners and modern technology resulted in big changes to the Inuit diet and way of life.

An educated adult might have just learned something about the Inuit. But here's the same passage without the words that are unlikely to be familiar to many third-graders:

In one of the most ████ places in the world, the ████████████, a people have ██████ over a ████████ years. They are the ████. For the ████, the ████ is a place ██████ with life. Depending on how far north they live, the ████ find everything from ████ ████ and ████████ to ████████████. The ████ have ██████ themselves to the ████ ██████ they ██████. At one time they were considered to be among the healthiest people in the world. This is no longer the case; the Inuit ████████ has changed ████████ over the past ██████. The ██████ of ████████ ██ and modern ████████ resulted in big changes to the ████ ██ and ████████.

Even if some of the words are explained in the text—like "Inuit"—or can be inferred, the effort involved in reading this paragraph makes it hard to grasp its meaning.

When we try to make sense of what we read, we rely on what cognitive scientists refer to as *working memory*, something Willingham has called *the staging ground for thought*. Another definition might be *consciousness*. It's the process whereby we take in new information and combine it with the facts and procedures stored in our long-term memory. The key thing about working memory is that it has a limited capacity. And information in working memory is lost if it isn't quickly "rehearsed"—perhaps articulated or written about. By one estimate, the limit is just fifteen to thirty seconds.

So time is of the essence when trying to assimilate new information. If we can relate it to something we already know, it speeds up the process considerably. If we need to stop and look up every other word, or puzzle them out from context, we're far less likely to be able to understand and retain what we're reading.

Background knowledge, Willingham explains, also enables a reader to engage in something called *chunking*. Let's say the text in the 1987 baseball experiment said that the shortstop threw the ball to the second baseman, who threw the ball to the first baseman, resulting in two runners being out. The students who knew a lot about baseball could "chunk" those actions by recognizing them as a double play. But those who knew little about baseball would have to try to remember each step in the series of actions described, which occupies more space in working memory.

Scientists also use the word *schema* to describe this process. A schema is a mental framework constructed from accumulated information and experience and stored in long-term memory. When people already have a schema for a topic, new information on that topic has something it can stick to. If knowledge about baseball helps readers understand a text about baseball, it follows that knowledge about the world in general equips readers to do well on a test that covers a variety of subjects. And that's exactly what experiments have shown.

Reading tests, Willingham has written, are really "knowledge tests in disguise." Test-takers don't need deep understanding; a passing familiarity with pneumonia or Greek mythical heroes will do. The tests don't directly assess content knowledge; they simply draw on it to try to assess comprehension. And those with the broadest knowledge have the best chance of demonstrating their comprehension.

If KNOWLEDGE ALWAYS trumps abstract skills, Willingham asks, what explains the many studies showing that instruction in reading comprehension strategies boosts test scores? The answer, he suggests, is that strategies function like a reminder to check your work. They may help you realize that you don't understand what you're reading, but they won't help you understand it.

Imagine that you buy a disassembled piece of furniture, he's written, and the instructions are merely generic: "Put stuff together. Every so often, stop, look at it, and evaluate how it's going. It may also help to think back on other pieces of furniture you've built before." That's not going to help you figure out that part A of your desk is supposed to attach to part C rather than part B.

Some studies have called strategy instruction into question. One found that asking open-ended questions about content—like "How does all this connect with what we read earlier?"—had more positive effects on comprehension and recall and led to richer discussion. "In doing strategy instruction," said one of the authors, "kids aren't going directly for the meaning of the text. They're going through, okay, how do I do a summary? Or how do I predict? They have to go through a kind of routine. And we think that sometimes there could be, for many kids, more focus on what that *routine* is than what the content of the text itself is."

As for the studies that show strategy instruction has a positive impact, Willingham speculates that some kids don't realize the point of reading is to make meaning from text. They may think that if they just manage to "decode," they're done. Strategies let that subset of students know they're actually supposed to understand what they're reading. And students don't keep getting better with practice: fifty sessions of strategy instruction yield no more benefit than ten.

What Willingham doesn't mention is that there's no evidence at all behind most of the "skills" teachers spend time on. While teachers generally use the terms *skills* and *strategies* interchangeably, reading researchers define *skills* as the kinds of things that students practice in an effort to render them automatic: find the main idea of this passage, identify the supporting details, etc. But *strategies* are techniques that students will always use consciously, to make themselves aware of their own thinking and therefore better able to control it: asking questions about a text, pausing periodically to summarize what they've read, generally monitoring their comprehension.

Instruction in reading *skills* has been around since the 1950s, but—

according to one reading expert—it's useless, "like pushing the elevator button twice. It makes you feel better, perhaps, but the elevator doesn't come any more quickly." And even researchers who endorse strategy instruction don't advocate putting it in the foreground, as most teachers and textbook publishers do. The focus should be on the content of the text.

In short, it makes sense to teach strategies as a means of helping students understand a particular difficult text, but not to spend a lot of time on them—certainly not the daily practice many schools engage in. Spending less time on strategies would free up more time for building knowledge in subjects like history and science, where there's no upper limit on the benefits. Ideally, schools will adopt a curriculum that builds that knowledge in a logical sequence from year to year, balancing familiar and fresh content so that students are challenged but not overwhelmed, and revisiting concepts periodically to reinforce learning.

There aren't yet any reliable studies showing that such a curriculum will outperform either a skills-focused curriculum or a content-focused one that lacks coherence. Still, says Willingham, it's reasonable to assume that's the case.

THERE'S A FUNDAMENTAL FLAW in Willingham's plan to take cognitive science directly to teachers: no individual teacher is in a position to ensure that schools adopt the kind of curriculum that is likely to be most effective. A lone teacher here or there changing his approach probably won't do the trick. So, while some teachers have gotten Willingham's message about the importance of teaching content, it's not always clear what they can do about it.

That's a particular problem for teachers at upper grade levels, where students often arrive with huge gaps in their knowledge. Stephanie Tatel, an elementary reading specialist in Charlottesville, attended a talk Willingham delivered there to an audience largely made up of teachers. For her, there were some practical takeaways, like the realization that pulling kids out of science and social studies to give them extra help in reading skills is actually "the worst thing you can do." But some found Willingham's talk disheartening.

"You know, like, *we* don't have control over that," Tatel said. "How are we supposed to make up for years of lack of background knowledge?"

It's not impossible to compensate for lacunae when students are older. But it's difficult, and it takes an intensive schoolwide effort that individual teachers may—again—be powerless to effect. Without the cooperation of principals, school districts, states, and schools of education, we're unlikely to see fundamental change.

In the end, Willingham is a typical scientist—a role that confers both strengths and weaknesses. His message carries weight with many teachers because it's clear he doesn't have any particular axe to grind, and he's not trying to sell them snake oil. But he's not endorsing any specific instructional method or setting out a clear path to success. It's up to others to figure out how to counter the entrenched beliefs and assumptions that have put American education on a collision course with the realities of how children actually learn.

SEPTEMBER 2016

"Are you ready for a *big* first-grade word?" Ms. Arredondo asks her students. The kids chorus a mild "yes."

"That doesn't sound very excited," Ms. Arredondo chides playfully.

"YES!" the kids scream.

A digital screen called a Promethean board—a space-age version of the traditional chalkboard—displays the first vocabulary word of the day: "Curious: eager to find out about things." But students aren't familiar with the word *eager*. So Ms. Arredondo explains: "Eager means that you really, really, really want to know."

Today's lesson will revolve around a story in the class's basal reader, *Journeys*, called "Curious George at School." Before the kids tackle the simple text, Ms. Arredondo has various other words to introduce them to: *paints*, *mess*, and *job*. And then one more: *genre*.

They've already talked about fiction and nonfiction, although it's clear some kids are still hazy on the distinction. Today's story, she tells them, is "fantasy," which she defines as "a story that could not happen in real life." It might have animals that talk and act like people, she says, encouraging the students to think of stories that fit that description. After some rambling discussion, Ms. Arredondo asks her culminating question: "Would fantasy be fiction—made-up—or nonfiction?"

"Nonfiction," one girl answers confidently.

With only a trace of exasperation, Ms. Arredondo leads the class through a train of reasoning that eventually brings them to the conclusion that fantasy must be *fiction*.

The skill-of-the-week, according to the basal reader, is "sequence of events," and Ms. Arredondo tells the students that after they've read the Curious George story with a partner, they should write down three events, or "things that happened." Her plan is to have each pair write down a sequence of events, mix them up, and have other students try to put them in the right order. But many have trouble just reading the story. Two boys are trying to read a sentence that repeats the word *mix* over and over, but they consistently read it as *max*.

The plot isn't complex: Curious George sings and entertains the kids at school by balancing lunch boxes on his head. But then, while the children are doing an art activity, he sees some open cans of paint. George being George, he starts pouring paint on the floor and making a mess. Then he tries to clean it up with a mop and makes an even bigger mess. The kids pitch in, and the mess gets cleaned up. The end.

But the sentences in the book don't tell the story that clearly. The text on the first page reads, "This is George. He can help a lot." The second page reads, "George can sing. He is funny." While the accompanying illustrations depict the events, the sentences themselves don't.

This makes it hard to follow Ms. Arredondo's directions to write down the sequence of events. The first "event," for example, might be "George goes to school." But there's nothing that says that. And, given the students' difficulty with reading and spelling, most have simply copied sentences from the book instead of using their own words. As a result, when they try to put their classmates' sentences in the correct order, it isn't always clear what should come first. Should "George can sing" come before "This is George. He can help a lot"? Neither of them are, strictly speaking, "events."

Given the difficulties, students begin to get fidgety. "You're just showing me right now you don't know sequence of events?" Ms. Arredondo says. "This is on the test. And can we read a story if we don't know what order it happens in?"

Like most basal readers, *Journeys* is so overstuffed with material that it's impossible for teachers to cover all of it. One thing Ms. Arredondo has decided to omit is the "Essential Question" that goes with the Curious George story: "Why is going to school important?" Figuring it didn't have much to do with the story, she had the kids discuss it during morning meeting instead.

She's also skipped the nonfiction text paired with the story. In an attempt to comply with the Common Core's requirements that children read more nonfiction and that instruction be focused more on content, the publisher has organized each unit around a theme and provided both a fiction and a nonfiction text. The ostensible theme for this unit is "school," and the nonfiction text is called "School Long Ago." Only a few paragraphs long and written at a first-grade level, it doesn't provide much information beyond the facts that students used to write on slates rather than paper and carry books and supplies in their arms rather than in backpacks.

Theoretically, Ms. Arredondo could bring in additional material about what school was like in the past and read it aloud to expand students' knowledge and vocabulary. But the fiction selections are generally easier for students to read on their own, and with so many kids in the class reading below grade level, she feels they should spend the bulk of their time reading—and trying to practice comprehension skills like "sequence of events."

Ms. Masi's second-graders at Center City are tackling some new words of their own: *conquer, suffering,* and *enlightenment.*

While they have time for reading at their own levels, they also spend at least forty-five minutes every day on the classroom rug, listening to information-packed Core Knowledge texts. Today they'll hear the story of Siddhartha, the historical figure who came to be known as the Buddha after attaining—yes—*enlightenment.*

"Enlightenment!" Ms. Masi says, while putting her hand to her head in a kind of salute, widening her already huge dark brown eyes, then sweeping the hand outward and upward. Just as Ms. Bauer does when teaching words like *summarizing*, teachers at Center City often have kids learn hand gestures along with vocabulary, to help cement the words in students' memories.

Enlightenment, Ms. Masi tells the kids, means "a greater understanding of life," and it's an important part of Buddhist belief. She turns to the vocabulary chart she's made, taped to the whiteboard behind her. (While her students sometimes work on computers, there's no fancy technology like a Promethean board.) Next to the word *enlightenment* she writes, "Buddhist belief. Greater understanding of life." The kids copy the definition onto smaller versions of the chart, which they have on clipboards.

Earlier they copied down definitions of *conquer* ("to defeat, overcome by force") and *suffering* ("pain"). Students themselves suggested *defeat* and *pain*, words they've learned in previous lessons. Next to each word, Ms. Masi adds a simple illustration; *suffering* has a stick figure who looks to be in distress. The kids copy those too, or come up with their own drawings.

Ms. Masi creates hand-drawn posters and charts to go with each read-aloud—one every day for second grade and another for third, for which she also serves as the literacy teacher—and by now the classroom walls are crowded. Yesterday's poster, taped to a closed venetian blind, tells the story of the Hindu holiday Diwali. Before launching into Siddhartha, Ms. Masi prods her students to review what they remember about it. One boy recalls that Hindus believe in dharma, which he defines as "they want to do the right thing." A girl explains that the lights associated with Diwali symbolize "light over darkness and good over evil." Ms. Masi leads the rest of the class in a cheer for the students who provided the correct answers.

Then she calls the kids' attention to the Essential Question they'll answer at the end of the lesson, written at the top of today's poster: "How did Buddhism begin, and how did Asoka help spread its message?"

Ms. Masi begins to read: Siddhartha, a young prince who had led a sheltered life, was shocked to discover how much suffering there was in the world. After sitting under a fig tree for seven weeks, meditating on how to bring happiness to people, he achieved enlightenment. Now known as the Buddha, he was able to come up with rules to prevent unhappiness, such as "be kind to others." A king named Asoka became a convert to Buddhism and set out to spread its teachings. As she reads, Ms. Masi flips the pages of a large book of illustrations displayed on an easel.

Despite their mostly grade-level skills, the children couldn't read this text themselves. They do, however, have worksheets with strategically chosen excerpts, which they consult when Ms. Masi pauses to ask questions like "What did Siddhartha's parents do to protect him?" During the read-aloud, the students answer these questions orally. Ms. Masi writes down versions of their answers on her big chart, which they copy onto their clipboards.

After the read-aloud, the children return to their desks and tackle written answers to the Essential Question—now divided into two parts: "How did Buddhism begin?" and "How did Asoka spread the message of Buddhism?" Like virtually all children at this grade level, they can express themselves far better when speaking than in writing. Trying to answer the first question, one student writes, "Siddhartha reached enlightenment," but doesn't explain how. Another writes, "He begin rich then he was sad becas peopl were criying he bigon to think."

Ms. Masi still sometimes has her doubts about the curriculum. "It's a lot of stuff to take in," she told me.

But the next day, when she reviewed the material with students, she was amazed to discover how much they'd understood and remembered. When she gave them riddles—for example, "I sat under a tree for seven weeks to discover how to conquer suffering and end unhappiness. Who am I?"—the kids all scored 100 percent. When she gave them worksheets, they found answers in the charts and drawings posted on the walls, incorporating words the class hadn't even focused on. Ms. Masi overheard them having conversations using their new vocabulary and engaging in "cool arguments" about definitions.

Students' writing sometimes reveals misunderstandings, but it also shows how much they've absorbed. When the kids imagined living in ancient India, one wrote of "a bustling city" (*bustling* having been a vocabulary word), while others mentioned "iragation canals" and trading food for "gold, steel, corn and dimonds."

Only six weeks into the year, Ms. Masi is already exhausted from teaching Core Knowledge to two grade levels—and creating daily posters for each—while also trying to lead guided reading and a separate writing block. But looking at the words her students are using, it seems that maybe all that hard work is paying off: these kids are *getting* it.

CHAPTER 4

The Reading Wars

I N THE EARLY 1950S, a nationally known expert on readability and clear writing offered to tutor a friend's son, Johnny, who had been held back in sixth grade because he couldn't read. The expert, Rudolf Flesch, started by giving Johnny what he thought was an easy word for a twelve-year-old: *kid*.

"He stared at it for quite some time," Flesch later recounted, "then finally said, 'kind.' I tell you, it staggered me. Nobody born and raised on the continent of Europe can easily grasp the fact that *anyone* can mistake *kid* for *kind*."

To help Johnny learn to read, Flesch used the same technique as his own teachers in Vienna: teaching the sounds of each letter of the alphabet, or certain letters in combination. Within six months, Johnny was reading—not perfectly, but on track to catch up to his peers in a few months. He was "happy again," Flesch observed, "a changed person."

Flesch's experience prompted him to look into "this whole reading business," as he put it. After extensive research, he announced his conclusion: "The teaching of reading—all over the United States, in all the schools, in all the textbooks—is totally wrong and flies in the face of all logic and common sense. . . . Johnny's only problem was that he was unfortunately exposed to an ordinary American school."

What Flesch discovered was this: instead of teaching children to read through letter-sound correspondences—phonics—American teachers encouraged their students to memorize whole words. If they came across words they didn't know, teachers urged them to guess, using context clues. This approach had held sway since about 1935.

At the time Flesch was writing, the most common exemplar was the Dick-and-Jane series, which used short sentences repeating the same simple words, along the lines of:

> *Come, Dick.*
> *Come and see.*
> *Come, come.*
> *Come and see.*
> *Come and see Spot.*

Children could read these kinds of books largely because they were able to memorize the few words they contained. But confronted with an unfamiliar word, they might be stymied.

All cultures that used an alphabetic writing system, Flesch railed, had relied on phonetic methods to teach reading, going back to the ancient Egyptians, Greeks, and Romans. But for some reason, twentieth-century American educators had decided to teach our alphabet as if it were hieroglyphics. Not only did this condemn many children to illiteracy, it also deprived them of the experience of enjoying literature. For example, a classic nineteenth-century introduction to mythology, *The Age of Fable*, uses the words *nymph*, *deity*, and *incantations*. "If a child that has gone to any of our schools faces the word *nymph* for the first time," Flesch wrote, "he is absolutely helpless because nobody has ever told him how to sound out *n* and *y* and *m* and *ph* and read the word off the page."

Instead, children like Johnny got "horrible, stupid, emasculated, pointless, tasteless little readers, the stuff and guff about Dick and Jane or Alice and Jerry visiting the farm and having birthday parties and seeing animals in the zoo and going through dozens and dozens of totally unexciting middle-class, middle-income, middle-I.Q. children's activities that offer opportunities for reading 'Look, look' or 'Yes, yes' or 'Come, come' or 'See the funny, funny animal.' During the past half year I read a good deal of this material," Flesch concluded wearily, "and I don't wish that experience on anyone."

THE BOOK in which Flesch vented his outrage, published in 1955, was called *Why Johnny Can't Read*, and it created a sensation. Partly thanks to Flesch's highly readable style—he was, after all, an expert on readability—the book sold sixty thousand copies in five months and remained on the bestseller list for six weeks. It also tapped into Cold War anxieties about whether American children were keeping up with their counterparts in the Soviet Union. Johnny's inability to read became a frequent topic of conversation at dinner parties, and excerpts were printed in a range of publications. Even now, more than sixty years after it first appeared, the title is frequently used as a catchphrase attached to any number of perceived ills. Google "Why Johnny can't," and you'll get everything from "Why Johnny can't ride a bike" to "Why Johnny can't code."

Flesch's intended audience was parents, and many embraced his message gratefully. Reviews in the mainstream press were favorable, and some publishers revised their textbooks to feature phonics. The vast majority of educators, however, rejected his argument, and some excoriated him personally. After publishing an article in 1979 titled "Why Johnny *Still* Can't Read," Flesch reported that he received letters from educators calling him a liar, a criminal, and a demagogue.

Far from settling the debate over how best to teach reading, Flesch's book turned out to be the opening salvo in a bitter, long-running conflict known as the Reading Wars, which reached its peak in the 1990s. A decade after *Why Johnny Can't Read*, the Dick-and-Jane method began evolving into a related philosophy called "whole language," and a few decades later it morphed into "balanced literacy"—a label that most reading teachers in the United States would probably use to describe their approach today, although they don't always agree on what it means.

Proponents of balanced literacy maintain that it's significantly different from what preceded it, incorporating and "balancing" the best features of whole language and phonics. But critics argue that it suffers from the same fundamental flaw as its predecessors: it doesn't rely primarily on the systematic instruction in foundational skills that many children, and especially those from less educated families, need. The Reading Wars aren't really over. They've just gone underground.

To UNDERSTAND HOW teachers view literacy—and why they so often overlook the importance of building knowledge—it's important to understand why their beliefs about the best way to teach reading have persisted despite overwhelming scientific consensus to the contrary.

Reading, it is generally agreed, is all about making meaning. Cognitive scientists would say that decoding—the part of reading for which phonemic awareness and phonics skills are essential—is a necessary stepping-stone in the process of making meaning from written text. But the whole-language/balanced-literacy camp maintains that if you're not making meaning, you're not reading. Phonics exercises don't involve making meaning; therefore, they have nothing to do with reading. Sure, you can throw in a quick lesson on phonics here and there, in response to questions kids raise. But there's no need to bore them by drilling in a systematic way. In fact, they have argued—relying primarily on their own observations and beliefs rather than on research—too much phonics will kill a child's interest in reading. (Hence the frequently heard expression "drill and kill.") Whole-language theorists say children will naturally pick up the ability to read and write if allowed to choose books and topics that interest them.

It's true that some children will learn to read without systematic phonics instruction—probably somewhere between half and a third, according to reading experts. But all children can benefit from it, and many won't learn to decode well without it. That includes children with learning disabilities, those learning English, and a disproportionate number of children from disadvantaged homes. Some have argued that children who speak a nonstandard dialect of English are at particularly great risk. Kids who have grown up in language-poor homes are also less likely to have been encouraged to look for patterns, in language and elsewhere, a practice that could prime them to pick up phonics on their own.

Phonics patterns are best taught systematically because it's easier to keep track of which students have yet to master which ones—or which students missed certain patterns because they were absent or late. As for the claim that phonics instruction is deadly dull, proponents respond that, on the contrary, it can be fun. Phonics can be taught through songs, videos, and activities like scavenger hunts for pieces of paper labeled with different vowel sounds, which I saw in Ms. Bauer's classroom. While a systematic phonics curriculum does constrain teachers' autonomy by prescribing a certain instructional sequence, teachers can exercise their creativity in coming up with engaging ways to teach it. To those who argue phonics will prevent kids from developing a love of reading, the answer is that children who can't decode are unlikely ever to become avid readers.

Scientists also disagree with whole-language advocates on how difficult it is for children to learn to read. The whole-language theory rests on the assumption that learning to read and write is a natural process, akin to learning to speak. But oral language has been with us for hundreds of thousands of years, scientists point out, while written language was invented somewhere between four and six thousand years ago—too recently for our brains to have evolved an innate capacity to master it. There are plenty of adults who speak one or more languages fluently but cannot read. There are even entire societies, throughout history, that never developed a written language.

Another area of conflict is so-called decodable texts, which provide children with practice reading words that conform to the phonics rules they have been taught. Whole-language advocates argue they're artificial and unnecessary, preferring to surround children with *authentic* texts—books written for the commercial market, not specifically to teach reading, which they believe are higher-quality. Reading scientists, on the other hand, argue that children become confused if they see too many words that don't conform to the rules they know. Besides, they say, many authentic texts at beginning reading levels—sometimes called predictable texts—are also repetitive and insipid.

Rudolf Flesch and the leaders of the whole-language movement agreed on the end goal: introducing children to the delights of literature. Psychology professor Frank Smith, one of the most prominent whole-language advocates, dismissed decodable texts with titles like *Jen's Hen* in terms similar to those Flesch used to excoriate the Dick-and-Jane readers: "fragmented, decontextualized, and trivial." What they disagreed on was the route that was necessary to get children to the point where they could gain access to literature. Both sides also overlooked the need to build knowledge and vocabulary. Flesch may have been right that children had to learn phonics to sound out *nymph*, but it apparently didn't occur to him that many children would have no idea what the word meant once they sounded it out.

THE DEBATE OVER phonics dragged on for decades. In the late 1960s, an influential book by a Harvard education professor named Jeanne Chall concluded that explicit phonics instruction was indeed the best method of teaching beginning reading, especially for children who were less likely to be exposed to books at home. But critics pushed back, eventually founding the whole-language movement.

Frank Smith argued that the best way to become a skilled reader was simply to read, without any particular guidance. "My own recommendation for how reading and writing should be taught is radical," he wrote. "They should not be taught at all." That view meshed well with the philosophy, still prevalent in education schools, that learning proceeds best when it unfolds naturally, in response to children's curiosity and interests. As one frequently invoked mantra puts it, the teacher should be a "guide on the side, not a sage on the stage."

Meanwhile, the evidence continued to mount that instruction in phonics was the most effective way of teaching reading. By the mid-1990s, one researcher observed that it was "one of the most well established conclusions in all of behavioral science." But whole-language proponents dismissed the research on the ground that it was conducted by cloistered academics who knew little of the realities of the classroom. Most classroom teachers were simply unaware of the data.

From a teacher's perspective, it may look as though young children are getting the hang of decoding without explicit phonics instruction. Often, though, they're just guessing from illustrations, relying on their memories of repeated readings of the same text, or using their background knowledge to figure out words they can't decode. When those students reach higher grade levels where texts aren't predictable and vocabulary is more sophisticated, they're often lost. In secondary school, decoding problems can lead to a lack of fluency in reading, which interferes with comprehension. One Florida study found that almost 71 percent of the tenth-grade students assessed were disfluent readers.

At an elementary school I visited in Reno, Nevada, the fifth-grade teachers had recently been shocked to discover, after administering a new reading test, that most of their students had never learned to decode. The students—mostly low-income and Hispanic—had always scored low on reading tests, but the tests had never distinguished between comprehension and decoding. This one did, showing that 88 percent of the fifth-graders were well below grade level on foundational skills; only 5 percent were where they should have been. One teacher was so stunned she wondered if she'd administered the test incorrectly.

"They know a lot of words by sight," another teacher told me, "but they might be stumped by a word like *pipe*." Somewhere, the ghost of Rudolf Flesch was banging his head against a wall in frustration.

The fifth-grade teachers believed the roots of the decoding problem at their school had been addressed, thanks to a new principal. But shortly after I spoke with them, I met a kindergarten teacher who told me she didn't believe in systematic phonics and was instead relying on her usual "mishmash" approach. As far as she could tell, it was "working beautifully."

In the 1980s and 1990s, many early-elementary teachers felt the same way, and the whole-language approach took over classrooms at a breathtaking pace. "Pick your metaphor," wrote one reading expert in 1989, "an epidemic, wildfire, manna from heaven—whole language has spread so rapidly throughout North America that it is a fact of life in literacy curriculum and research." The leading whole-language theorists addressed practitioners in easily understandable terms and stressed the importance of teacher autonomy, a message that resonated with many who were tired of the routine prescribed by basals: snippets of insipid text, followed by questions designed to test understanding. Students were often bored, and teachers were bound to mind-numbing scripts. It was a lot more satisfying to teach children to read using high-quality authentic texts—or at least, to appear to teach them to read.

In 1987, whole language appeared to score a major victory when California adopted a curriculum framework based on the approach. Publishers began producing whole language–oriented basal readers for the state's enormous market, which influenced the textbook industry as a whole. Although the majority of American schools continued to use basal readers, many started freeing teachers to use authentic children's literature to teach—or, in whole-language terms, *facilitate*—reading.

But a few years later, California's performance on national reading tests plummeted: 56 percent of its fourth-graders had "below basic" reading skills. Although it wasn't clear that whole language caused the drop, the media took the occasion to highlight the plentiful research supporting phonics. California changed course, scrapping its whole-language textbooks and returning to a more phonics-focused approach.

The debate over phonics again erupted into the national conversation, and now the rhetoric was even more vicious and political. The push for phonics had long been identified with the right, while whole language was an offshoot of a philosophy called progressive education, associated with the left. One phonics advocate charged that the whole-language crew wanted to turn "American children into little socialists." Whole-language theorist Ken Goodman accused the phonics camp of not wanting students to become literate, fearing that "they would have easy access to information that may empower them."

State governments began to enter the fray. By 1997, thirty-three states had enacted legislation stressing the importance of teaching phonics. The federal government was also funding research showing that direct instruction in phonics increased the chances that children would be reading on grade level by third grade.

Then, in 1998, President Bill Clinton appointed the National Reading Panel, the blue-ribbon group whose voluminous report unequivocally endorsed systematic phonics along with four other "pillars" of reading instruction. Four years later, President George W. Bush launched a program called Reading First, which conditioned $4 billion in federal grants on the adoption of phonics-based programs. Together, the two developments appeared to hammer the final nail into the whole-language coffin.

Ultimately, Reading First provided grants to about 10 percent of all public elementary schools. Some school districts reported significant benefits, especially for poor and minority students. "Reading First is the most effective federal program in history," the Alabama superintendent of education wrote. African American fourth-graders at Reading First schools in that state made more than twice as much progress on a standardized reading test as African American students at other schools. Some other states saw similar results.

But Reading First was short-lived. Congress declined to extend the program in 2008 after studies showed it was having no effect on students' reading comprehension. That didn't necessarily mean that phonics had failed to teach students how to decode. Rather, it reflected the fact that the designers of Reading First—like the National Reading Panel—failed to take into account the need to build knowledge and vocabulary in order to boost children's comprehension.

One lasting effect was that—in combination with pressure from the testing requirements of No Child Left Behind—Reading First increased the amount of time teachers spent on reading as a self-contained subject. That led to a corresponding decrease in the amount of time spent on subjects that could have built knowledge and comprehension. In 2004, a third-grader named Zulma Berrios gave a reporter the following account of her school day: "In the morning we read. Then we go to Mrs. Witthaus and read. Then after lunch we read. Then we read some more." The reporter noted that aside from time for math, recess, and art or PE, Zulma's summary was accurate. Generally, teachers believed that as long as they taught children to read accurately and fluently, "comprehension [would] pretty much take care of itself."

"Once they learn the fundamentals of reading, writing, and math," commented the superintendent who oversaw Zulma's school system, "they can pick up science and social studies on the double-quick. You're not going to be a scientist if you can't read."

DESPITE THE OVERWHELMING evidence that systematic phonics is the best way to ensure that all children learn to decode, there are still many educators—like that kindergarten teacher in Nevada—who choose not to use it or are unaware of its importance. Some education schools continue to teach approaches to decoding that aren't backed by evidence or to encourage students to form their own philosophies about the best way to teach reading; some prospective teachers graduate without ever having heard the word *phonics*. To researchers, whole language appears to be something out of a science fiction movie: The Thing That Wouldn't Die.

It's not just in the area of phonics that educators and scientists have conflicting perspectives. Another widely held view—both among teachers and the general public—is that students have different "learning styles," such as auditory or visual. In fact, numerous experiments have shown there's no evidence to support the idea. If we want to maximize the chances that educators will embrace the scientific consensus on the importance of building knowledge, we need to understand why they sometimes resist findings backed by data.

A basic problem is that it can be difficult for teachers to distinguish theories that are valid from those that are not, especially when new ones are thrown at them all the time. On average, urban school systems launch a significant reform initiative once every three months. More than half of teachers surveyed in 2017 said they had experienced "too much" or "way too much" change in the preceding two years. Understandably, even programs that claim to be backed by evidence raise suspicions.

"The term 'research-based' over time has become the teachers' nightmare," said one teacher. "We view it as, okay, we've got a bunch of people who think they know what they're doing, but they've never been in a classroom. They're throwing out a bunch of jargon, and then they want us to buy into it."

When it comes to phonics, specific factors may be at work. In addition to their assumption that phonics drills are inherently tedious, many teachers believe they already *are* teaching phonics, not realizing the need to do it systematically. Resistance may also stem from the emphasis by scientists and policy makers on its importance; teachers know there's more to reading than decoding, but they haven't heard enough about the components *beyond* phonics, so they dismiss the mandate to teach it as overly simplistic.

For some, the antipathy to phonics is so strong they may reject even evidence they see with their own eyes. In the 1990s, before Reading First, a teacher at a high-poverty elementary school wanted to experiment with a reading program that relied on systematic phonics. Like many other schools at the time, this one had embraced whole language. The principal, Anthony Pedriana, didn't have any doubts about the method, but he was puzzled by the school's inability to boost reading proficiency beyond 30 percent. So he told the teacher, Gayle Gorman, to go ahead.

Gorman was given a group of twenty-two second-graders, all struggling readers. Normally, Pedriana recounts, the school would have tried various "special interventions": individual counseling for students in foster care, vision and hearing screenings, behavior plans for disruptive kids. Gorman's students got none of that. Nevertheless, after a year of systematic phonics, she managed to get all but one reading on grade level. The following year, the same students scored proficient or advanced on the state reading test. The benefits not only to students' reading but to their self-esteem were enormous, and Pedriana decided to adopt phonics schoolwide.

But the plan ran up against resistance. The kindergarten teachers protested that the phonics drills were developmentally inappropriate, and others were loath to follow a largely scripted program. The very words Pedriana used to describe the new approach—*direct, intensive, systematic*—"were enough to cause allergic reactions among whole-language purists and others who purported to uphold the spirit of child-centrism," he writes. "Showing the efficacy of such an approach was not a message they were willing to accept under any circumstances. It was like asking a Christian fundamentalist to embrace the spirit of Allah."

When new information is inconsistent with our existing beliefs, we experience mental discomfort—which we resolve by rejecting the information, regardless of the evidence. Psychologists call this tendency *confirmation bias*, which can be explained by another well-established psychological concept, *cognitive dissonance*. That tendency can be reinforced if those around us also reject the information, as much of the education community has done with phonics. And members of the helping professions—like teachers—may find it particularly difficult to accept evidence that undermines their self-concept. If you've devoted much of your life to improving people's lives, and information comes along to suggest you're actually harming them, that can be an extremely difficult pill to swallow. Doctors in mid-nineteenth-century Vienna, for example, refused to accept the strong evidence presented by one of their colleagues that washing their hands before delivering babies would reduce maternal deaths from what was called "childbed fever." Instead, they got rid of the colleague, Ignaz Semmelweis.

Of course, many teachers are receptive to scientific findings once they've been introduced to them. For the others, one approach psychologists warn against is the one taken by Semmelweis—to tell people experiencing cognitive dissonance they're stupid, irrational, or cruel. Better to focus on their existing goals and values and explain how evidence-based practices will serve them.

Teachers who reject phonics surely want their students to learn to appreciate literature, acquire knowledge independently, and love reading. I'm not sure how to convince skeptics that the most effective route to accomplishing those objectives is to teach phonics systemically while building knowledge through read-alouds and discussion. But I do know that far too often, teachers are simply told to do things without having the underlying reasons explained—and without enough of an opportunity to explore and investigate these reasons for themselves. That's no more likely to change beliefs and behavior than Semmelweis's harangues about handwashing in nineteenth-century Vienna—or, for that matter, the harangues of another irate Viennese in the twentieth century, Rudolf Flesch.

OCTOBER 2016

Ms. Arredondo is seated behind a kidney-shaped table across from five students, ready for guided reading.

Every day for ninety minutes, students are divided into three groups: the Dolphins, the Tigers, and the Turtles. One reads under her guidance for half an hour while the other two alternate between working independently at computer stations or reading books of their choice at their individual levels. The groups rotate at thirty-minute intervals, so that by the end of the literacy block each group has had a turn reading with Ms. Arredondo.

Today's book—the first one of the year—is the classic *Brown Bear, Brown Bear, What Do You See?* The first page repeats the question in the title, to which the brown bear answers, *I see a red bird looking at me.* On the next page there's an illustration of a red bird with the question, *Red Bird, Red Bird, What do you see?* The red bird sees a yellow duck, the yellow duck sees a blue horse, and so on.

Yesterday, Ms. Arredondo introduced the book and went over the vocabulary. Today, the children will be reading it for the first time and responding in their journals. She asks a few preliminary questions: What's the title? Who's the author? What does an author do? Then she demonstrates how to read in a "whisper voice."

When students are done, they copy their favorite picture from the book or read a page aloud while Ms. Arredondo listens for mistakes. Tomorrow they'll reread it, add some written responses to their drawings, and work on the week's comprehension skill, "main idea."

Given that nothing much happens in *Brown Bear*, I ask Ms. Arredondo what the "main idea" could possibly be. She acknowledges there really *isn't* one, but that's a problem with a lot of books at beginning reading levels. What she's planning, she says, is to guide students to seeing the "pattern of the book," which she identifies as the idea that "these were animals with different colors."

Although Ms. Arredondo is supposed to spend a little over half an hour teaching either social studies or science two days a week, so far she has found time for only one social studies unit, which extended over two days—a grand total of only about one hour devoted to anything other than reading or math. I had asked her to alert me to opportunities to observe a social studies lesson, but I only heard about this one after the fact.

The subject was mapping. The class read a story about a girl who visits various shops in her neighborhood—which the students plotted on a map—and another about a girl who maps her bedroom and the places her dog likes to visit. They also watched videos of songs about the continents and talked about them. Finally, they made maps of the world by coloring labeled cutouts of the continents and pasting them onto paper.

Most of the maps, displayed on the class bulletin board, have the continents in approximately the right places, but others are highly idiosyncratic. One has Africa situated below North America, South America in the top right corner, and Antarctica off to the left, parallel with Africa. Ms. Arredondo isn't sure whether her students grasped the concept of continents. "I don't think they have the idea of countries or states yet," she says. "We don't test it, so it's hard to know."

But continents weren't really the point. The mapping unit, like Ms. Arredondo's lesson on captions, was part of an effort to acquaint students with the concept of labels—just as Ms. Bauer's lesson about flags at Reeves Elementary was more an effort to teach about symbols than anything substantive about flags or history. And from that perspective, the lesson was successful.

"I think they got the idea that maps are things that represent something else," Ms. Arredondo says.

Ms. Masi's second-graders are also working with maps. Today, it's maps of ancient Greece that they've labeled with various locations they've learned about, like Athens and Sparta.

"What was something *unique* about civilizations in ancient Greece?" Ms. Masi asks, calling on them to compare Greece to the other ancient civilizations they've studied, while using a recent vocabulary word.

"Something unique was that they weren't near a river and they didn't have any fertile soil," says one boy, "so it was difficult for them to farm."

Ms. Masi began today's lesson by reminding students of what they've learned about kings and queens and explaining that things worked differently in Athens. Then she orchestrated a mock election, with students voting for one of three Greek gods (Athena, Poseidon, or Apollo) to be "president" of the class. This, she told them, is how rulers are chosen in a *democracy*, one of today's vocabulary words. Given that this class is taking place shortly before the 2016 election, the topic is timely.

When Athena was declared the winner, with Poseidon a close second, the result was greeted by a mixture of cheers and groans. That's how it works in a democracy, Ms. Masi explained, asking students if they know who the two main presidential candidates are (they do). Some people will be happy and others won't, but "the point is that in a democracy you have the opportunity to give your vote and for your vote to be heard."

The read-aloud is a story about two friends who walk around their hometown of Athens, commenting on its architecture and statues and passing their elected leader, Pericles. The text mentions that women couldn't vote and that boys—but not girls—had the right to attend school. Ms. Masi pauses to ask if that was fair and then asks what *fair* means.

After a couple of false starts, a boy named Amir—whose behavior is often disruptive—raises his hand. "Fair means like, if I gave Joshua some chips, and I get more . . . that's not fair."

"Why not?" Ms. Masi prods. "Because fair means . . ."

"Because it means equal."

"Thank you," Ms. Masi says. "Because fair means equal. So if we say some people get to go to school and others do not, that doesn't sound fair to me."

Later, Ms. Masi leaves a Post-it on Amir's desk that says, "When you are focused you are an amazing example—like when you explained what fair means." Earlier, Amir had been making rude noises with his lips and occasionally wandering around the classroom. But after seeing the Post-it from Ms. Masi, he sits quietly, paying close attention.

The read-alouds provide students with more than just information.

They can be jumping-off points for discussions about topics like fairness, and they can build students' self-esteem by enabling them to show off their knowledge and—as in Amir's case—the insights they're capable of contributing.

They also provide opportunities for students to engage in one of the comprehension strategies beloved by balanced-literacy teachers: making text-to-self connections. In a typical elementary classroom, teachers often "prepare" students to read a text by asking about relevant personal experiences beforehand. If the story is about a family reunion, the teacher may first ask if any students have attended one. These discussions may ramble and last longer than the reading and discussion of the text itself. But in Ms. Masi's classroom, the connections can emerge naturally from the content—during or after reading the text rather than before.

In one recent class, Ms. Masi tells me, the discussion centered on whether Alexander the Great's "ambitious nature" was "an inspiration or a flaw." Some students argued he was wrong to invade other people's lands, but Ms. Masi observed that if you were his follower, you might consider that a *good* thing. At that point, she said, some of the students of Ethiopian descent—who comprise about half the class—started "making comparisons to Ethiopia, where people were coming in and taking land away."

Ms. Masi wasn't sure what events they were referring to. But she was amazed by their ability to extract the concepts of ambition and conquest—and fairness—and apply them to an experience close to their own lives.

"I had thought that maybe we don't give their culture enough attention," Ms. Masi said, "but here they were, making a connection."

On another day, I listened as the students thoughtfully debated strategy at the Battle of Thermopylae, when the Greeks held off the much larger Persian army by trapping it in a narrow pass. But later that day, during a guided reading lesson in comparing and contrasting, some of the same students missed the fact that Canadians celebrate Thanksgiving in October rather than November.

Does that mean they need more practice in "skills" like comparing and contrasting? Or should they spend more time comparing and contrasting, for example, what they've learned about ancient Athens and

Sparta? (Their written answers about the differences between the two city-states revealed some misunderstandings.) Maybe they were just less interested in the simple text about Thanksgiving and were paying less attention: readers actually learn better from more complex text, as long as they have sufficient background knowledge on the topic, perhaps because the challenge engages them.

Ms. Masi isn't sure why students missed the point about Thanksgiving being celebrated in different months. But if she had her druthers, she would spend more time on text sets—groups of books organized around a single topic, like the set on mummies her students read last year. In conjunction with the Core Knowledge units on ancient Asian and Greek civilizations, students are now reading books about life in the ancient Indus River Valley and the creation of the Greek alphabet.

True, most of the time the students are listening and following along as Ms. Masi reads aloud rather than reading the texts themselves. But they're also acquiring the knowledge and vocabulary that will enable them to make sense of the increasingly sophisticated material they'll confront as they progress through school.

CHAPTER 5

Unbalanced Literacy

ONE JANUARY MORNING IN 2003, a Columbia University education professor named Lucy Calkins was sitting in an empty auditorium in Brooklyn, waiting for a press conference to begin—and wondering where everyone else was. She was also wondering why she'd been summoned there.

All she knew was that she'd gotten a call a few days before from the office of New York City's schools chancellor, Joel Klein, asking her to attend. She also knew Klein would be announcing the literacy curriculum he had chosen for elementary and middle schools throughout New York's sprawling system. Calkins had dressed in black, expecting the worst: one of the textbook-based programs distributed by major publishing companies—in other words, a basal reader.

By 2003, the basals—which were still being used in half or more of American schools—had embraced a phonics-focused approach to decoding. Calkins, a whole-language veteran and leading balanced-literacy theorist, held the basals, and phonics instruction in general, in low regard. Against the background of the Reading Wars, "balanced literacy" came to signify a peace treaty: children would learn the correspondence between sounds and letters of the alphabet, but they would also be exposed to rich literature for meaning and pleasure. The flag of whole language was quickly lowered, and educators rushed to gather proudly under the banner of balanced literacy. After all, who could oppose either *balance* or *literacy*?

But the movement's leaders have primarily been educators who, like Calkins, were fervent advocates of whole language. They've preserved its opposition to systematic phonics while maintaining they *are* teaching phonics, whenever the need seems to arise. And they continue to believe fervently in giving children their choice of "authentic" literature rather than requiring them to read any particular texts—including decodable ones. Critics have charged that balanced literacy is little more than the same old approach with a new label. Some defenders of whole language have candidly agreed.

Still, balanced literacy is far more structured than whole language. Instead of giving children free rein, balanced-literacy teachers confine their choices to books at their "just right" level. Rather than roaming at will through classroom centers, children rotate at set intervals. There's also a writing component, pioneered by Calkins, that stresses free choice and individual self-expression. And, of course, there's daily instruction in comprehension skills, a practice originally associated with basal readers and one that whole-language theorists opposed.

Calkins's base is the Columbia Teachers College Reading & Writing Project, which she founded in 1981. By the time she was waiting for Klein's press conference to begin, a couple of hundred New York City public schools, many in affluent areas, had adopted her version of balanced literacy. Around the world, thousands of teachers had been trained by her and her team. An intense, energetic woman who speaks passionately about inspiring children with a love of reading and writing, Calkins had many devoted followers. But as far as she knew, Klein was not one of them.

He had been installed as chancellor the year before, after newly elected mayor Michael Bloomberg managed to obtain complete control over the city's schools—all 1,400 of them, with their 80,000 teachers and 1.1 million students. The problems were obvious: almost half the city's fourth-graders and two-thirds of its eighth-graders were reading below grade level. Only about 50 percent of high school students managed to graduate on time. In the spring of 2002, New York State had for the first time released test scores that were broken down by race and ethnicity, revealing that black and Hispanic students in the city were doing far worse than white and Asian ones. Bloomberg had campaigned on a promise to improve these figures and was willing to accept the responsibility for delivering—but only if he could run the schools as he saw fit.

Klein had no background in education, but his experience had convinced him of its life-changing potential. He had gone from the New York City public schools to Columbia University and then to Harvard Law School and a glittering career as a top antitrust lawyer and successful businessman. Like Bloomberg, he felt a sense of mission about shaking up the entrenched interests—particularly the teachers' union—that he believed were blocking a similar trajectory for many students. One problem that struck Klein right off the bat was that schools were using what he called a "chaotic mishmash" of curricula—not uncommon in a large district. Determined to quickly identify a single high-quality literacy curriculum for all elementary and middle schools, he had convened a committee of local education officials to make recommendations. Now he was about to unveil his decision.

Calkins had every reason to fear Klein would choose a basal program that incorporated phonics. In a speech the week before, Bloomberg had called for just that, and the George W. Bush administration—bolstered by the National Reading Panel's report—had tied federal funds to that approach. Besides, balanced literacy was considered to be at the liberal end of the political spectrum, and Bloomberg and Klein—in the context of New York politics—were conservatives, or at least traditionalists.

As Calkins was waiting for the event to start, a Klein aide ran in and said, "Oh, *there* you are, Lucy. Come on!"

Calkins was rushed upstairs to the correct room and directed to stand between Carmen Fariña, a regional superintendent and a good friend, and Randi Weingarten, the head of the New York City teachers' union.

"Why am I the bridesmaid at this wedding?" Calkins remembers thinking. "And then the cameras start, and Joel announces that the Teachers College Reading and Writing Project is the curriculum for New York City."

Calkins was dumbstruck—as were the advocates of phonics. Why would Bloomberg and Klein suddenly throw their weight behind a touchy-feely pedagogical method that was unlikely to work for the city's neediest kids?

Eventually, Klein was forced to adopt a supplementary phonics program to avoid losing millions in federal funds. Years later, he would say that choosing Calkins's balanced-literacy curriculum was the only regret he had about his tenure as chancellor. And not just because it gave short shrift to phonics. Ultimately, he concluded that balanced literacy's fundamental flaw was that it prevented low-income students from acquiring what they needed most: knowledge.

BALANCED LITERACY HAS come to be defined by two practices that were alien to whole language: leveled reading and reading comprehension instruction.

The roots of leveled reading lie in a famous "study" in the 1940s, whose very existence has been challenged by a modern-day reading expert. But it didn't become significant until the 1980s, when teachers began tossing aside their basal readers and replacing or supplementing them with commercially available books. To determine which books were right for each student, they began conducting periodic "running records," listening for the number of mistakes a student makes while reading a passage. A pair of education professors named Irene Fountas and Gay Su Pinnell developed a system that analyzed the complexity of commercially available books according to ten different factors, including sentence structure and vocabulary, and assigned them letters of the alphabet corresponding to students' reading levels.

Under the basal system, all students read texts deemed to be at their grade level. But with balanced literacy, students are confined to books at their individual levels. A balanced-literacy teacher might find that a second-grader can't read beyond Level D with the required 95 percent accuracy and comprehension and direct the student to a basket of *D* books—a kindergarten level. The second-grade levels are K through M. The theory is that struggling readers will gradually move up the ladder of text complexity until they catch up.

One problem for beginning readers is that leveled readers don't conform to whatever phonics rules they may have been taught. Since the books are "authentic" children's literature—and therefore not aligned to any particular sequence of phonics instruction—that kind of limitation is impossible. Nor do reading-level tests try to match students with books on subjects they know something about.

Despite their wide use, measures like Fountas and Pinnell's don't reliably predict comprehensibility, and different formulas can result in different classifications for the same texts. In fact, there's evidence that leveled reading not only fails to boost children's learning, it can inhibit it. Under the leveled-reading system, teachers don't *teach* students the content and vocabulary they need to access more complex text. Instead, books themselves are expected to do that work, even though students are limited to books that largely consist of words and concepts they already understand.

But, balanced-literacy advocates like Lucy Calkins respond, students who work with leveled readers aren't just *reading*. They're practicing the comprehension skills and strategies that—in theory—will enable them to glean more and more meaning from their leveled texts. And that brings us to the other major component that distinguishes balanced literacy from the original concept of whole language: the enthusiastic embrace of reading comprehension strategies.

Basal readers have included questions designed to assess comprehension since the late nineteenth century. In the 1920s, the emphasis shifted to developing comprehension rather than just testing it. Basals began to include activities to help students practice discrete "skills" like finding the main idea and drawing conclusions. By the 1950s, the approach was deeply entrenched. Still, academics debated whether comprehension was something that could be taught as opposed to something that arose naturally from a combination of intelligence and experience.

By the '80s, declines in SAT scores and other measures had made the question urgent. Studies focused not on the skills taught in the basals but on "strategies" skilled readers used naturally: the idea was to guide poor readers to use the same techniques to monitor and control their thinking, a process called *metacognition*. Results were promising. But at least one expert—P. David Pearson, a professor of education at Berkeley—still entertained doubts about whether comprehension could be taught. What about the abundance of research showing that background knowledge was the most important factor in understanding any text?

"If this is true," Pearson and a coauthor mused in 1988, "then one way to improve reading comprehension might be to help students learn more about everything. . . . If teachers put the focus on helping students deal with the content, perhaps comprehension skill acquisition will occur almost incidentally." There was also a "final sobering possibility," he continued. "What if teachers make the task far more complicated than it really is? We have to consider the possibility that all the attention we are asking students to pay to their use of skills and strategies and to their monitoring of these strategies may turn relatively simple and intuitively obvious tasks into introspective nightmares."

The same year, one of the godfathers of whole language, Frank Smith, dismissed the idea of teaching comprehension in the abstract. "We can only infer, predict, and think critically with respect to specific subject matter," Smith wrote, "and if a subject is foreign to us then we will not be able to demonstrate any thinking ability."

But many teachers were already heading in a different direction. By the late 1980s, the whole-language movement had begun to take on a more institutionalized flavor. Teachers and "staff developers" were publishing books that drew other teachers like moths to a flame, fueling the movement's rapid growth. They wrote in voices that were direct, intimate, and passionate—not an out-of-touch expert issuing dictates from an ivory tower but a fellow teacher sharing anecdotes, experiments, and missteps.

One such teacher-author was Lucy Calkins, who advocated that elementary students be encouraged to write freely in "writers' workshops." A few years later, she was joined by Nancie Atwell, a middle school English teacher who wrote an enormously influential book detailing how she had abandoned teacher-led instruction in favor of "readers' workshops," in which students simply read books of their choice and thereby discovered a love of reading. Calkins and her team, along with like-minded educators, led training sessions for teachers around the country at Columbia University's Teachers College.

One place where the readers' and writers' workshop model quickly took root was Denver. Teachers there were soon reveling in their freedom from basal readers and fill-in-the-blank worksheets. Students were sprawling on classroom rugs and curling up in comfy chairs, reading for long stretches, choosing "just right" books. Student-created writing and projects covered the classroom walls and spilled out into the hallway. Life was good.

And yet some educators were uneasy. "Nagging questions started keeping me up at night," recalled a teacher named Debbie Miller. "As I planned for the week ahead, I'd wonder, 'Am I really teaching kids everything they need to know about reading?' I kept thinking that something was missing: surely there must be something more for them, and me."

Ellin Keene, a staff developer in Denver, heard these doubts from Miller and other teachers. "The record remained stuck on the same groove," she wrote: " 'I'm not teaching these children how to read, how to read, how to read.' "

Essentially, whole-language teachers had talked themselves out of a job. If all that was required for kids to learn to read was to just *read*, what was their role? Another problem was that not all students were able to understand what they were reading. Still, teachers didn't want to return to basals and comprehension skills. They needed to find something else.

One day in the early 1990s, Ellin Keene gave Debbie Miller an article she'd come across coauthored by none other than P. David Pearson, by now—in an about-face of unknown origin—an enthusiastic advocate of reading comprehension strategies. At first, wrote Miller, "my eyes glazed over. Who were these guys, anyway? And what did they know about teaching real kids in real classrooms? Yes, I knew something was missing in my readers' workshop. I'd been saying I wanted rigor. And yes, I trust Ellin. But come on! This stuff seemed way too ivory tower to me."

And yet the article seemed to provide the very solution she had been seeking. Pearson and his coauthors listed seven strategies used by "expert" readers: connecting new and existing information, for example, or synthesizing information across texts. Most involved activating prior knowledge or schema, but Pearson's point was that proficient readers understood instinctively that they needed to draw on their existing knowledge to make sense of what they were reading; poor readers often did not. The good news was that poor readers could be *taught* to do so.

Miller and Keene put aside their suspicion of ivory-tower academics and eagerly embraced Pearson's assertion that these strategies were a different animal from the old comprehension skills. Rather—in words that would resonate with any progressive educator—Pearson promised they would enable readers to "construct their own meaning."

Keene interpreted the research to mean that teachers should model one strategy at a time, spending weeks on each, and teach them year after year beginning in kindergarten—but in fact, no studies endorsed that approach. Teachers in Denver not only began introducing kids to strategies like activating schema, they tried using them in their own reading and found it could be annoying and distracting. But Keene decided that this "hyperawareness" was necessary to "empathize with the frustrations of our developing readers."

It's possible, though, that by pushing students to constantly be aware of their schema, teachers were unintentionally making reading *more* frustrating—turning "relatively simple and intuitively obvious tasks into introspective nightmares," as David Pearson had once worried. Certainly the experience of constantly monitoring your thinking doesn't conform to the ideal reading experience described by cognitive scientist Daniel Willingham—a process of which you're *un*aware, like looking through a clear pane of glass. Metacognition can be one more thing a reader's overloaded working memory has to juggle.

As MUCH AS she appreciated the power of schema and prior knowledge, Keene focused only on *activating* the knowledge that children already possessed rather than systematically trying to augment it. For some students, that wasn't a problem; Keene recalls a slightly obnoxious fifth-grader who showed her up by knowing more about the demise of the Anasazi people in the southwestern United States than she did. For others, though, it was a serious obstacle, especially when teachers decided to add nonfiction to the agenda.

Teachers in Denver were mystified by their students' lack of understanding when they turned to nonfiction. "These kids are fluent readers and many of them really like to read," they would tell Keene, "but it's as if this fog bank rolls in when they're hit with challenging nonfiction." Nonfiction, Keene explained, is "inconsiderate" text, meaning that it doesn't allow for deficiencies in background knowledge. But rather than suggesting building that knowledge, she decided to double down on strategy instruction.

Keene describes encountering a fifth-grader named Jeremy who is struggling to understand an encyclopedia entry on the American Revolution. She and Jeremy's teacher advise him to use the strategy of identifying which sentence is most important. Jeremy points to one that begins with the word *ammunition*, explaining he chose it because he likes guns. But, he adds, he doesn't understand the last half of the sentence, which includes terms like "Committee of Safety" and "provincial assembly." Rather than explaining their meaning, Keene agrees it can be hard to decide what's important in nonfiction. But, she advises, just do what "great readers" do: they "listen to that mental voice tell them which words, which sentences or paragraphs, and which ideas are most important."

Afterward, Keene and the teacher wonder if telling Jeremy to listen to his mental voice was no more helpful than the old, ineffective basal approach of telling students to practice the skill of "finding the main idea." But no, they decide: "We helped him to know specifically on what he should concentrate. Although it is a strategy used in many reading situations, proficient readers must focus on what is important as they find their way through inconsiderate text."

Over time, the distinction between the old reading skills and the new strategies has fallen away. While some reading experts continue to maintain that they are "very different things," most teachers now use the terms interchangeably.

In the 1980s and 1990s, Lucy Calkins was just one of several prominent balanced-literacy gurus. More recently, she has become by far the best known. *The Art of Teaching Writing*, originally published in 1986, is one of the most frequently assigned books in schools of education. Her most recent book, *Pathways to the Common Core*, reached number seven on the *New York Times*' list of bestselling education books in 2013.

Many elite private schools use her approach and send teachers to her workshops, as do many charter schools, including some in the nationwide KIPP network. According to her organization's website, her writing curriculum has been adopted by "thousands of districts, including many large cities." In addition, the organization partners with "scores of schools" in the New York City area, as well as in every state in the country and "a dozen very large US school districts."

To a large extent, Calkins owes her prominence to Joel Klein. During a transformative trip to San Diego around the time he became chancellor, Klein heard of a district in—of all places—New York City that seemed to be benefiting from a new approach called balanced literacy. He proceeded to surround himself with devotees, which was not hard to do: most of the city's thirty-two superintendents were in that category. Soon he installed Lucy Calkins's close friend and protégé, Carmen Fariña, in a key administrative position.

The only problem for Calkins was that, at the time of Klein's announcement in 2003 that New York City schools would adopt her curriculum, she didn't have a curriculum to offer. Balanced literacy was simply an instructional approach, largely reliant on training and coaching. Its components weren't codified in writing the way basal programs were. Calkins had written several books, but they were too discursive and general to serve as guides to classroom instruction. In fact, one of the tenets of balanced literacy was that it was impossible to teach in a scripted way. Teachers needed the flexibility to respond to the needs of individual students and the autonomy to exercise their own judgment. The very idea of mandating a curriculum—hers or anyone else's—was something to which she was philosophically opposed.

But she wasn't about to turn down the opportunity. After she recovered from the shock of hearing Klein announce that he'd chosen her "curriculum," she spent three weeks creating one. That project ultimately evolved into a series called the Units of Study, which by 2017 had grown to include three or four modules in both reading and writing for each grade from kindergarten through eighth, plus supplemental materials. They are in wide use not just in New York but across the United States. A researcher in Mississippi told me that Lucy Calkins is "big" in that state and that the Fountas and Pinnell leveled-reading system—with which her approach is often linked—"is in every school I go to."

In some ways, Calkins's Units of Study are even more skills-focused than the basals she scorns. The passages in the basals may be of uneven quality, but they're deemed to be on grade level and all students are exposed to the same ones. And while the basals emphasize skills over content, teachers can choose to focus on the content if they're so inclined. Calkins's curriculum, on the other hand, only provides teachers with a sequence of skills and strategies to briefly model, using whatever "authentic" text they want, before students scatter to practice on books *they* choose, at their individual reading levels—which may be far lower than their grade level. That makes it much more difficult for teachers to focus on content even if they want to, and it's less likely that struggling students will be exposed to grade-level text.

As a result of her content-agnostic approach, Calkins's "teaching points" and discussion questions are all framed in generic terms, on the theory that they can be applied to any text. That's true even of the non-fiction units she has recently produced in response to the demands of the Common Core. In a unit on the American Revolution for fourth-graders, for example, the lessons aren't actually *about* any events or figures of the era. Instead, their titles are phrases like "The Role of Emblematic Detail in Nonfiction," or "Readers Study All Parts of a Text to Determine Main Ideas." The idea is that some other topic could easily be substituted.

Subject-matter knowledge has its place, Calkins says—namely, in the social studies and science classes that elementary schools are often providing only in theory. Rather than seeing comprehension and analytical skills the way cognitive scientists do—as abilities that grow *from* knowledge and are inextricably intertwined with it—she believes they can be taught in the abstract and transferred to other subject matter. But a child who develops a feel for "the role of emblematic detail" in a book about the American Revolution is unlikely to understand a book about ancient China or even nineteenth-century American history if she knows nothing about those topics.

Calkins's curriculum shares one feature with basal readers: it can feel pretty scripted. After Klein mandated its use, one teacher complained, "Administrators expect all our reading and writing workshops to adhere to an unvarying and strict script. For example: 'Writers, today and everyday you should remember to revise your writing by adding personal comments about the facts.' Sometimes I feel like I'm a robot regurgitating the scripted dialogue that's expected of us day in and day out."

This surely wasn't what Calkins intended—although her Units of Study are full of such statements. But these days, many teachers who believe they're using balanced literacy engage in a variety of practices that those who created the movement wouldn't condone: looking to upcoming tests to decide what skill to focus on, for example, or having kids practice skills without monitoring their own thought processes. Most have added components that have little connection to the metacognitive techniques that so captivated Ellin Keene and Debbie Miller: literary concepts like setting and character, nonfiction "text features" like captions and glossaries, and old basal standbys like sequence-of-events and cause-and-effect.

In 2013, Keene herself expressed dismay at what had happened to reading strategy instruction since the publication of her influential book *Mosaic of Thought* in 1997. She complained that many teachers had adopted a "lockset—and boring—emphasis on identifying and naming the strategies," teaching them in a "rigid, formulaic fashion." She placed the blame on "scripted, packaged programs that leave no room for thoughtful discussion, exploration of passions, or a commitment to encouraging thinking."

It's not clear Keene meant to include Calkins's program in that category, and certainly Calkins can't be held responsible for every sin committed in the name of balanced literacy. But the Units of Study have greatly expanded her influence, which was already significant. Having emerged from a movement that frowned on "scripted, packaged programs" produced by commercial publishers, Calkins now sits atop a publishing empire of her own.

Scripts themselves aren't the problem. They can be valuable resources for novice teachers. And the kind of boring and formulaic recitation of strategies that Keene decried is no doubt occurring in many balanced-literacy classrooms where teachers *aren't* following a script. The real question is whether the script foregrounds skills and strategies at the expense of knowledge.

WHILE CALKINS'S CURRICULUM was spreading across the country, Joel Klein—the man who had sparked its creation—was beginning to have his doubts. He and others were questioning whether students, and especially those at the lower end of the socioeconomic spectrum, were getting anything of value from it. Although the city's fourth-graders were showing improvement on national tests, scores for eighth-graders hadn't budged. Klein saw that teachers were often prioritizing having students make text-to-self connections rather than analyzing content.

"What caused the war?" asked a teacher in a class on the Civil War. "Slavery," a student answered.

"And what caused slavery?" the teacher continued.

"Racism," said another child.

"When the teacher then asked, 'Has anyone here experienced racism recently?'" Klein wrote, "half the students raised their hands and started talking about their own personal experiences. The class never got back to discussing the Civil War."

At the same time, Klein was beginning to pay attention to the ideas of an English professor and education theorist named E. D. Hirsch Jr., who had been arguing for twenty years that children from less-educated families needed a knowledge-building curriculum.

And then, Klein told me, "a weird thing happened." As he recalls it, in 2007, the head of Hirsch's Core Knowledge Foundation, Linda Bevilacqua, wrote an email to Hirsch in which she referred to something she'd seen in the news suggesting that Klein had taken an interest in a knowledge-focused approach. Somehow, Klein says, Bevilacqua inadvertently copied Klein on the email.

"It was something like, 'Wow, look who might be interested,'" Klein recalls. "It was clearly an email that was not intended [for me]—it was tongue-in-cheek about me. But that, as they say in *Casablanca*, was the beginning of a beautiful relationship. Because I wrote back and literally said to them, not only am I interested, I really want to learn a lot more."

Neither Hirsch nor Bevilacqua remembers the email incident, but they do recall that Klein contacted them. They were delighted; they had been trying to raise money to create a literacy curriculum and thought Klein might be able to help.

For many years, the Core Knowledge Foundation had been producing materials that schools could use to create their own content-focused curricula, but that required a lot of work. Hirsch had been hoping that publishers of basal readers would begin producing programs that incorporated richer material, but that hadn't happened. So Hirsch and Bevilacqua decided to create their own. If language arts was squeezing out history and science, they would bring history and science to language arts.

The result of Bevilacqua's errant email was a privately funded $2.4 million pilot that would test a content-rich approach in ten New York City schools—a forerunner of the Core Knowledge Language Arts curriculum now used by Center City. It incorporated the principles of systematic phonics instruction, including decodable readers, and covered a range of topics in some depth.

The pilot lasted three years, following a thousand students from kindergarten through second grade. In 2008, the same year the pilot began, Klein rescinded his mandate that all schools use Calkins's curriculum. When the results were released in 2012, they showed that students in the Core Knowledge schools scored significantly higher on reading comprehension tests than those in the comparison schools. They also came out ahead on tests of social studies and science knowledge.

Calkins objected that she hadn't personally worked with the comparison schools, and there was no way of knowing how faithfully any of them had adhered to her model. Nevertheless, after the results of the study came out, the city's Department of Education omitted her program from its list of recommended curricula.

BY THAT TIME, Joel Klein was no longer New York's schools chancellor. Now a firm believer in the need for content-focused curriculum, he says that if he'd still been in office when the study was completed, he would have moved "much, much more" toward a Core Knowledge approach. That is, if he could have.

"I mean," he says, "I had a hard time even just getting the pilot off the ground. Because New York is a balanced-literacy kind of town."

Indeed it is. When Bill de Blasio succeeded Michael Bloomberg as mayor of New York in 2013, his choice for schools chancellor was Carmen Fariña, who had helped convince Klein to adopt balanced literacy and then served as its chief enforcer. Taking the helm, Fariña sounded a retreat from Core Knowledge. Facts are learned "maybe to take tests," she observed, "but we learn thinking to get on in life." And she asserted that the leveled-reading approach is particularly well suited to students who know little English. "They're going to feel frustrated, alienated," Fariña said. "You need to put them on something they can accomplish and do fluently."

Within months, Fariña had arranged for Calkins to hold seminars for hundreds of the city's principals and teachers. In early 2015, she required dozens of the city's lowest-performing elementary and middle schools to implement Calkins's approach. The schools were told to set aside forty-five minutes a day for "just-right" reading, and to send their "best and brightest" teachers to be trained by Calkins's program. And the test-score gaps in New York continued to grow.

I WANTED TO see how Calkins's version of balanced literacy worked in practice, and she graciously arranged for me to visit a couple of New York City schools she's worked with that serve largely low-income populations. The teachers and administrators I spoke with were uniformly enthusiastic about Calkins's approach and credited it for raising test scores. But much of what I observed gave me pause.

In one classroom, a second-grade teacher was leading a small group in a nonfiction lesson, whose focus was described on a nearby sign as "figuring out topic," using a book called *Ponies*. The way to figure out a topic, she told the students, was to look at the title and then at words that repeat in the text. She turned to a chapter titled "Wild Ponies" and asked the students to listen as she modeled a "think-aloud."

"Wild Ponies," she read. "Okay, got it. Now I'm going to read and look for repeating words." She softly read at a fast clip, mumbling words like *Chincoteague* and *Assateague* in passing—words the kids themselves were unlikely to know. The only words she emphasized were *wild ponies*, which popped up many times.

"What words are repeating?" she asked. Before the students had a chance to answer, she reread the two pages for good measure, this time only saying aloud the words *wild ponies*: "Wild ponies . . . wild ponies . . . wild ponies . . . wild ponies. . . . So I think our topic is about . . . ?"

"Wild ponies," the kids replied.

In a fifth-grade class, the lesson focused on "author's perspective," using a book about the ways animals defend themselves. During her think-aloud, the teacher told the students, she would try to determine the author's perspective on scientists.

"So, I'm noticing that the author says [a scientist] 'tricked' a mantis shrimp," she mused. "Hmm, I like those word choices." She pointed to "the fact that the author adds information about scientists" and a photo in which the scientist was smiling, both of which, she said, indicated that the author "feels positive about the scientist."

It's hard to believe that students got much of value—or of interest—out of these lessons. Meanwhile, they didn't get a chance to learn anything much about ponies, scientists, or the mantis shrimp. (Which, according to one website, is "one of the most interesting crustaceans found in the ocean." Who knew?) Granted, I visited only two schools—albeit ones that Calkins's team had worked with directly, so presumably they were implementing her approach faithfully. But regardless of how well teachers generally conduct these lessons, a central problem remains: there is no *there* there.

Calkins points to data her organization has collected showing that New York City schools that use her approach do better on state reading tests than schools that don't—and that schools she's worked with directly do even better. But while the statistics she offers are disaggregated by race, ethnicity, and disability, they don't separate out students who are low-income—an odd omission, since schools are required by law to collect that information. And her methods have apparently never been evaluated by independent researchers—unusual for a program that is decades old.

The other evidence Calkins cites to prove her method's success is its popularity. Schools are clamoring to work with her and her team, she says, including many high-poverty ones. Popularity, however, is not equivalent to success. Balanced literacy and Calkins's Reading & Writing Project have both been around for at least thirty years—longer, if you count their close ancestor whole language. And yet the test-score gaps between racial and socioeconomic groups have remained as wide as ever. Now, with the advent of the Common Core and its demand that students read—and be tested on—complex and "inconsiderate" nonfiction text, those gaps are only becoming wider.

Many in the balanced-literacy camp say it's unrealistic to expect struggling students to read grade-level text, as the Common Core requires. But perhaps it's only unrealistic because the content-averse approach they have championed is what is holding those students back.

NOVEMBER 2016

Charts on the walls of Ms. Arredondo's classroom at Star Academy explain the difference between nouns, verbs, and adjectives and give examples, and a diagram that looks like a rudimentary drawing of a dachshund shows a long horizontal oval labeled "Main Idea" with two stubby legs for "Details." Other posters provide rhymes designed to help students remember the short *a* and short *e* sounds. At the front of the room are the same samples of student writing that have been there for weeks—sentences using the word *pal*. *A pal can help you wrok*, one reads. *A pal can be Dad*, says another. Yet another reads, cryptically, *A pal can play at the preu.*

I've scheduled a visit hoping to see a science lesson, since I missed the one social studies unit. But the school, concerned about reading and math scores, has suspended all science and social studies, as well as the two weekly half-hour sessions that are supposed to be devoted to writing. They want teachers to use the time to test students' reading levels using the Fountas and Pinnell system, a process that should theoretically have taken place at the beginning of the school year.

But because she hasn't yet received the materials to conduct reading tests, Ms. Arredondo is testing students in math. While she assesses small groups, the rest of the class is working independently on iPads or computers.

When I take a look at the math problems kids are working on, I begin to see how a lack of vocabulary can affect children's performance in subjects other than reading. A boy named Kevin is staring at his iPad screen, which reads, *Combine 8 and 3*. He presses the "listen" button but doesn't try to provide an answer.

"Do you know what *combine* means?" I ask.

He doesn't, so I explain that it means "add." Then—satisfied that I've put Kevin on the path to success—I walk around to observe what other students are doing. I see iPads displaying sentences like *Round 119 to the nearest ten* and *Find the area of the following triangle in square units.* If

Kevin doesn't know the meaning of *combine*, I wonder, can other kids understand words like *round* and *area*?

Then I see a boy named Marcus staring at a screen that reads, *What number comes before 84?* I watch as he puts in *85* and gets a try again message. He tries 86, then 87, and keeps getting the same response.

I crouch down beside him. "What comes before four?" I ask, thinking that the problem might be the size of the number.

"Five?" he guesses. No, I explain, that comes *after* four. What number comes *before* it?

Six? Seven? Eight?

It occurs to me that Marcus doesn't understand the meaning of *before*. So I jot down a number line for him on a piece of paper—1, 2, 3, 4—and write the words "before" on the left side and "after" on the right, then read them aloud as I point to them.

"Ohhh," Marcus says, the light dawning. He immediately clicks 83.

I decide to check back with Kevin to see if he's been able to combine eight and three yet. I find that he's just drawing bright pink lines on the iPad with his finger—one of the gizmo's numerous distracting capabilities.

"Can you answer the question?" I ask him.

"I don't want to," Kevin says with a sigh. "Can I play a game?"

By mid-November, Ms. Masi's classroom walls are a riot of posters and charts, attesting to the bounty of information the class has covered since the beginning of the year. It's easy for me to identify which Core Knowledge domain the students are now in the midst of: Greek myths, which comes after ancient Greek civilizations.

There's one poster for Arachne, the Weaver ("Why is Arachne transformed in this myth?"); another for Prometheus and Pandora (with vocabulary words including *foresight* and *terrifying*); one for Theseus and the Minotaur ("According to the myth, how did the Aegean Sea get its name?"); and one for Demeter and Persephone (*pine*, *despair*, *retrieve*).

There are also posters on past topics like Alexander the Great, Julius Caesar, the Punic Wars, and Daily Life in Ancient Rome, along with charts listing gods and goddesses and other characters in Greek myths.

On the wall displaying student writing, there are explanations of "how farming was important to the development of ancient civilizations," with accompanying illustrations. While it's clear that students are continuing to have difficulty with writing conventions, they seem to be grasping the content.

"Greece uses olive to cook and light lamps," one boy has written. "They used grapes to make wine."

Today is a "pausing point," intended to help students consolidate the knowledge they've acquired. Ms. Masi has divided the class into three groups that will rotate through a series of activities every twenty minutes. One group is working with a computer program called Lexia, which has nothing to do with what the class has been studying and is designed to improve general literacy skills. One screen reads, "The boy looked sick. He was . . ." The choices given for the end of the sentence are:

> *as green as a frog*
> *as green as the flu*
> *as green as mud*

I find all of these similes odd, but I assume the correct answer is the first.

A second group is engaged in a writing assignment that Ms. Masi has devised: Retell your favorite Greek myth in your own words, list at least three reasons why it's your favorite, and then change the ending. For example, she says, she would choose the myth of Daedalus and his son Icarus, but instead of having Icarus die after his wax wings melt off when he flies too close to the sun, she would have his father swoop in and rescue him.

Ms. Masi gives her students a list of five myths to choose from and coaxes them to start by retelling the myths orally, but they have trouble translating their thoughts into writing. It strikes me that she's underestimated the challenge of the task she's set for these kids, all of whom are still struggling with spelling and vocabulary, let alone sentence structure and the organization of paragraphs.

The Core Knowledge curriculum has its own writing component, but educators at Center City felt it was lacking and adopted a writing curriculum called Write Steps instead. At the beginning of the school year Ms. Masi was hopeful that she would be able to simply insert the Core Knowledge topics into the Write Steps program, but that's turned out to be difficult. And no one at Center City seems particularly happy with Write Steps anyway.

Things are going more smoothly out in the hall, which is being supervised by Ms. Masi's assistant teacher, Alexis Fields. Eight or nine students are rehearsing a play about Demeter and her daughter, Persephone, that Ms. Masi found online. The script portrays Persephone—who is abducted by Hades, the god of the underworld—as a rebellious teenager and Demeter as a doting mother. Hades says things like, "You're mine! All mine!!"

"Help me, Mother," the girl playing Persephone reads without expression.

After some coaching from Ms. Fields, Persephone manages to read the line again with more feeling. The girl playing Demeter stumbles over several words—*precious, rebels, darling*—but Ms. Fields provides help where needed.

Practicing their lines—and learning to say them with appropriate pronunciation and expression—is not only helping these kids acquire vocabulary but also developing their fluency. At the same time, they're reviewing what they've learned about the myth of Persephone. And despite the challenges, they seem to be enjoying themselves.

CHAPTER 6

Billions for Education Reform, but Barely a Cent for Knowledge

IN THE FALL OF 1993, Bill Gates—already one of the world's wealthiest men at the age of thirty-eight—took a long walk on a deserted, pristine beach in Zanzibar with his then fiancée, Melinda French. It was the first time either had been to Africa, and the longest Bill had ever spent away from Microsoft, the company he founded at nineteen. The couple wanted to see Africa's exotic animals and dramatic landscapes. But then something unexpected happened.

"What really touched us, actually, were the people, and the extreme poverty," Melinda French Gates recalled during a TED Talk in 2014. "We started asking ourselves questions. Does it have to be like this?"

The walk on the beach led to the creation of what ultimately became the world's largest private foundation, with assets of more than $40 billion and nearly 1,500 employees. In 2015 alone, it gave away over $4 billion, funding organizations in more than one hundred countries and all fifty states and the District of Columbia. The foundation came to have two main focuses: global health and poverty, an interest sparked by that visit to Africa; and, in the United States, education.

"Both of us have had amazing educations," Bill Gates said during the TED Talk, "and we saw that the way that the US could live up to its promise of equal opportunity is by having a phenomenal education system. And the more we learned, the more we realized we're not really fulfilling that promise."

The Bill & Melinda Gates Foundation is only one of many foundations that aim to improve public education. But Gates has been the leader of the pack, dispensing an average of about $300 million every year. It has funded so many different education groups and causes that, as one researcher observed, "it's easier to name which groups Gates doesn't support than to list all of those they do."

Still, as Bill Gates is quick to point out, his foundation's contributions are a tiny fraction of total spending on public education, which amounts to more than $600 billion a year. All the money philanthropists spend on K–12 education—about $2 billion annually—is only three-tenths of 1 percent of the total. To leverage that relatively minuscule amount, Gates wants his foundation to act as a kind of R&D lab, doing the research that no one else has an incentive to fund, in hopes it will lead to breakthroughs that schools across the country will replicate.

There's nothing new about American philanthropists pouring their resources into education. What *is* different about twenty-first-century philanthropists like the Gateses is that instead of just supporting and expanding existing institutions, they hope to fundamentally transform what they see as a broken system. Funding after-school arts or tutoring programs doesn't cut it anymore. Applying the ethos and lingo of their generally high-tech business backgrounds, they want to see returns on their "investments." They want to be "disruptive" and data-driven. And they're willing to put massive amounts of money where their mouths are.

The Gateses soon settled on one bedrock principle: making sure that every student is taught by what education reformers call a "highly effective" teacher.

"The fundamental key," Melinda said during the TED Talk, "is a great teacher in front of the classroom. If you don't have an effective teacher in the front of the classroom, I don't care how big or small the building is, you're not going to change the trajectory of whether that student will be ready for college."

The TED audience, lit by blue lights in the darkened auditorium, burst into thunderous applause.

In 1994, just a year after Bill and Melinda's fateful walk on the beach, an Indiana University graduate student named Doug Lemov also had an epiphany. While pursuing an advanced degree in English, Lemov took a part-time job tutoring the university's football players. A sweet, eager-to-please student named Alphonso was a particularly difficult case. When Lemov asked him to write a brief autobiography to introduce himself, the paragraph he produced didn't contain a single complete sentence and was virtually incomprehensible.

Indignant, Lemov assumed the university had bent the rules to admit a star player. But no, he discovered, Alphonso had been admitted on the strength of his academic qualifications. Not only had he been promoted year after year at his high school in the Bronx, the school had anointed him with good grades and enthusiastic teacher recommendations. Alphonso had every reason to see himself as well-prepared for college. Lemov's outrage spread to encompass an entire system that was cheating Alphonso and who knew how many other students of the education they deserved.

Within a few weeks, Lemov had abandoned his graduate school plans and embarked on a new career as a teacher and education reformer. He helped found a renowned charter school in Boston and later became managing director of a highly regarded charter network, based in the northeastern United States, called Uncommon Schools. Schools like Uncommon came to be called "no excuses" charters, in part because they refused to accept poverty as an excuse for poor academic performance and in part because of their strict behavioral code. The schools often managed to boost test scores. But Lemov felt something was still missing.

As he knew from his own experience, teachers didn't just naturally know how to maintain order and foster engagement in the classroom. The professional training most of them got wasn't much help. When Lemov had been a young teacher, he'd heard lots of lofty but vague advice, like "Have high expectations for your students," or "Teach kids, not content." But he couldn't figure out how to translate those maxims into action.

What did help were concrete tips from more experienced or proficient teachers. One colleague, for example, advised standing still when giving students directions: "If you're walking around passing out papers, it looks like the directions are no more important than all of the other things you're doing." Lemov tried the technique and found it worked. He decided to identify highly effective teachers—partly on the basis of their students' test scores—and learn from their "moves." That project ultimately became an international bestseller called *Teach Like a Champion: 49 Techniques that Put Students on the Path to College*.

It's hard to overstate the book's influence. Reading *Teach Like a Champion* for the first time, I had a sensation familiar to readers of Shakespeare: oh, I kept thinking, so *that's* where that came from. There's Technique 32, the ubiquitous direction to "SLANT" (Sit up, Listen, Ask and answer questions, Nod your head, Track the speaker); Technique 43, Positive Framing (instead of admonishing a student for looking at a friend, say, "Keana, I need your eyes forward"); and Technique 35, Props (public but brief accolades for students who have done something praiseworthy, like "Two claps for David").

Lemov came to the same basic conclusion as Bill and Melinda Gates: the fundamental building block of education reform is the teacher. Whether the solution is weeding out the bad teachers or trying to improve those who are subpar, make them better, the argument goes, and you'll improve education outcomes. Another way of putting it is that the reason poor kids do so much worse on standardized tests is that their teachers are inferior to the ones serving affluent kids.

That's the theory on which billions of dollars have been spent. But maybe it's only part of the story. Teacher quality is important, to be sure, but even the best teacher can get only so far in a system that has put knowledge beyond the reach of the kids who need it most. Perhaps the *what* of teaching—the content of the curriculum—is more significant than the *how*, the techniques that individual teachers use. Some observers now believe that the way to make a teacher truly effective is a method that has rarely been tried: making sure he has the best possible materials to work with.

BILL GATES STARTED with high school, because that's where the problems were most obvious. As he put it in a 2005 speech to governors attending the National Education Summit, "high schools are a crucial intervention point for equality because that's where children's paths diverge—some go on to lives of accomplishment and privilege; others to lives of frustration, joblessness, and jail."

His first foray into education was to help establish more than two thousand small high schools across the United States, affecting nearly eight hundred thousand students and spending more than $650 million, on the theory that students in small schools were more likely to develop personal relationships with teachers. But after several years, those schools showed only a slight improvement in reading scores and a decline in math.

One possible reaction would have been to look to middle and elementary grades, to see if children's paths begin to diverge long *before* high school. But the Gates Foundation decided it needed quicker and more disruptive results, something that would have nationwide impact. In 2007, it turned to teacher effectiveness. Traditionally, teachers were hired and promoted on the basis of their credentials: a bachelor's degree, state licensure and certification, coursework or a passing grade on a standardized test in a subject area. Their jobs were secure, barring some egregious offense. And nearly all got positive ratings from their principals, even if their students didn't seem to be learning much.

Casting about for a new direction, officials at Gates seized on research that identified a different measure of effectiveness: how a teacher's students performed on standardized tests. Studies showed that some teachers "added value": their students showed average or above-average gains as compared to students with similar demographics and previous test scores. Having one of the best teachers instead of the worst four years in a row, one group of researchers wrote, "would be enough to close the black-white test score gap."

"Ultimately," their paper concluded, "the success of U.S. public education depends upon the skills of the 3.1 million teachers managing classrooms in elementary and secondary schools around the country. Everything else—educational standards, testing, class size, greater accountability—is background, intended to support the crucial interactions between teachers and their students. Without the right people standing in front of the classroom, school reform is a futile exercise."

Gates officials recruited one of the paper's authors—Thomas Kane, an economist at the Harvard Graduate School of Education—to head their research department. The foundation turned to developing ways to track teacher performance and making it easier to fire the ones who didn't measure up.

At the same time, it was influencing government policy. Under President Barack Obama, some of the top hires at the Department of Education either came directly from Gates or had ties to it—including Education Secretary Arne Duncan, who had led the Chicago public school system at a time when it received $20 million from the foundation. Under Duncan, the Department of Education provided powerful incentives for states to begin evaluating teachers and principals partly on the basis of value-added measurements. By 2015, the number of states requiring that such data be considered in teacher evaluations had almost tripled, rising from fifteen to forty-three. States have also been required to report the percentage of students at each school who score proficient on tests— broken down into racial and socioeconomic subgroups—and legislation in effect during the Obama years specified a series of consequences triggered by failure to make progress.

Tying tenure and compensation to performance certainly seems to make more sense than simply hiring teachers on the basis of paper credentials and then paying little attention to what they're actually doing. But figuring out how to evaluate effectiveness accurately and fairly proved to be trickier than the researchers anticipated. Once the worst teachers were eliminated, reformers found themselves confronting much the same situation as before: the vast majority of teachers were rated effective or highly effective, even though student achievement hadn't made discernible progress. Teachers also complained that their ratings could vary signifi- cantly from one year to the next and that tests can't measure all learning.

It's not just teachers who have been evaluated using reading and math scores. Under No Child Left Behind, schools were rated that way as well—and simply on the basis of the percentage of students who scored proficient, as opposed to the "growth" measures used to evaluate teachers. Given the test-score gap, it was virtually impossible for schools serving lower-income students to win ratings that equaled those given to schools serving a more affluent population. Legislation that replaced NCLB in 2015 gave states some flexibility in rating schools and teachers, but most have chosen essentially to preserve the status quo.

Perhaps the most damaging consequence of this system is that it's sent the message that subjects other than reading and math aren't im- portant. That leads many teachers to focus on the supposed skills that appear to be tested on reading assessments. Even in the rare instances when some school officials try to communicate the futility of skills- focused instruction to teachers—as is the case in Washington, D.C.— the continued use of test scores to evaluate success can make it hard to get the message across. One fourth-grade teacher who was charged with teaching both literacy and social studies told me she'd like to focus more on social studies, "but there are no consequences attached to under- standing or misunderstanding the content." Even when teaching social studies, she foregrounds comprehension skills over content; perhaps that's why during a unit on European explorers—on a day when, as luck would have it, she was being observed by an administrator—a student confidently declared that the country Columbus discovered was China.

Still, she said, "What counts for teachers at the end of the day is that students need their strategies. They need to be able to tackle difficult texts. The test isn't going to be a quiz about where the Navajo people resided, or is this a sedimentary rock, or whatever. . . . On the [test], none of the passages had anything to do with what we studied."

There's another huge problem with using scores as a lever to boost teacher—and student—performance: they can't tell an ineffective teacher how to improve. As the education journalist Dana Goldstein has written, "The hope that collecting more test scores will raise student achievement is like the hope that buying a scale will result in losing weight." And the reformers' initial theory that they could simply fire their way to a more effective teaching force ran up against the reality that there are more than three million teachers in the country. Most—the good-but-not-great ones—need to be helped rather than replaced.

The Gates Foundation recognized this relatively quickly. Around the time Doug Lemov's book *Teach Like a Champion* came out, in 2010, the foundation also hit upon the idea of observing and filming successful teachers. Rather than intending to provide tips directly to teachers, as Lemov did, Gates hoped to advise education policy makers. And while Lemov did his research on a shoestring, enlisting a wedding videographer to travel around with him, Gates officials had ample resources at their disposal. They spent $50 million on a three-year randomized controlled trial that filmed some three thousand teachers, producing videos of more than thirteen thousand lessons that were analyzed by dozens of trained experts. They also undertook five-year partnerships with several school districts and charter networks that were open to changing the way they hired, evaluated, and compensated teachers, at a total cost of $575 million, about a third of which was borne by Gates.

The results of the filming project, however, were inconclusive, and certainly less helpful to teachers than Lemov's taxonomy of effective classroom "moves." Teachers who were effective one year were also effective the next, so they were doing something right; it just wasn't clear *what*. As for the partnership effort, a five-hundred-page report concluded that it failed to boost teacher quality or student learning; one education policy analyst argues the data even shows a "significant and negative overall effect on test scores."

SCHOOL SYSTEMS HAVE long had their own way of increasing teacher effectiveness—or trying to—with massive amounts of on-the-job training, called *professional development,* or *PD.* American school systems spend as much as $18 billion a year on PD, which can translate into $15,000 to $20,000 per teacher. The problem with PD is that it hasn't worked. Teachers often see it as a waste of time, and studies back that up. Most PD, the Gates Foundation reported, is "highly fragmented and characterized by key disconnects between what decision-makers intend and the professional learning teachers actually experience." In 2015, an education reform nonprofit called TNTP studied three large public school districts and one charter network and concluded there was no evidence that any particular kind of PD helped teachers become more effective.

"As much as we wish we knew how to help all teachers improve," the authors of the report wrote, "we do not. . . . Every development strategy, no matter how intensive, seems to be the equivalent of a coin flip. . . . The pervasive beliefs that 'we know what works,' that more support for teachers is inherently good regardless of the results, and that development is the key to instructional excellence have all contributed to a vision of widespread teaching excellence just over the horizon that is mostly a mirage."

But some observers discerned a glimmer of hope amid those bleak findings. The PD provided by the charter network Achievement First had a far greater effect than that provided by the three traditional public school districts. Using multiple measures of teacher effectiveness—including value-added and classroom observations—the report found that seven out of ten teachers improved each year at Achievement First, as compared to three out of ten elsewhere. The report didn't place much weight on those results because the researchers hadn't been able to find a "magic formula of teacher supports that we can link to that growth." But Doug Lemov felt the key to Achievement First's success lay in the network's "culture": an ethos of continual improvement, fueled by regular in-class coaching and feedback as opposed to a series of disconnected one-off PD workshops with little follow-up. Rather than getting six pieces of advice—some of it conflicting—from six different sources, teachers at Achievement First were getting clear, consistent direction from one or two individuals.

Rachel Leifer, then an education-focused program officer at the Leona M. and Harry B. Helmsley Charitable Trust, also saw some positive takeaways. For her, the explanation lay in the fact that administrators and instructional coaches at Achievement First not only advised teachers *how* to teach; they also told them *what* to teach, and then they grounded their advice on pedagogical technique in that content. That's very different from most PD, which might advise teachers on, say, how to foster critical thinking in general. Content-specific PD would focus on fostering critical thinking about invertebrates or Greek myths—or whatever the curriculum calls for. In other words, traditional PD has suffered from the same defect as elementary literacy instruction: it has tried to develop skills disconnected from content. That approach hasn't worked any better with adults than with children.

Recent evidence indicates that Lemov and Leifer were both right: for PD to be effective, it has to be part of a cycle of continuous improvement, *and* it has to be embedded in specific content—preferably content that is part of a coherent, cumulative curriculum.

It's true, as education reformers like Gates and Lemov initially assumed, that the best way to improve education is to improve the effectiveness of teachers. But it turns out that the best way to do *that* is to coach teachers in how to deliver content. That means schools need to provide that content in the first place, so that teachers can focus their energies on delivery. In many schools, teachers are responsible for figuring out both what to teach *and* how to teach it—a nearly impossible task.

Things have only gotten worse with the advent of the Common Core. Because existing textbooks and instructional materials often aren't aligned with those standards, teachers have to scrounge for classroom materials, usually online, and try to come up with their own lesson plans. "It's like expecting the waiter at your favorite restaurant to serve your meal attentively while simultaneously cooking for twenty-five other people—and doing all the shopping and prepping the night before," observes education commentator and former teacher Robert Pondiscio.

A SMALL but growing band of education funders—including Rachel Leifer—has concluded that the place to start is curriculum. Without a high-quality curriculum, no amount of PD or coaching will work, and even a great teacher will eventually hit a wall. In countries that perform well on international tests, like Singapore and Finland, teacher preparation is based in detailed, content-focused curricula, and new teachers aren't expected to develop lessons from scratch. But in the United States, schools of education have no standard curricula in which to ground training, and in any event, their prevailing philosophy is opposed to the very concept; some professors even discourage teacher-candidates from relying on textbooks, encouraging them to create their own materials. With high-poverty schools losing 20 percent of their faculty every year, providing inexperienced teachers with good materials and content-specific training could have a huge impact.

Still, most American education philanthropists haven't seen much value in curriculum. Leifer recalls telling an education reform "thought leader" about the strategy she was spearheading at the Helmsley Charitable Trust to provide teachers with content-rich materials. The reaction was, "Why would you do *that*?" In fact, education funders have paid little attention to *anything* that goes on inside classrooms. They've been far more likely to focus on measuring results, usually in the form of test scores, or on giving students and families "choice" by supporting charter schools and tuition vouchers. And despite their ostensible focus on narrowing the test-score gap, hardly any philanthropists or reformers have focused on the dearth of high-quality curriculum where it has the greatest potential to level the playing field: elementary school.

The reason, some say, is the lack of data. Where are the "proof points"— schools getting vastly different results with low-income kids that can be traced to a content-focused curriculum? But philanthropists have invested in many initiatives without proof points. Some, including Gates, invested millions in the Common Core without any evidence the standards would boost achievement. And Gates's description of his foundation as a kind of R&D lab implies that its function is to come up with hypotheses and try them out. One researcher concluded that most foundations "work on and advocate for programs with little or no research basis for their activity. They appear confident they know what is good and just want to do it."

Besides, there *is* evidence that curriculum can make a huge difference. Nine countries that consistently outrank the United States on international assessments all provide their students with comprehensive, content-rich curricula. On the domestic front, studies have shown that the impact of a high-quality curriculum can be greater than that of a highly experienced teacher, and the weakest teachers are likely to get the biggest boost. Curriculum reform is also cheap: the best costs no more than the worst. But the US studies have focused on math curricula, which are easier to compare: "math" covers a much more defined set of concepts than "reading." There are also few content-rich literacy curricula out there to conduct research *on*, and those that exist may not bear fruit in the form of standardized test results for years. It takes time to build children's knowledge to the point where they can understand texts on a wide variety of topics.

Aside from the supposed lack of data, reformers have been inclined to leave decisions about instruction to the professionals and focus on management and administration. Many have a business background and trust that data about measurable outcomes will tell them whether a system is working. Like the education professionals whose judgment they rely on, they're unlikely to be familiar with the cognitive science demonstrating the importance of building knowledge from an early age. And it can be hard to grasp how much some kids simply *don't know*.

"When you grow up with knowledge," says Doug Lemov, "you can't really see the *role* of knowledge. The reverse knowledge gap for people on the privileged side of the achievement gap is that they have no idea how they got there."

Even reformers who are aware of the problem may find it difficult to do anything about it, either because of opposition from educators or simply a lack of interest or familiarity. One philanthropist who hoped to fund a preschool program using Core Knowledge in the mid-2000s gave up after she couldn't find any takers. Generally, curriculum has been seen as a script administrators impose when they don't trust teachers to do a good job. As a result, some educators are hostile to the idea of curriculum, period.

Then there's politics. When Michelle Rhee arrived in D.C. in 2007 to take the job of schools chancellor, with an agenda that focused on getting rid of individual teachers deemed ineffective, she was asked if she was also planning to make sure those teachers were provided with good curriculum, or any curriculum at all.

"The last thing we're going to do," she replied with a chuckle, "is get wrapped up in curriculum battles."

Foundations and philanthropists in the education reform world have also suffered from groupthink: if no one else is focusing on curriculum, it's unlikely to occur to anyone that it's important. Even their opponents have failed to identify the problem. The most influential is Diane Ravitch, an education historian who has denounced the charter movement as part of a plot to privatize American education and mocked funders like Bill Gates as members of "the Billionaire Boys Club." She's been a vocal critic of just about every reform initiative, from charters and school vouchers to No Child Left Behind and the Common Core. And she's a social media star who blogs fast and furiously. To Ravitch, reformers' reliance on testing and free-market principles is not only misguided and futile but part of a deliberate conspiracy to destroy public education.

Ravitch argues there's nothing wrong with the American education system as a whole. Our more affluent students are doing fine; it's only the schools serving poor kids that need help—an assertion that has been challenged. But even assuming she's right, there's still the question of what kind of help to provide. Rather than focusing on the knowledge gap, she says that "poverty is a bigger problem than curriculum" and that standardized tests "reflect family income, not knowledge or learning."

Ravitch's failure to highlight the need for content-focused curriculum is particularly puzzling because in the 1980s and 1990s she took a leading role in trying to bring that very issue to the attention of the public. Once a vigorous proponent of teaching history to young children, she now ridicules Core Knowledge as developmentally inappropriate, singling out the unit on Mesopotamia as "a circus trick, an effort to prove that a six-year-old can do mental gymnastics."

The idea that in order to fix education, we need to fix poverty first is a frequent trope among those who oppose reform, but it's unlikely to bring much cheer to poor families. While it may be true that our education system hasn't done much to reduce inequality, the fact is that we've never attempted to provide a content-focused, knowledge-building elementary curriculum on a large scale. And opponents of reform have overlooked the cognitive science on the importance of knowledge, just as reformers have. It's disingenuous to say education can't have an impact until we've experimented with the one strategy we have yet to try.

PERHAPS WHAT IS most puzzling is that high-performing charter schools have generally failed to focus on content. Unlike foundation officials who disburse multimillion-dollar grants from offices that are nowhere near the troubled neighborhoods their efforts target, charter school administrators and faculty are in the trenches. The obstacle posed by the knowledge gap stares them in the face on a regular basis.

Beyond that, many charter schools pride themselves on rejecting the gospel of progressive education on issues like phonics and discipline, blaming it for holding back the achievement of low-income students. Many of their leaders and staff were not trained in conventional schools of education and are therefore unlikely to have been indoctrinated in the belief that teaching skills is good and teaching facts is bad. And yet most charters have embraced skills and strategies with even more enthusiasm than the traditional public school sector. For years, that approach appeared to be working.

Then, beginning in 2013, more rigorous Common Core–aligned tests arrived, and some previously high-performing charters saw their scores plummet. Some large networks—including KIPP, Uncommon, and Achievement First—noticed that a few schools with a more content-focused approach hadn't suffered the same drop. So they began retooling their elementary curricula to focus more on content.

Doug Lemov went through a similar evolution. Originally, he put his faith in skills, and *Teach Like a Champion* was content-agnostic. On the assumption that "it doesn't matter what questions you're asking if the kids are running the classroom," Lemov designed his techniques to be used by any teacher teaching any subject. Now a firm believer in the primacy of content, he says the skills-focused approach confuses correlation and causation. Sure, good readers may make inferences, visualize what they're reading about, and so on. But that doesn't mean that having kids imitate those practices will *make* them into good readers.

"Look," he says, "good readers often relax with a glass of wine, but I don't think we're talking about that being an instructional strategy for third-graders."

Lemov's latest book, *Reading Reconsidered*, urges English language arts teachers to build students' knowledge by assigning more nonfiction and historical fiction, providing contextual information, asking content-based as well as skills-based questions, and using text sets focused on a particular topic. The best hope is for schools to implement content-rich curricula that progress logically across grade levels, Lemov acknowledges.

Even that, however, won't be enough. It's often hard for teachers and administrators to shed their old habits. Teachers may *think* they're focusing on content, but often they're still talking primarily about skills.

I saw this in action at one highly regarded charter network, the Brooke Charter Schools in Boston, which has been held up as a model of knowledge-building. In a fifth-grade social studies class, the teacher asked what "the author's purpose" had been in including a diagram of a caravan in a text about the Silk Road. Students offered reasonable answers that focused on the diagram's content, but the teacher kept rejecting them. "You guys need to get your brains working!" she said. Eventually she revealed the answer she wanted, so obvious that students may not have thought it worth mentioning: to show us what a caravan looks like.

A third-grade teacher began by asking about the "text features" of an article on the early domestication of animals and then, after reading only the first paragraph aloud, about the author's "argument." While I was in the classroom, she never asked a question about the subject matter, like: "Why did people start domesticating animals? Just to kill and eat them? What else could they use them for?" (Having bought into the progressive education shibboleth that history is developmentally inappropriate for young children, the school doesn't offer social studies before third grade.)

When I ask Lemov and one of his *Reading Reconsidered* coauthors, Colleen Driggs, why charter schools embraced skills in the first place, there's such a long silence at the other end of the line that I begin to wonder if I've lost the connection.

Finally Lemov says, "Colleen and I are looking at each other hoping the other one is going to answer that."

They have a few theories: Because charters teach decoding as a set of skills, perhaps it seemed logical to continue that approach when it came to comprehension. Or maybe it had to do with the fact that charters scored their biggest successes in math; teachers may have assumed that similar skills-focused instruction would also work with reading. And many charters pride themselves on their "data-driven instruction," continuously consulting the numbers gleaned from standardized assessments and adjusting their instruction accordingly. That data is entirely focused on skills, so the plans to improve achievement are as well.

Ultimately, Lemov says, the idea of teaching reading by teaching skills is "a beautiful dream": all you have to do is give kids a set of transferable techniques, and they can unlock any text and gain all the knowledge they want.

"It's a lot more compelling than, 'Actually, we have to teach all the details and facts and do all the legwork, and there is no shortcut,'" he says. "It's a very seductive notion, the alternative to which is gruelingly hard work that a lot of people scorn, that you don't really know how to execute in a day-to-day sense."

THE EDUCATION REFORM movement has produced plenty of success stories, and many kids have gotten a better education than they otherwise would have. But because of the lack of large-scale progress, reformers and philanthropists have started searching for a new approach. Their ideas have included cultivating character and "grit," along with fostering a "growth mind-set" by telling students they can get smarter if they work at it. Some have tried making the school a hub for health care and other services for the surrounding neighborhood and reaching out to parents through text messages and home visits.

Concerned about the high rate of suspensions and expulsions—and the evidence that students who experience those punishments are more likely to end up in prison—some schools have pinned their hopes on restorative justice, where the emphasis is on discussion and making amends. Others are trying out curricula intended to develop social and emotional skills, or bringing psychologists and psychiatrists into schools to treat students' mental health problems.

An increasingly popular academic approach is "project-based learning," which calls for students to investigate a problem for an extended period, gaining knowledge and skills along the way. At some project-based schools, students "choose their own curriculum and teachers are more like mentors guiding them through activities and topics of interest." One organization that trains educators in the technique has seen a surge of interest: in 2010, they trained five hundred teachers; in 2016, fifteen thousand. But studies extending back at least thirty years have found that low-income students—and any novice learners—generally do best when they receive direct instruction. Even advocates warn project-based learning can be difficult to do well, especially for teachers who lack experience or deep knowledge of the content.

The initiative that has captivated today's philanthropists the most is *personalized learning*, a concept that often overlaps with its cousin, *blended learning*. Personalized learning—like balanced literacy—is a slippery concept, but the idea is to tailor learning to individual students and have them demonstrate mastery of each component before moving on to the next. Blended learning refers to combining traditional face-to-face instruction with technology that can be used to personalize instruction—for example, having different students use different software, depending on their needs.

The approach has proved immensely appealing to tech titans like Mark Zuckerberg and Bill Gates. Zuckerberg and his wife, Priscilla Chan, have made it the prime focus of their own education initiative, planning to invest "hundreds of millions of dollars a year" toward the goal of providing "every student with a customized education." So far, the research on its effectiveness has been inconclusive. But, says Zuckerberg, "The model just intuitively makes sense." (So much for proof points.)

Even more troubling is that for many—including Gates and Zuckerberg—part of the vision is that students will determine not only the pace of their learning but also its content, as in some versions of project-based learning. "If allowed to choose my own content in elementary school," one critic has observed, "I would have become an expert in princesses and dogs."

Personalized learning is simply a delivery mechanism. If technology enables students at different levels of ability to access the same high-quality content, personalization could work. But if it's attached to a skills-focused curriculum, it won't work any better than the skills-focused instruction we have now. If it immerses each student in different content, we'll lose the essence of the school experience: the opportunity for group discussion, the excitement of bouncing ideas off fellow students, and the guidance that a teacher ideally provides.

The notion of putting students in charge of their own learning is alluring. For high-achieving self-starters like Gates and Zuckerberg—both Harvard dropouts—part of the appeal may be the memory of their own school days, when they would have leapt at the chance to move at their own pace. But that doesn't mean the approach will work for students who have acquired less knowledge and fewer skills.

Many of the avenues reformers are exploring are worthwhile. But if these new initiatives fail to inject content into the school day, they're unlikely to boost performance. In fact, injecting content may be the only way to achieve their goals. The author who helped put "grit" on the map, Paul Tough, has argued that what really promotes perseverance and a growth mind-set is grappling with meaty ideas rather than practicing basic skills, as students at high-poverty schools spend the bulk of their time doing. Students' mental health and self-esteem are also more likely to improve when they're congratulated for demonstrating knowledge they've acquired than when they're chastised for once again failing to grasp concepts like "captions" or "sequence of events."

Teachers at schools that have implemented a knowledge-focused approach tell me they've seen disciplinary incidents decrease sharply, because students are more engaged. And if children came home chattering about something they'd learned, it could be far easier for schools to forge connections with parents. How many kids come home eager to explain the strategy of making inferences?

RECENTLY THERE HAVE been signs that education reformers are at last beginning to change course. That includes the Gates Foundation, which installed a new director of K–12 strategy, Robert L. Hughes, in 2016. Shortly after his appointment, Hughes had a conversation with Ken Wagner, the education commissioner for Rhode Island.

"Gates has screwed up a lot of things," Wagner says he told Hughes, "but one thing they've done really well is mosquito nets."

Wagner was referring to a phenomenally successful initiative in the foundation's global health strategy, an effort to combat malaria by distributing mosquito nets treated with insecticide in countries where the disease is endemic. Between 2007 and 2017, the number of annual deaths from malaria—one of the world's biggest killers—was cut in half.

"It's a high-impact, low-tech model that saves people's lives," Wagner told Hughes. "We need a mosquito net for education, and curriculum is it. It will save lives."

A few months after Hughes joined Gates, Rachel Leifer—who had long been a lonely voice in the philanthropy world calling for investment in curriculum—was hired to be a senior program officer. And in the fall of 2017, Bill Gates announced that he would be shifting away from teacher evaluation. We know, he said, "that high-quality curricula can improve student learning more than many costlier solutions, and it has the greatest impact with students of novice and lower-performing teachers. We also know it has the greatest impact when accompanied by professional learning and coaching."

Overall, Gates said, he expected the foundation to invest close to $1.7 billion in education over the next five years, with 60 percent of that going to support "the development of new curricula and networks of schools that [will] work together to identify local problems and solutions." All of this should be music to the ears of anyone who understands the importance of curriculum.

On the other hand, when Gates mentioned grade levels, he spoke only of middle and high schools. And when the foundation identified the subjects it would focus on, the list included only English, math, and science—no history or social studies. If Gates chooses to direct his $1.7 billion only toward higher grade levels and omits subjects that lay the groundwork for an informed citizenry, his new initiative may prove to be anything but the educational equivalent of mosquito nets.

DECEMBER 2016

"So, the United States and *who* are going to go to war?" Ms. Masi asks her second-graders as a siren wails on the busy street outside. A number of hands are already wiggling in the air, but Ms. Masi repeats the question, waiting for more. "The United States is declaring war on *who*?"

The class has moved from Greek myths and the birth of democracy in ancient Athens to the War of 1812. While many American adults would be hard pressed to explain what that conflict was all about, these seven- and eight-year-olds are already fairly well versed in the subject. And they can draw on what they learned in years past.

In another lesson, when the word *surrender* came up, a girl volunteered that "when someone surrenders they put up a white flag." Yes, Ms. Masi said, surprised. Where had she heard that? The girl, named Yolanda, explained that she remembered it from first grade—the British used a white flag to surrender at the end of the Revolutionary War—as other kids, their memories jogged, began to call out, "Yeah! Yeah!"

Ms. Masi is constantly amazed at the connections these kids are able to make. Many are still talking about Greek gods and goddesses—a domain they loved—and she often hears them using their vocabulary words: *greedy, merchant, cargo, goods, foresight, conquer.* During a lesson on the life cycle of plants, I saw kids retrieving information from kindergarten about a honeybee named "Polly the Pollinator," along with words like *nectar, nutrients, soil,* and *roots.*

At last Ms. Masi calls on a student to tell the class what country the United States declared war on in 1812. Great Britain, she answers. Why? Ms. Masi wants to know. She reminds them that Americans hadn't wanted another war so soon after the Revolution.

"They were destroying a lot of things that were *costly* in America," a boy volunteers, trying out a new word.

It's not quite the answer Ms. Masi was looking for. Pressing for clarity and specificity, she eventually gets the kids to articulate that the Americans believed the British were arming Native Americans on the frontier so they could attack settlers.

The class collectively fills in a chart of the challenges and successes the United States experienced at the start of the war. The "challenges" pile up: it had a smaller army and navy; it lost to the British first in Canada, then around the Great Lakes; a British blockade was in effect. The kids are getting concerned, and they start trying to come up with ways the United States could win. One boy suggests that maybe the Americans "could just make another army," but Ms. Masi explains it wasn't that easy to replace soldiers who were killed or wounded. When she reads about the USS *Constitution*, which got the nickname "Old Ironsides" because cannonballs shot from a British ship bounced off its strong sides and smashed back into the ship they'd come from, the kids burst into cheers.

The story she's reading explains that when Americans declared war on Great Britain in 1812, they assumed British resources would be diverted to the Napoleonic Wars in Europe, giving the Americans a better chance of winning. But by 1814, the end of the Napoleonic Wars was in sight. She pauses to ask whether that would be a challenge or a success for the United States. "A challenge," a student answers.

"How was that a challenge?" a boy asks. Ms. Masi suggests he call on a friend, who explains that now the British could "put all their attention and fight on the United States." No one mentions it, but the friend has just successfully "made an inference"—as the students have been doing all along, using their knowledge of history.

After hearing that America was almost out of money, the kids' worries about America's chances increase. "I hate Britain," one mutters. Yolanda suggests that maybe the United States could ask France for help, or the Native Americans. After a pause, she raises her hand again. "Who won the Napoleonic Wars?" she asks, in a soft but clear voice.

Ms. Masi admits she doesn't know but will try to find out. I can't resist raising my hand.

"Great Britain won," I tell the class.

The news is greeted by a wave of disappointed *Aww*s.

———

WHATEVER IS GOING ON at Star Academy during December, I'm not there to see it. Ms. Arredondo keeps putting me off. Perhaps in January, she writes, "things will calm down and there will be more of a steady rhythm."

But in early January, after I text her seven times, Ms. Arredondo finally tells me she doesn't want me to visit anymore, explaining that "having visitors can become a bit of a distraction for the students and me, and I think it would be best for me to focus on my teaching."

I suspect her decision has more to do with the fact that her students' behavior seems to be getting worse rather than better. I don't hold her responsible for that. In fact, I think a fundamental reason for it is that her students aren't particularly interested in what she is required to try to teach them.

I'll spend the next several months looking for another teacher using a skills-focused curriculum. Since that's true of the vast majority of elementary teachers in the United States, you might think it would be easy to find one. But many are understandably wary of having a total stranger spend months in their classroom, observing their instructional methods and interactions with their young students—and then going off to write about it.

PART TWO

How We Got Here

The History Behind
the Content-Free
Curriculum

CHAPTER 7

Émile Meets
the Common Core

IN RURAL EIGHTEENTH-CENTURY FRANCE, there lived a boy named Émile. An orphan from a wealthy family, Émile was entrusted from birth to the care of a tutor who took a highly unusual approach. The tutor, Jean-Jacques, was determined that Émile would learn only from nature and his own experience. He would never be compelled to learn anything in particular, and Jean-Jacques would always be on the alert for signs of boredom.

Jean-Jacques might ask a series of questions to guide Émile to the right answers, but he avoided teaching anything outright or even correcting errors. It was better for the boy to discover things for himself. Far from adopting the role of an authoritarian taskmaster, as many tutors did, Jean-Jacques would be Émile's friend and playmate, pretending to have no greater skill than his pupil and to be learning alongside him.

Émile spent much of his childhood happily playing outdoors. The concepts of history, geography, and science were entirely unfamiliar to him, because Jean-Jacques was confident that children couldn't handle such abstractions. He derided books as "the instruments of children's greatest misery," believing that youngsters weren't actually thinking when they read; they were just learning words that had little meaning for them.

Émile did learn to read eventually, but only because he wanted to—or rather, because his tutor provided him with sly incentives. Instead of sitting the boy down and teaching him the alphabet and the sounds that letters make, Jean-Jacques arranged to have little notes sent to him, inviting him on tempting excursions. Voilà! Because he was motivated, Émile figured out how to read.

By the age of fifteen, Émile was happy, healthy, possessed of sound judgment and a good heart—but also ignorant of anything beyond his own direct experience. This was just as Jean-Jacques had planned. At the very stage in life when his peers were ending their formal education, Jean-Jacques declared proudly, it was at last time for Émile to begin his.

ÉMILE NEVER EXISTED. But the book his "tutor," Jean-Jacques Rousseau, wrote about this grand, if fictional, experiment—*Émile, or Treatise on Education*, published in 1762—has had a profound influence on the way educators in the United States have seen their mission over the past hundred years.

Not that most teachers today have read Rousseau. Nevertheless, his ideas and those of later European Romantic thinkers—including some who worked with real children rather than fictional ones—gradually filtered into the American education establishment during the nineteenth century. In reaction against the view that children were born into a sinful state that required harsh correction, the Romantics believed that the child was a naturally good, even mystical, being who entered the world "trailing clouds of glory," as the English poet William Wordsworth put it.

The idea that books should be withheld until students are fifteen never caught on—fortunately. But Rousseau's influence is apparent in the prevailing view that education should be child-centered—driven by a child's choices and interests—rather than teacher-directed. Rousseau would also feel right at home with the widely held precept that it's better for children to discover things for themselves than to be given information. For some progressive educators, that holds true even for "an arbitrary convention, such as how to address an envelope, where to put a footnote, or the fact that September has thirty days." Directly providing that kind of information might be okay, one prominent education theorist has written, but "the burden of proof should be on the teacher to show that students can't, or for some reason shouldn't, find these things out themselves."

Giving students free rein might make sense at upper grade levels, if they've already acquired a base of knowledge about the world that enables them to make informed choices about what to study and to understand and retain what they read. But it's elementary classrooms that have been shaped the most by Rousseauian ideals.

The American education establishment's aversion to teacher-directed, content-focused instruction was originally a reaction against late-nineteenth-century public schools that went through eighth grade. Using textbooks like the popular McGuffey's Readers, these "common schools" exposed children to excerpts from classic literature and stories from American history, creating a shared pool of references that helped knit the nation together across class lines. The common schools were also seen as engines of social and economic mobility, equipping poor and working-class students to better themselves.

These schools were clearly an improvement over what had preceded them, which was little or no education for those who couldn't afford private schools or tutors. But they were designed to impart no more than basic skills—which, at the time, were sufficient to prepare many students to earn a decent living in agriculture, business, or manufacturing—while instilling the traits of good character and good citizenship. More problematic in the eyes of reformers, though, was the fact that the schools used harsh discipline and techniques of drilling and rote memorization.

This approach was premised on "faculty psychology"—the theory that the mind consists of various faculties, the most important of which is memory, that can be developed through repeated practice. Teachers might, for example, have students memorize and recite passages in

Latin, regardless of whether they could actually understand or appreciate what they were reciting. The idea was that this exercise would endow them with a strong memory that could be applied in other contexts. The more unpleasant and difficult the task the better, in order to develop discipline and perseverance.

To train teachers, nineteenth-century reformer Horace Mann established "normal schools." While these institutions were, like the common schools themselves, an improvement over the void they replaced, they created their own problems. Mann deliberately recruited women as students, partly on the theory that they would be more nurturing—an important qualification in the eyes of the Romantics—and partly because they were less expensive. Until the early twentieth century, teachers-in-training generally went straight to normal schools from grammar school, meaning that they often had only the equivalent of a sixth- or seventh-grade education. Later, most normal schools became state colleges of education, but they continued to have low admissions standards and to focus on teaching pedagogical skills and methods rather than content.

Partly as a result, the American teaching profession went in a radically different direction from its counterpart in continental Europe: more female, less prestigious, less academic, and more focused on skills. Undergraduate education students often don't acquire much in the way of subject-matter knowledge because their curriculum focuses on teaching methods. And because of the gulf that separates them from the rest of academia, their professors are largely unaware of developments in other disciplines, like cognitive psychology, that run counter to what they are teaching.

By 1900, the theory of faculty psychology was falling by the wayside, setting the stage for the emergence of the progressive education movement. Many assume that *progressive* connotes liberalism, as it now does in the political context, and left-leaning teachers often proudly identify as progressive educators. But originally, the term was used to encompass a host of aims, not all political; philosopher John Dewey, considered the father of the movement, used it to signify that a child's experience at home and at school should build "progressively." And twentieth-century educational progressivism—like the Progressive Era itself—encompassed some strains that today sound thoroughly reactionary: for instance, the idea that only elite students should take academic courses, while the majority should be funneled into vocational, general, or basic tracks based on their mental capacity as measured by IQ tests.

The strand of progressive education that lives on today is the child-centered one, which found its greatest proponent in John Dewey. He said and wrote many things about education—many of them opaque, ambiguous, and contradictory. But his basic educational philosophy, as summed up by a friend, was: "If you provide a sufficient variety of activities, and there's enough knowledge lying around, and the teacher understands the natural relation between knowledge and interested action, children can have fun getting educated and will love to go to school."

That description overstates the case a bit. Dewey's own Laboratory School in Chicago emphasized hands-on activities but also followed a content-rich curriculum. Some of his followers, however, emphasized the "activity" part and downplayed—or omitted—the subject matter. They stressed that children should be free to follow their own interests and engage in "projects," perhaps choosing to make a dress or put on a play. Some, echoing Rousseau, went so far as to dismiss the need for children to learn to read and write at all.

Dewey may not have subscribed to these interpretations of his pedagogy, but he didn't disavow them. Nor did he stress the vital role played by the transmission of knowledge, particularly for disadvantaged children. Unlike some other progressives, he did see education as a means of changing society, believing his methods could engender habits of mind that were conducive to democracy. But it's doubtful that his approach could ever have equipped children from low-income families to move up the ladder, at least on a mass scale. The conditions at his school were impossible to replicate in the public school system: small classes, well-trained and carefully selected teachers, and—perhaps most important of all—students who were absorbing all sorts of knowledge and vocabulary from their highly educated parents.

Outside of the private schools that catered to the wealthy, teachers and parents generally resisted the child-centered approach; many parents *wanted* their children to learn how to read, spell, and do math. And the few public schools that did embrace progressivism found they needed to spend part of the day in old-fashioned drills. But other changes were holding back disadvantaged students. Many public elementary schools were abandoning phonics in favor of books like the popular Dick-and-Jane readers, which made it less likely that students would be able to sound out unfamiliar words when they moved on to upper grades. At the same time, the commonly used readers that contained excerpts from classic literature were disappearing. Beginning in the 1930s, fables, Greek myths, and tales of heroes from American history were replaced by "social studies" texts that focused on the present and introduced children to a series of "expanding environments" that didn't expand very far: home, family, neighborhood, school, and community. The goal was to build on children's real-world experiences rather than the "less-connected content of history, civics, and geography."

The result was that children were no longer exposed to material that could help them make sense of allusions they were likely to encounter in sophisticated literature—for example, phrases like "Achilles' heel" and "the tortoise and the hare." Instead, they got the kind of social studies curriculum that elementary schools still deliver, to the extent that they deliver one at all: a series of disjointed lessons on mundane topics like street signs or the concepts of *family* and *neighborhood*.

The justifications varied depending on the decade. During the Depression, tales of "the days of old when knights were bold" were considered to be an unhealthy escape "from the realities of this world in which we live"—realities that had to be confronted even by six-year-olds. In the 1940s, when the expanding environments curriculum was nearly universal, it was simply seen as modern. In the 1950s, it was considered essential to teaching citizenship. By the 1960s and 1970s, the theory was that children needed to build self-esteem by learning about themselves first.

By the 1980s, when Jean Piaget's theories had become influential, teachers assumed that the old curriculum had been tossed out because its historical bent was "developmentally inappropriate." But Diane Ravitch reported that she consulted "a dozen leading scholars in the fields of cognitive psychology, child development, and curriculum theory. None knew of any research justifying the expanding environments approach; none defended it. All deplored the absence of historical and cultural content in the early grades."

Although child-centered progressivism didn't have much effect on public schools in the early twentieth century, it did have a huge impact on teacher-training programs. Columbia University's Teachers College became a bastion of progressivism and the country's most influential school of education—a position it arguably still holds today. The seeds of child-centered progressivism would lie dormant within American teacher-training institutions through the middle of the twentieth century, ready to bloom when watered with the effusions of the do-your-own-thing counterculture of the 1960s.

THE OTHER STRAIN of American progressive education might be called *social efficiency*. Both strains rejected rote learning and the traditional curriculum of the nineteenth and early twentieth centuries, which often included such ostensibly useless subjects as Latin. Both emphasized prioritizing students' interests, teaching through hands-on activities, and connecting the school to the larger society. Generally, both rejected the idea of using schools to transmit any particular body of knowledge. But the social efficiency progressives ended up going in quite a different direction from the child-centered ones—and for a while at least, they had a much greater impact.

For the most part, the social efficiency progressives focused on secondary education, while the child-centered ones trained their sights on the elementary grades. And although at least some child-centered progressives saw education as a means of improving society, if not necessarily furthering social and economic mobility, their social efficiency cousins were concerned with ensuring that education fit the needs of society as it existed. As they saw it, the traditional high school curriculum was narrowly designed to prepare students for college. This one-size-fits-all approach, they argued, was ill matched to an increasingly diverse student population that included few who were headed for further education. Rather than try to equip all students with academic knowledge, they changed the curriculum so that most students wouldn't need that kind of knowledge in order to graduate.

These innovations were partly a reaction to an explosion in high school enrollment in the early twentieth century. Between 1870 and 1940, the population of the United States tripled, but the number of students in secondary schools increased by a multiple of almost ninety, rising from eighty thousand to seven million. Educators found themselves dealing with a sudden influx of students who hadn't necessarily chosen to be there and weren't prepared for high school–level academic work. In urban areas, many were immigrants or children of immigrants, still struggling with English. African American children, especially in the South, were the products of an inferior education network.

Faced with large numbers of poorly equipped students, the social efficiency progressives advocated nonacademic tracks to keep students in school and prepare them for the jobs that would be open to them. In the 1930s, some high schools began to submerge English and social studies into courses that focused on questions like how to get along with others or be a smart consumer. They adopted separate curricula based on prospective vocations: agriculture, business, clerical work. While most high schools retained an academic track for the small number headed to college, the bulk of students might be taking units like "Language Activities" and "Health and Happiness."

To sort students, high schools resorted to IQ testing, believing the tests measured innate and immutable capacities. They saw no point in wasting an academic education on students whom it would never benefit. By the 1960s, students were routinely assigned to different tracks based on tests that were largely dependent on general knowledge and vocabulary. The result was that students from better-educated families usually ended up in the academic track, while others were relegated to vocational or general tracks.

There were critics, but they had a hard time making themselves heard. Black parents who wanted their children assigned to an academic track were dismissed as being unfamiliar with the tenets of progressive education and unduly suspicious that white educators were trying to hold them back rather than help them enter the workforce.

DURING THE CULTURAL UPHEAVALS of the late 1960s, the child-centered progressivism that had flourished before World War II enjoyed a rebirth—now wedded to a more explicit concern for social justice, fueled by the burgeoning civil rights movement. But the marriage proved to be a difficult one, given that educational models that prioritized free choice and deemphasized content failed to give most children what they needed—and what many parents wanted.

The first warning shot appeared in 1960, with A. S. Neill's book *Summerhill*. Neill described the boarding school he had founded in England some forty years before as a Rousseauian paradise. Students were free to do whatever they wanted, whenever they wanted—or to do nothing at all. One student, Neill boasted, had spent thirteen years at Summerhill without attending a single class. Perhaps going even further than Rousseau, Neill argued that the child "is innately wise and realistic. If left to himself without adult suggestion of any kind, he will develop as far as he is capable of developing."

Summerhill didn't make much of a splash when it first appeared, but as the decade progressed, its message began to resonate with a society that was increasingly focused on individual freedom and opposed to authority. By 1970, it was selling two hundred thousand copies a year and was required reading in at least six hundred university courses. During the late 1960s and early 1970s, other popular books criticized the repressive nature of traditional education and urged the elimination of curricula, grades, and homework. Many focused specifically on the plight of poor, mostly African American children but overlooked lack of knowledge and vocabulary as a root cause. And when some of the more extreme approaches of the 1960s were tried on children from less-educated families, as opposed to the affluent students who boarded at Summerhill, the results were far from encouraging. At one school that was led by political radicals, teachers refrained from teaching children to read until they asked. The result was that no one learned to read. "The severest critics of the school," according to one account, "were the black parents, who wanted their children to learn academic subjects and 'to rise in American society, not remake it.'"

More influential was the open-classroom model, based on the British infant school, in which children roamed freely from one "interest center" to another, engaging at will in art projects, number work, sand and water play, and independent reading in cozy armchairs. At some schools, even separate grades were abolished. To facilitate the free movement of students and teachers, school districts across the country began knocking down classroom walls and commissioning new open-plan buildings. (The walls in my own neighborhood elementary school were knocked down as part of this trend and replaced only a few years ago.) There was no set curriculum, since students never did anything as a group. As leaders of the movement put it, "children's own experiences are the subject matter—the content—of their learning."

But the approach wasn't a big hit with parents who wanted their children to learn about something *beyond* their own experiences. At one predominantly African American urban school, an attempt to introduce the open-classroom model soon turned to disaster, with disruptive kids and disgruntled parents.

"You have had a certain kind of educational experience," one parent chided a teacher, "teacher as source of knowledge and control, child as respectful and obedient responder, and you made it. If our children have the same kind of educational experience, *they too* will make it."

By the mid-1970s, the open-classroom movement had begun to fade, but its basic elements live on in early-elementary school classrooms: children moving from one center to another (now in set groups and at set intervals), free choice in reading material (albeit constrained by a student's reading level)—and the absence of any coherent content.

IN THE LATE 1970S, reports that SAT scores had been steadily declining for fifteen years set off national alarm bells. A panel appointed by the College Board, which administers the SAT, determined the source of the problem: textbooks had been getting simpler. Sentences were shorter, vocabulary less complex. Reading passages on the SAT had also been dumbed down, but not as much as the books students were reading in school. Calls for reform ensued, focused largely on America's high schools.

At the same time, the nation's schools of education were reinforcing beliefs and practices that made it difficult for many students to tackle high school–level text. While new names and justifications were attached, the prevailing pedagogical theories of the 1970s and 1980s were fundamentally the same as those propounded by child-centered progressives before World War II and the radical reformers of the 1960s: teachers should engage in as little direct instruction as possible; children should learn through a natural process of discovery; and *what* they were learning wasn't all that important. Those theories persist today as "constructivism," which is premised on the belief that students must be active participants in constructing their own knowledge rather than passive receptacles.

It's true that we all construct our own knowledge, in the sense that we don't just store facts we've heard verbatim. We need to interpret and synthesize to achieve true understanding. But that's not the same as discovering *facts* for ourselves, which is a potentially endless and inefficient process that isn't well suited to most subjects. We also construct knowledge when we listen to someone talking or reading aloud and think about or discuss the content—or even better, *write* about it.

Constructivism, like progressivism, takes a dim view of memorization, often characterizing it as "rote." But that implies students don't understand the facts they're memorizing. When students are not just memorizing, say, the date "1787" but connecting it to the Constitutional Convention and also to 1776, 1783, and 1789, learning isn't rote at all. It's hugely important to building knowledge and expertise. Another trope is that it's pointless to teach students factual information because it's constantly changing. Although the argument may sound fresh in the "just Google it" era, it has been surfacing in various forms for decades and is firmly embedded in mainstream teacher training.

This disdain for factual knowledge has been reinforced by a framework of "educational objectives" that teachers-in-training are required to memorize, called Bloom's Taxonomy. Created by education theorist Benjamin Bloom in the 1950s, the taxonomy ranks different thinking tasks, beginning with the less complex and more concrete—*knowledge* and *comprehension*—and ending with the more complex and abstract: *analysis*, *synthesis*, and *evaluation*. Usually the taxonomy is represented as a pyramid, with *knowledge* at the bottom and *evaluation* at the top. That graphic has led many educators to conclude that the "lower-order" tasks should be passed over as quickly as possible, or even eliminated, because they're inferior to those at the top. In fact, Bloom meant that knowledge and comprehension are *prerequisites* for higher-order thinking, and that teachers should never ask students to start analyzing or evaluating a topic until first ensuring they have a solid understanding of it.

Cognitive science has since provided scientific support for Bloom's intended approach; we can think critically only when we have factual information at our fingertips—or to be more precise, stored in our long-term memory. That enables us to devote the limited space available in working memory to analysis. Memorizing and understanding is a crucial step to developing so-called twenty-first-century skills like critical thinking. The more you know about a particular topic, the better able you are to think about it critically.

Far from developing higher-order skills, skipping over basic, concrete aspects of learning denies many students the opportunity to realize their full potential. A lack of familiarity with history and the world beyond one's own experience might not have been such a terrible handicap for a young eighteenth-century aristocrat like Émile. But for a teenager today, it can represent a serious obstacle to success.

DURING THE LAST FIFTY YEARS, education has once again been heralded as the prime ladder out of poverty. That view has spurred federal aid to schools that serve poor children, and it's a large part of what has fueled the modern education reform movement. But what we are asking schools to do is unprecedented. In the nineteenth and twentieth centuries, no one expected schools to prepare the majority of students for college. When high school enrollment expanded, twentieth-century reformers made the curriculum less academic for all but the elite. Instead of a ladder, school was seen as a multipronged funnel directing students to the paths determined by their existing socioeconomic status.

Since the 1960s, it is fortunately no longer socially or politically acceptable to openly use our educational system to perpetuate inequality. Efforts to equalize opportunity for disadvantaged students have reached their apotheosis in the Common Core standards, which aim for *all* students to graduate "college- and career-ready," defined in terms more rigorous than any we have previously adopted.

There's unavoidable tension between that worthy aspiration and the realities of providing an academic education to students who, on the Rousseauian plan, have been deprived of the opportunity to acquire essential knowledge. Tightening graduation requirements inevitably results in more dropouts and lower high school graduation rates—which inevitably results in an outcry for higher graduation rates. Today's reformers no longer have the escape valve available to their predecessors: openly lowering standards. The foul odor clinging to the concept of tracking is so strong it has put many school systems off the concept of vocational education altogether, depriving some students of what could be a meaningful experience that prepares them to enter the workforce. At the same time, most teachers say that some form of de facto tracking persists.

Even something as ostensibly objective as the Advanced Placement program, which administers tests graded by outside examiners, is susceptible to gaming. In recent years, reformers have urged that AP courses be open to all students regardless of grades or teacher recommendations. Partly as a result, enrollment in AP and other college-level classes nearly doubled in the decade after 2006, and the percentage of students who earned a passing score on AP exams increased from about 14 percent to 22 percent.

Schools often tout their AP numbers, sometimes with good reason. Any student who is genuinely eager to tackle advanced work should have that opportunity, with appropriate support. But AP classes at high-poverty schools, where many students are years below grade level, rarely resemble those at more affluent schools. Students may be assigned to them simply because of scheduling constraints or the need to fill the class. At some schools, no students receive passing scores on AP tests. At others, virtually all tests are given the lowest possible score, which could mean students failed to answer any questions whatsoever. Many who get As or Bs in their AP classes end up failing the exams.

Unlike the social efficiency progressives, who were at least aboveboard about their intentions, we are only pretending to provide many low-income students with an adequate education. "Should reform start with American high schools, community colleges, or both?" one article asked.

The answer, of course, is neither: reform should start in elementary school, if not before.

Perhaps the most powerful belief teachers absorb during their training is that education should be a natural, pleasurable process and that learning or (heaven forefend) *memorizing* is inherently boring and soul-destroying. And if teachers directly impart information, progressive and constructivist educators argue, they will produce automatons who can regurgitate disconnected facts but are unable to think critically about them.

While fact-focused instruction certainly can be boring and ineffective, is that necessarily the case? From what I saw at Center City and other schools that have embraced content-rich curricula, the answer is no. But to really see a "traditional" school in action—one that unapologetically embraces knowledge-building and even memorization—I traveled to England.

That's not because teachers in the United Kingdom are any less "progressive" than those in the United States. On the contrary, progressive education is well entrenched in the land that gave us *Summerhill* and the open classroom. But the Michaela Community School has bucked those long-standing beliefs with a vengeance. Founded in 2014 as a "free school"—the British version of a charter school—Michaela opened with the equivalent of a sixth-grade class and will eventually go all the way through the equivalent of twelfth grade. When I visited in the spring of 2017, it had three grade levels and about 350 mostly low-income students, many from immigrant or non-white families. The school accepts students on a first-come, first-served basis.

Michaela employs the kind of strict discipline commonly found in high-performing American charter schools. It also systematically inculcates kindness and gratitude, having students volunteer to deliver "appreciations" of other individuals at the daily communal lunch, for example. (I got one the day I visited, for having informed the kids at my table about American education.) But its instructional approach differs significantly from most charters, and most schools of any kind in the US or the UK.

Students at Michaela not only spend a lot of time listening to teachers, they memorize dates, events, key concepts, and even entire poems—classics like Percy Bysshe Shelley's "Ozymandias" and W. E. Henley's "Invictus," which they recite chorally. Homework focuses on self-quizzing, and teachers don't skip over factual questions to get straight to "higher order" skills.

I saw one teacher prepare students for a novel set during the civil rights era by asking for an explanation of *Brown v. Board of Education*. After getting a correct answer, he wrote a summary, which students copied: "Brown v. Board of Education was about segregation in schools. As a result, schools were forced to integrate." When he asked for the word used to describe marriage between people of different races, the students chorused, "Miscegenation."

In a sixth-grade-level history class, students were preparing to write paragraphs on how religion had led to the development of England as a nation by 1066. They had collectively filled out an outline that was being projected on a screen. One student asked if the first sentence should be an "ideas" sentence. Yes, the teacher responded, the sentence should begin with, "Ideas such as religion . . ." After the students had written for fifteen minutes, the teacher projected some of their paragraphs to have them critiqued by the class as a whole.

I also dropped in on one of the after-school "reading clubs" Michaela requires its weakest readers to attend four days a week for half an hour. Thirty or so students sat at rows of desks, following along as a teacher read from *Jane Eyre*. The passage focused on Jane's experience at a harsh nineteenth-century boarding school, where students were berated for transgressions like dirty fingernails—never mind that the water in their pitchers that morning had been frozen solid! The situation seemed remote, and much of the vocabulary and syntax were archaic. But there was no chatting or fidgeting. The students used clear plastic rulers to keep their place in the text and never lifted their eyes from the page. This practice, used across the curriculum at Michaela, helps students develop fluency and familiarizes them with texts too complex for them to read independently.

As far as I could tell, students were far from unhappy. When I had lunch with a polite, inquisitive table of "Year 7s"—sixth-graders, in our system—all six agreed they were learning more than they had at their previous schools and didn't mind the additional work. They were clearly proud of the knowledge they had acquired: one boy compared Mary Shelley's poetry unfavorably to her husband's (not as good as "Ozymandias," he opined), but allowed that she did write *Frankenstein*. Another told me he spent four hours a night on homework. "You could get it done in two," he said airily, "but that wouldn't be Michaela." Like the others at the table, he couldn't think of anything about the school he would change. "We're not perfect, but . . ." He shrugged and left the sentence unfinished.

The general assumption among educators has been that if you focus on teaching analytical skills, knowledge will follow. But Michaela's founder, Katharine Birbalsingh, says it's the opposite: Once students have grasped the facts, they naturally learn to analyze them through discussion or writing. Birbalsingh says that visitors who read students' essays—on topics like the causes of Macbeth's downfall or the origins of the English civil war—often ask, "But how have they learned this analysis? How have they been able to evaluate?"

"And I say, well, because they've written the essay, about the stuff they learned," she continues. "They say, yes, but how have you *taught* them? And I say, well, they're just *doing* it. If you just teach them the knowledge, that other stuff happens."

What makes the essays even more remarkable is that many of Michaela's students entered the school at the age of eleven reading and writing years below grade level—some at the level of six-year-olds. Within two years, the school had managed to catch all of them up, and the results were almost as good in math.

Birbalsingh, familiar with the Matthew effect theory, was surprised. "I used to be of the opinion that at age three there's this massive gap," she told me, "and by the time they get to us at age eleven, you can't do that much. But you can do a lot."

When I was there, Michaela hadn't been in operation long enough to have results on national tests, given when students reach the equivalent of tenth grade. But shortly after my visit, the school had its first government inspection and got the top rating—"outstanding"—in all five categories. "From their starting points, all groups of pupils make rapid progress in a wide range of subjects," the inspectors reported. "Disadvantaged pupils make substantial progress and achieve as well as other pupils."

And, the inspectors went on, "Teaching is reliably lively and engaging. It captures and holds pupils' attention."

IT'S UNLIKELY many American schools will embrace the "traditional" model as intensively as Michaela, given how deeply principles of progressive education are engrained. So our best bet is to focus on filling the knowledge vacuum at the elementary level.

A key step will be for progressive educators to recognize their common ground with those they have labeled traditionalists. At least some of the latter agree with progressives that in the past twenty years we've placed too much emphasis on standardized tests. Both groups believe that education should provide a ladder out of poverty. And both want students to learn some facts and develop analytical thinking skills; the disagreement comes down to what to put in the foreground and how much time to spend on each.

Change will also require progressive educators to accept the findings of cognitive science from the past thirty years or so. That won't be easy, because those findings have undermined many of the theories they have cherished—including those behind both the whole-language approach to decoding and the skills-and-strategies approach to comprehension.

Some progressives are also loath to acknowledge, at least publicly, that students from less-educated families have different needs or less knowledge of the world than other students, fearing they'll be labeled racist or reactionary. But ignoring or denying that fact puts them in the position of ascribing the undeniable gap in test scores—and in educational achievement generally—simply to "poverty," as though it were poverty itself that prevents poor kids from achieving at the levels of their wealthier peers. The very real ills associated with poverty—hunger, housing instability, exposure to violence—can make it difficult for children to learn. But as schools like Michaela are demonstrating, knowledge-focused education can do an enormous amount to narrow the gap *despite* those significant handicaps and can increase the chances that students will eventually escape them.

Today's child-centered progressive educators—and the many who have unconsciously absorbed the movement's shibboleths—sincerely want our education system to function as an engine of social and economic mobility. Many are working diligently to that end. But by denying less-privileged children access to knowledge, they are doing just as much to perpetuate existing inequities as their distant cousins who invented tracking: the social efficiency progressives.

JANUARY 2017

Now in the midst of their domain on Westward Expansion, Ms. Masi's second-graders have heard about a fictional family's arduous journey on the Oregon Trail and Robert Fulton's invention of the steamboat. They've listened to the journal of a fictional twelve-year-old who helped his father transport goods on the Erie Canal. Most recently, they've learned about the Cherokee chief Sequoyah and how he invented a written language for his people in the early nineteenth century—and about how some years later the government forced the Cherokees to give up their land in Georgia and travel to Oklahoma on a journey so difficult it was given the name the Trail of Tears.

A large map of the United States hanging at the front of the classroom displays two lines of Post-it notes, one marking the route of the fictional Morgan family from Indiana to Oregon, and one showing the Trail of Tears. On a bulletin board are students' drawings and compositions in response to the question "Would you have wanted to travel west in a covered wagon?"

Most have answered in the negative. "You have to walk for 6 months," one wrote. "You are going to be hungry. You will need water. You need to sit." Another observed that "it mite be pretty boring." But some see it as an adventure: "I will see new things," one girl wrote. A boy observed that a covered wagon would protect him from bad weather.

Today the students are divided into three groups, preparing to write two-paragraph essays in the voices of one of the people they've learned about: Fulton, Sequoyah, or a member of the Cherokee tribe. Ms. Fields is out in the hall with the Robert Fulton group. Lenee Washington, a teacher-in-training who is spending several months working alongside Ms. Masi, is with the group reviewing Sequoyah's invention of the Cherokee alphabet—a project that some students are trying to emulate, coming up with their own writing systems. Ms. Washington reminds them that the other Cherokee chiefs were *skeptical* of Sequoyah's work and asks if they remember what *skeptical* means. The kids have trouble saying the word, but they get the meaning: the chiefs didn't believe it would work.

Ms. Masi is with the group that will be writing as Cherokees. She's given them a list of questions to answer, including "Who is Andrew Jackson? How do you feel about him?"

The students have encountered Jackson before, as the heroic general who won the Battle of New Orleans during the War of 1812. But as president of the United States, he's sided with the white settlers who covet Cherokee land and businesses in Georgia. He's sent soldiers to force the Cherokees to relocate and provided the tribe with so little in the way of provisions that many die during the journey. The Core Knowledge curriculum teaches children about the heroes and triumphs of American history, but it doesn't shy away from its darker aspects.

"The Trail of Tears and other forced movements of Native Americans are some of the saddest events in the history of the United States," the read-aloud observes, "but that is why we need to remember them. It's important to remember the sadder parts of history to prevent them from happening again."

Other teachers who have used this curriculum have told me their second-graders have been shocked to realize that the Andrew Jackson who fought the Battle of New Orleans and the Andrew Jackson responsible for the suffering of the Cherokees were one and the same. One class had a heated debate over whether Robert E. Lee could be considered a hero: he fought for his country in the Mexican-American War and for his state during the Civil War, but on the other hand he was fighting for slavery. It's an early introduction to the complexities of historical figures.

Ms. Masi's group, when asked to describe how they feel about Jackson and the soldiers who came to enforce his orders—imagining themselves as Cherokees—settle on *mad* and *sad*.

CHAPTER 8

Politics and
the Quest for Content

ONE DAY IN 1978, a group of about two hundred students filed into a large classroom at the J. Sargeant Reynolds Community College in Richmond, Virginia, each receiving a test booklet at the door. While the passages printed in the booklets all covered the same content, half had versions that were written well and the other half versions that were written badly. The students—virtually all of them African American, from modest economic backgrounds—received the booklets randomly: one was handed version A, the next version B.

The man giving out the booklets was E. D. Hirsch Jr. Rather than trying to test students' reading ability, he was conducting a writing experiment. He wanted to provide writing instructors at the University of Virginia in Charlottesville, where he was a professor of English, with scientifically based general principles of good writing. The point was to see if the students who got the well-written versions—which had logical organization and parallel sentence structure—read and understood them more quickly.

With funding from various government agencies, Hirsch had been assembling one or two hundred students at a time. He would put a digital scoreboard clock at the front of the room—the kind you see at athletic events, tracking time down to the second—and have students note the exact times they began and finished each passage. Ultimately, he would test more than seven hundred individuals.

He had begun the experiment at the elite UVA campus, where the data largely supported his hypothesis: the "speed of uptake" was faster for students who got the well-written versions. There had been only one exception, when the subject was Hegel's conception of logic as metaphysics. In that case, the speed of uptake was the same for everyone. Hirsch concluded that most UVA students just weren't familiar with the topic. If you didn't have enough background knowledge, it seemed, writing quality made little difference; you would have a hard time understanding the passage no matter what. Then someone suggested that Hirsch bring his experiment to a community college. So there he was at J. Sargeant Reynolds, his scoreboard clock installed at the front of the room.

One pair of passages had been adapted from a student-written essay about the benefits of friendship. The other, describing Robert E. Lee's surrender at Appomattox, was from a well-regarded history of the Civil War. Hirsch had created a "degraded" version by introducing features that violated his hypothetical principles of good writing.

Students read the good version of the passage on friendship significantly faster than the bad one, as expected. But for the other passage, the quality of the writing made no difference. Looking at the data, Hirsch recalls, "was a shock." Given the results on the friendship texts, he knew the problem wasn't a lack of reading skills. And when Hirsch had used the Civil War passages at UVA, they had produced the expected results. The only possible explanation was that the Civil War was as unfamiliar to students at the community college as Hegel had been to students at UVA. Hirsch was appalled. "These kids had been cheated," he said years later.

Hirsch's background had primed him to take this realization to heart. As an English professor, he had dissented from an influential school of thought called the New Criticism, which held that the only thing that mattered was the text itself. Hirsch had countered that a reader's comprehension depends on his own knowledge and experience. The experiment seemed to provide real-world confirmation. Then there was the emotional baggage Hirsch carried from his childhood. A political liberal who has described himself as "practically a socialist," Hirsch had grown up in the 1930s and '40s in Memphis, where his wealthy family had "largely looked the other way" rather than confront segregation. It wasn't until he read Gunnar Myrdal's analysis of "the Negro problem," *An American Dilemma*, as an adolescent that his eyes were opened to the racism surrounding him. Now, Hirsch was determined to become the voice that called attention to the less-visible racism that persisted: the withholding of what he would come to call "cultural literacy"—the knowledge that elite Americans take for granted—from minority and low-income students.

That wasn't how things turned out. To his surprise, Hirsch was the one who found himself accused of racism. The book he published in 1987—*Cultural Literacy: What Every American Needs to Know*—came under immediate attack from the left, who charged Hirsch with trying to foist a Eurocentric and reactionary vision of culture down the throats of black and brown children.

HIRSCH ABLY DIAGNOSED the root cause of our educational inequity, but he made several missteps. While the Richmond community college students who had sparked his outrage made a brief appearance in his book, they and their peers essentially got lost in a scholarly and discursive narrative. What struck readers more than Hirsch's calls for fairness was his emphasis on the need to transmit some core of knowledge from one generation to the next to forge a sense of national identity. Schools, he argued, were necessary vehicles of acculturation. "Only by accumulating shared symbols, and the shared information that the symbols represent," he wrote, "can we learn to communicate effectively with one another in our national community."

Perhaps his greatest misstep was to be extremely specific about what the core of knowledge should consist of. He and a couple of UVA colleagues undertook to catalogue the exact information that Americans needed to participate in civic life and move up the socioeconomic scale. The three academics scanned newspapers and magazines for frequent phrases and ran them past hundreds of people whose jobs required them to communicate with the public: newspaper reporters and editors, trial lawyers who argued before juries. "Which words and concepts do you assume people know?" they asked. The responses they got were remarkably similar.

The result was an appendix to *Cultural Literacy* that came to be known simply as "the List." It included almost five thousand words and phrases that reflected what Hirsch and his colleagues had found. Starting with a few significant dates—"1066" was the first—it moved on to "Aaron, Hank," and ended with "Zurich." In between were such items as "Ali, Muhammad" and "Confucius," but the list was dominated by snippets of European-oriented, traditional American culture: historical references like "Geneva Convention," sayings like "lemmings to the sea." There were also scientific terms like "genus" and literary allusions like "Shoot, if you must, this old gray head . . ."

The List soon came to overshadow the book itself, to the point that pirated editions of the List alone were in wide circulation. Those five thousand words and phrases became the basis for informal quizzes, with friends competing to see who knew the most. But the List drew critics as well. To some, it seemed Hirsch wanted students to memorize disconnected facts, when he was actually advocating for a curriculum that would *introduce* the words and concepts in their broader context. Many saw the List as Hirsch's attempt to set himself up as a cultural arbiter, and they thought he'd left a lot out. "Oh yeah," said a friend of mine when I asked him if he knew the name E. D. Hirsch. "I hate that guy." When I asked why, my friend—a jazz aficionado—replied, "He didn't have Charlie Parker on his list!"

For Hirsch—a genial man who admits he can be clueless in predicting people's reactions—the first inkling of what awaited him came at a press conference in San Francisco, just as the book was being published. An Associated Press reporter asked the first question: "Is Cinco de Mayo on your list?" Hirsch admitted he didn't know what "Cinco de Mayo" was. By the time he got back to his hotel room, there was a message from a TV station in Texas asking him if he was worried about all the things that were not on the list. He was now.

While the book garnered some favorable reviews—including one from the *New York Times*—many publications excoriated Hirsch as a "white male elitist" who wanted to turn education into a Eurocentric version of Trivial Pursuit. Hirsch's view of culture, opined two left-wing academics in the *Harvard Educational Review*, was "at odds with the notion of difference, and maintains an ominous ideological silence—an ideological amnesia of sorts—regarding the validity and importance of the experiences of women, Blacks, and other groups excluded from the narrative of mainstream history and culture."

Meanwhile, many on the right—including officials in the Reagan administration—embraced Hirsch as a kindred spirit who bemoaned what they saw as a threat to traditional American values from the rising forces of multiculturalism and political correctness. The enthusiasm from the right only confirmed to leftists and liberals that Hirsch was an arch-conservative.

"You don't like to be falsely accused," Hirsch says now, the wounds still palpable, "especially of being a Republican."

HIRSCH HAS GONE on to produce many more books, including a popular series directed at parents that outlines what children at each grade level should know. In 1988, a foundation he created began developing the Core Knowledge Sequence, a list of topics that teachers should cover from kindergarten through eighth grade. The foundation got input from university professors, parents, teachers, and a multicultural advisory committee. Later, in collaboration with then New York City schools chancellor Joel Klein, it began building a curriculum that became Core Knowledge Language Arts—the same now in use at the Center City charter network—which extends from preschool through fifth grade.

The number of schools that now use either the Core Knowledge Sequence or Core Knowledge Language Arts is hard to pinpoint, but it's in the thousands. Still, they're only a fraction of the sixty-six thousand public elementary schools in the United States. The commercially published version of CKLA has less than 1 percent of the share of the market for English language arts curricula, while the basal reader used by Ms. Arredondo, *Journeys*, is the top choice, at 19 percent. While Hirsch has not been without influence, his impact has been greatly limited by the mistaken perception that he's a right-winger.

Hirsch's foray into the world of education policy brought him face-to-face with a fundamental truth: the more specific you are about what all students should learn, the more likely that you'll unleash a political firestorm. That's a shame, because the evidence is clear that countries with specific, challenging curricula have education systems that are more successful and equitable than ours.

If teachers don't know what their students have learned in years before, they may omit important content or repeat material students have previously covered. Some children can pick up information at home to fill the gaps, but others are left to flounder. Even if individual schools create their own specific curricula, low-income students are at risk because they're more likely to switch schools frequently. A student may find herself studying the life-cycle of the butterfly for the third time or rereading *Charlotte's Web*—and never learning anything about the American Revolution. Vagueness about curriculum also makes it difficult to train teachers effectively, because it's impossible to predict what content they'll be expected to teach.

In virtually all other developed countries, the national government has the power to set curriculum or at least a framework of what students should learn at each grade level. Most have exercised that power. In the United States, education has always been a matter of local control. While some states recommend certain textbooks and programs for school districts to choose from, the majority leave those decisions entirely to the districts. And many districts have left those decisions largely to the schools—which sometimes leave them to individual classroom teachers.

That's not to say there hasn't been standardization. In the early grades, the standard approach is to focus on skills rather than content. At higher grade levels, textbooks do specify content. But to make the textbooks attractive to as many districts as possible, publishers stuff them full of so much material that no teacher can cover everything in a year. They have to pick and choose, and whatever they choose is likely to get only superficial treatment.

Usually, controversy flares up only when the government takes a prominent role in setting specifics. And it's generally history and subjects that touch on culture that have ignited the fiercest debates, with much of the firepower coming from the right rather than—as in Hirsch's case—from the left. In the 1930s, a series of textbooks written by a left-leaning education professor was denounced as "un-American" and swiftly yanked from classrooms. In the 1960s, another flap arose over an anthropologically oriented, federally funded fifth-grade curriculum entitled "Man: A Course of Study." Conservative activists falsely claimed it furthered a "hippie-dippie philosophy" that incorporated gun control, pornography, evolution, and communism, and schools quickly abandoned it.

Nevertheless, in the early 1990s, a conservative Republican administration came to embrace the idea of creating content-specific curricula that states would be free to adopt or not. The results were disastrous.

TEN YEARS BEFORE, as a result of alarm about the state of American education, a government panel had been appointed. Its report, released in 1983, caught the public's attention. "If an unfriendly foreign power had attempted to impose on America the mediocre educational performance that exists today," it declared, "we might well have viewed it as an act of war." Its title was just as dire: *A Nation at Risk*. Some critics scoffed that the report was attempting to manufacture a "mythical national crisis," but even they admitted there were serious problems at the lower end of the socioeconomic spectrum. Among minority youth, functional illiteracy was as high as 40 percent.

Within a little over a year of the report's release, forty-four states had ratcheted up their graduation requirements, forty-five tightened teacher certification and evaluation standards, and twenty-seven increased instructional time. But these measures still left a gaping hole: Exactly what were teachers supposed to be teaching, and what skills were students supposed to master?

The solution, some argued, was to develop a set of standards broadly defining these things. States could then use the standards to create curricula setting out what topics should be covered in what order and what materials should be used. Teachers could be trained in the content they would be teaching. To hold both teachers and students accountable, states could administer tests measuring whether students had mastered that content. Support was widespread—at least in the abstract: 70 percent of Americans wanted schools to conform to "national standards and goals," and 69 percent supported a "standardized national curriculum." In 1989, when President George H. W. Bush summoned the nation's governors to an "education summit" in Charlottesville, Virginia, all but one showed up.

Some observers were particularly concerned about how little American students knew of history. Diane Ravitch—who gave E. D. Hirsch the idea to write *Cultural Literacy*—coauthored a book called *What Do Our 17-Year-Olds Know?* that also appeared in 1987. The answer was: not much. For decades, history had been pushed out of the curriculum by social studies, which prioritized topics deemed more relevant to students' lives, like "interpersonal relations" or the boosting of self-esteem. The result was that on a national test of history and literature, only 32 percent of students could place the Civil War within the correct fifty-year period and 28 percent thought Columbus's voyage to the New World occurred between 1750 and 1850.

In the years following the release of *A Nation at Risk* and the education summit, additional reports were issued and more commissions were set up—including one with the unfortunate acronym NCEST (the National Council on Education Standards and Testing), which was pronounced just as you might imagine. In 1992, NCEST recommended that national standards be developed in a number of core subjects, including English, geography, math, science—and history.

By this time, Ravitch, a lifelong Democrat, had accepted a job as an assistant secretary of education in the Bush administration. "Surely education," she thought, "was a nonpartisan issue." Her mission was to promulgate content-based standards that could improve the sad state of curriculum in the United States. To abide by limitations on the role of the federal government, the standards would be strictly voluntary. And to make doubly sure that the government's role was limited, Ravitch's office would merely issue grants to private groups to develop the standards.

Lynne Cheney, the head of the federal National Endowment for the Humanities, chaired the task force charged with funding the history standards and encouraged UCLA education professor Charlotte Crabtree to apply for the grant. A few years before, Cheney's agency had supported an effort by Crabtree and a UCLA history professor, Gary Nash, to improve history instruction by forging links between university-level historians and classroom teachers. Not long after Cheney's task force met, Crabtree and Nash were selected to direct the project.

Like Hirsch, Crabtree and Nash had no idea that their work would ultimately spark intense outrage. "I didn't realize I was walking into a buzz saw," Nash later recalled.

BEFORE DAWN ON OCTOBER 20, 1994—a few weeks before the National History Standards were due to be publicly released—Nash and Crabtree were jolted from their sleep by ringing phones. At the other end were friends on the East Coast who had just read a startling op-ed by Lynne Cheney in the *Wall Street Journal*.

Much had transpired since work had started on the standards. Nash and Crabtree had convened councils, forums, and focus groups involving almost six thousand history professors, teachers, school district officials, and representatives of education, parent-teacher, and public interest groups in multiple drafts of three sets of standards. There was one for kindergarten through fourth grade and two others covering the higher grade levels—one for American history and the other for world history.

Things had changed within the federal government as well. In November 1992, Bill Clinton, a Democrat, had been elected to replace George H. W. Bush as president. As a result, Cheney had stepped down from the National Endowment for the Humanities and was now ensconced at the American Enterprise Institute, a conservative think tank. But before leaving the government, Cheney had followed the history standards' development and expressed nothing but approval. "What nice work you do!" Cheney wrote to Crabtree on one draft.

Cheney's op-ed struck a different tone. "Imagine an outline for the teaching of American history in which George Washington makes only a fleeting appearance and is never described as our first president," it began. "Or in which the foundings of the Sierra Club and the National Organization for Women are considered noteworthy events, but the first gathering of the U.S. Congress is not." She went on to deliver a withering account of the not-yet-public US history standards, saying that not a single one mentioned the Constitution. Such luminaries as Robert E. Lee, Alexander Graham Bell, Thomas Edison, Albert Einstein, and Jonas Salk—dead white males all—didn't make an appearance, she complained. Meanwhile, the Ku Klux Klan was mentioned seventeen times and Senator Joseph McCarthy or McCarthyism nineteen times. The standards admiringly described the lavish court of a wealthy African ruler, Cheney charged, but instructed students to conduct a trial of John D. Rockefeller for participating in "unethical and amoral business practices." While Cheney hadn't yet seen the world history standards, she had heard they gave short shrift to Western civilization. All in all, she said, the standards reflected an "unqualified admiration for people, places and events that are politically correct," and a disdain for the achievements of the United States.

Crabtree and Nash were flabbergasted. Cheney's name counts were misleading because the standards mentioned no individuals by name. For example, one required that students understand "the institutions and practices of government created during the revolution and how they were revised between 1787 and 1815 to create the foundation of the American political system." While George Washington wasn't mentioned, it would be hard to cover the standard without him.

Cheney's assertions had come largely from the extensive suggested teaching materials that accompanied each standard. Many references to historical figures were simply repetitions within the same question or activity. All nineteen mentions of McCarthy and McCarthyism appeared within the same two pages of "examples of student achievement" accompanying a sub-standard that asked students to "demonstrate understanding of the origins and domestic consequences of the Cold War."

Cheney claimed the standards had been altered since the early drafts she'd approved, charging that the election of Bill Clinton had "unleashed the forces of political correctness." Nash and Crabtree denied the accusation, speculating that the real reason for Cheney's change of heart was that her husband, Dick Cheney, was contemplating a run for the presidency and wanted to curry favor with the Republican Party's right wing. Conservative support for national education standards had largely evaporated due to concern about federal encroachment on local prerogatives, and Republicans were even clamoring to abolish the federal Department of Education.

More fundamentally, the differences between Nash's and Cheney's conceptions of history—and how it should be taught—mirrored divisions within the American public at large. Nash believed a curriculum should shift its focus from Western civilization to other cultures during eras when events in the West were relatively unimportant. Cheney argued that a consistent focus on Western civilization was essential to developing loyal citizens, a position that led her to mock the standards for treating "gender relations under India's Gupta Empire" as equivalent in importance to the Magna Carta. Nash also believed it was just as important for students to understand that George Washington was a slave owner as it was for them to know he was a great man. Cheney thought it was essential to present figures like Washington as "models of greatness" who would inspire students to become heroes themselves.

Perhaps most fundamentally, she felt students needed to be taught that America was unique in the world, "a beacon of opportunity to people everywhere."

"If we do not teach our children these things," Cheney has written, "they may well conclude . . . this nation deserves no special support."

Cheney's argument may sound reminiscent of E. D. Hirsch's, but there's an important difference. Hirsch's goal was to provide disadvantaged students with access to references understood by the elite—whatever they might be—and knit the country together through a shared culture that could and should change over time. Cheney, on the other hand, was making a value judgment: American history and culture were superior.

But it wasn't only right-wingers who were unhappy with the standards. Even Diane Ravitch, along with the distinguished liberal historian Arthur Schlesinger Jr., had reservations. Nor was it only left-wing academics who agreed with Nash that history should attend to ordinary people and their struggles. Many textbooks already in use reflected that view. A reasoned national conversation could have ensued about the purposes of teaching history and what children should learn about the past, just as Hirsch's *Cultural Literacy* could have prompted rational debate.

Instead, Cheney's op-ed sparked a media circus, led by conservative commentator Rush Limbaugh. Limbaugh declared that the history standards should be flushed "down the sewer of multiculturalism" and claimed they would teach students "that America is a rotten place . . . and they don't have a chance here." If the standards were implemented, he predicted on TV, the result would be "a bunch of embittered people growing up, robbing and stealing and turning to crime because they've been told all their young lives that there's no future for them." Taking Cheney's name counts literally and treating the voluntary standards as though they were a required text, Limbaugh dramatically tore up a history book. "Here's Paul Revere," he said, balling up a page and casting it on the floor. "He's gone. . . . Here's George Washington as president. . . . He's gone." There went Thomas Edison, J. P. Morgan, and the Wright brothers.

The controversy raged for months, with conservative commentators like Phyllis Schlafly launching invective and groups like the Christian Coalition rallying their troops. Nash and Cheney became frequent on-air debate partners. The final blow came in January 1995, when Republican senator Slade Gorton introduced a resolution condemning the standards. It passed the Senate 99–1.

The lopsided nature of the vote had more to do with procedure than substance, but the public perception was that everyone—even liberal Democrats—believed the standards were beyond the pale. Even after Nash and Crabtree's organization released a revised version that won the support of some who opposed the earlier draft—including Ravitch and Schlesinger—the Clinton administration wanted nothing to do with it. Any attempts by the federal government to inject content into academic standards, however indirectly, had become politically toxic.

DESPITE THIS DEBACLE, reformers who had joined what was now known as the standards movement weren't ready to give up. They pinned their hopes on the states, which—unlike the federal government—were subject to no legal constraints on their ability to specify curricular content. Thanks to a 1994 federal law that required all states receiving federal funding to adopt standards in reading and math, forty-three had developed standards in at least three subjects by 1998.

But these standards still shied away from specifics. Here's a typical United States history standard, which was in effect in Arkansas until 2006:

Students use experiences, biographies, autobiographies or historical fiction to explain how individuals are affected by, can cope with, and can create change. Students will compare past and present similarities and differences in daily life. Students will examine how actions of groups and individuals cause change. Students will know that events can cause change and that change can cause events. Students will analyze how events can cause change and change can cause events. Students will identify the dreams and ideals that people from various groups have sought, some of the problems they encountered, and the sources of their strength and determination.

English standards were no better, usually failing to specify any particular books or authors. Washington State, for example, merely required students to read "a variety of traditional and contemporary literature." A think tank that periodically grades state standards for clarity and specificity has given nearly all of them low marks. In 1998, the states got an overall grade of D+, and in 2000 and 2006 a barely improved C–. History and social studies standards are particularly dismal; half the states get Fs in US history and almost as many in world history.

There have been a few exceptions. In the 1990s, Massachusetts managed to adopt a set of "curriculum frameworks" that included specific content, along with new tests based on it. The state now comes out at or near the top on national—and even international—tests. The bad news is that the state's test-score gap has only *expanded* in recent years and is now the third largest in the nation. Boston suffers from the same high school–level disparities that afflict other urban school systems. The root of the problem may be that, as elsewhere across the United States, elementary classrooms in Massachusetts are still largely content-free zones. The curriculum frameworks for those grade levels, especially in history and social studies, are vague, and students aren't tested on those subjects until fifth grade. That has left a vacuum that many elementary teachers have filled with what they're used to teaching: comprehension skills. Even with more specifics, it would be hard to test, on a broad scale, how much very young children are learning. To reach the crucial early years, one group of researchers concluded, the state needs to help administrators choose content-rich, engaging curricula.

Despite decades of effort to put them in place, high standards alone haven't boosted overall outcomes or narrowed gaps. States that have adopted the Common Core or something like it are now deemed to have high standards, but test scores there are no better than in states with less-ambitious goalposts. The one thing the United States has in common with countries that outperform it on international tests is high standards. What those other countries have, but we don't, is a detailed national curriculum along with tests based on it—which include essays rather than just multiple-choice questions, so they measure not only students' ability to recite facts but to connect and analyze them.

One line of attack on this approach is that the choice of content is arbitrary. Is the Ming dynasty more worthy of study than the empire of Mali? How much will students even remember about the Ming dynasty in ten years? But learning about any topic isn't an end in itself. The concepts and vocabulary students acquire through studying the Ming dynasty will enable them to understand and analyze other material, even if they don't remember the details. (Not to mention that the Ming dynasty could be really interesting.)

States and school districts also avoid specifics for the same reason the federal government now does: politics. State governments may be legally free to set curriculum, but that doesn't insulate them from criticism. In 2017, Florida passed a law allowing residents to mount legal challenges to textbooks and instructional materials they find objectionable. Members of the conservative group that pushed for the law have a litany of objections, ranging from the treatment of Islam to discussions of climate change and evolution.

Those on the left have their own concerns, similar to those that greeted Hirsch in 1987. Even among educators who believe in the importance of building knowledge, a frequently raised question is: *Whose* knowledge? Who decides which topics to include and which to leave out? Will black and brown students see themselves and their experiences?

These disagreements aren't always easily resolved, especially as our society becomes increasingly polarized. Still, we can't allow them to be used as a justification for keeping information from the students who need it most. And the political obstacles may not be as high as many fear; after conservatives attacked a proposed revision of the AP US history curriculum, for example, a compromise was reached that appears to have left everyone satisfied.

There's particular cause for optimism at the elementary level, where content-focused instruction has the best chance of narrowing the knowledge gap. Lost in the conflict over the National History Standards was the fact that the materials for kindergarten through fourth grade attracted little controversy—and still exist for any state or district that chooses to adopt them. They seem to have struck an acceptable balance between the "great men" approach to history and the more multicultural "bottom up" approach. The Bantu migrations in Africa are covered, along with "the movement of Europeans and Africans to the Western Hemisphere."

Hirsch's Core Knowledge curriculum similarly extends to cultures around the world and minorities within the United States. First-graders learn about Mesopotamia, Egypt, and the African savannah, and the second-grade unit on the Civil War begins with the story of Harriet Tubman and a discussion of slavery. A unit called "Fighting for a Cause" shows "how members of very powerful groups have often excluded members of other groups from exercising certain rights." As we've seen, Andrew Jackson is presented in all his complexity—hero of the Battle of New Orleans but also perpetrator of the Trail of Tears.

When I've asked teachers at Core Knowledge schools whether faculty or parents have found the curriculum objectionable in any way, they've all said no. Nor have there been significant battles over content-focused curricula in the handful of jurisdictions that have adopted one at the elementary level. And schools can always tweak or supplement a curriculum with material that relates to the needs or backgrounds of their students.

When it comes to injecting content into elementary school, the challenge may be less political than ideological. In addition to arguing that subjects like history and non-hands-on science are developmentally inappropriate, progressive educators urge that children should learn primarily through play and self-direction. It's certainly important that young children have an opportunity to play. But arguments against teaching them about the world are based on assumptions that don't stand up to the evidence on how children learn—or, judging from classrooms like Ms. Masi's, what they enjoy doing.

Past political battles have left American policy makers so gun-shy that when it came time to draft the Common Core State Standards, released in 2010, no one even suggested they should specify any content beyond a few key historical documents at the high school level. The many states that have adopted the standards or something like them have, with only a couple of exceptions, failed to make up for that omission. But if local education officials want all students to have a chance at meeting the high bar set by the standards—and receiving a meaningful education—that's exactly what they need to do.

FEBRUARY 2017

"So," I ask the second-graders sitting with me in Center City's high-ceilinged lunchroom, echoing with the voices of dozens of children, "I remember the first thing you learned about this year was 'Tall Tales and Fairy Tales,' but what came next?"

I'm trying to see how much they've retained of the enormous volume of information lobbed at them over the past five months. My lunch partners include Laura, a soft-spoken African American student, and David and Silas, both from Ethiopian families. The others are all from Spanish-speaking families and classified as English language learners: Andrea, small and lively; Oscar, a serious boy who often speaks up in class; and deep-voiced Mario.

The kids have been getting more curious about me as the year has progressed. Word has gotten around that I'm writing a book, and when Ms. Masi announced who would be having lunch with me, there were groans of disappointment from the others. I'm now sitting at "the VIP table" with the six anointed ones as they dig into today's offering— "breakfast for lunch," they tell me: pancakes, eggs, orange juice, bananas.

The children have a little trouble getting started, but once I give them a few prompts they're off and running, verbally tripping over one another in their excitement. Oscar wants to tell me the story of King Minos, but David interrupts him to explain the Battle of Thermopylae, where the Greeks managed to defeat the Persians—thanks, as David puts it, to "the narrow pass where the opponents would get trapped." I recall watching that read-aloud, as Ms. Masi and Ms. Fields funneled the kids through a small passage they had formed by pushing together chairs and desks, to give them the idea of what a "narrow pass" meant.

But Oscar hasn't forgotten about King Minos. "In the beginning," he starts, "King Minos's son was going to visit him, and uh . . . he had a accident—"

"Minos wanted revenge," Andrea interrupts. Maybe she's frustrated by Oscar's pace, or maybe she's trying to be helpful. "So he built a labyrinth—"

"And then he found the Minotaur, and then he was beating the Minotaur up," Oscar interjects. This is *his* story. "And then, um, he forgot to change, uh, the color to white, because, um, if it's black that represents, um, that King, um, Minos had won, so . . ."

The others pile on, eager to explain. But what's really remarkable—in addition to the enthusiasm these kids are displaying—is the vocabulary: *opponents, revenge, labyrinth, represents.* And it continues. Excited as they are to tell me about Greek myths, they're possibly even more eager to talk about Paul Bunyan, Casey Jones, and other figures from the American tall tales they learned about many months ago. Andrea laments that Casey Jones—the legendary train engineer who died in a crash, trying to make sure the mail got through—"*sacrificed* himself for all the people." One of the boys remarks that Pecos Bill turned a snake into a *lasso*, which leads to an argument about whether that came before or after he tamed a mountain lion. Suddenly everyone is talking at once.

"Calm *down*, everyone!" bellows tiny Andrea. Taking advantage of the temporary lull, I observe that it sounds like everyone really liked the tall tales. "Were they true?" I ask.

"*No!*" the kids chorus emphatically.

"It's an *exaggeration*," Laura says, using a vocabulary word they've heard many times.

I'm about to try to explore their views on Andrew Jackson when lunch is over. It's time to clean up and move outside to the asphalt expanse that serves as the school's playground. But the kids want to keep talking.

"Can you go to recess with us?" several of them ask. "When are you coming back?"

PART THREE

How We
Can Change

Creating and Delivering
a Content-Focused
Curriculum

CHAPTER 9

The Common Core: New Life for Knowledge, or Another Nail in Its Coffin?

I N THE LATE 1980s, a Yale undergraduate named David Coleman volunteered to tutor at New Haven's James Hillhouse High School. The school was only a mile from the Yale campus, but its students, predominantly black and poor, inhabited a different world from undergraduates like Coleman, a philosophy major who had grown up in Manhattan as the child of an academic and a psychiatrist.

As when E. D. Hirsch gave his reading test to students at J. Sargeant Reynolds Community College, or when Doug Lemov tried tutoring Alphonso, Coleman's experience working at Hillhouse brought him face-to-face with the ways in which our education system has failed poor and minority students. He was dismayed to find, as he later put it, that "none of these students were close—not even close—to being ready for Yale. They'd had so little practice with commanding difficult text."

One day, Coleman handed out copies of the Langston Hughes poem "Harlem," which begins with the famous lines: "What happens to a dream deferred? / Does it dry up / like a raisin in the sun?"

What would be different, Coleman asked, if Hughes had made the fruit a plum instead of a raisin? He didn't have any particular answer in mind. That was the point. The question, he believed, put him and the students on an equal plane, despite the greater amount of academic knowledge he'd been lucky enough to accumulate. It was like a question Coleman's rabbi had put to him years before, when, at the age of twelve, he was preparing for his bar mitzvah. As part of the ceremony, Coleman was to discuss the biblical passage in which Joseph interprets Pharaoh's dream about seven "plump and good" ears of grain being swallowed up by seven other "thin and blighted" ones. Why, the rabbi asked, were the ears of grain described in such detail?

"Now, why ask a child of twelve that question?" Coleman says now, in his quiet but intense manner. "Because the kid doesn't know. And the only way I could try to figure that out was to reread the story. But [the rabbi] didn't say to me, you're a child, you have no expertise in this field, you have no chance, because your knowledge is trivial compared to mine—which was true. Instead, he invited me into a sense of mystery and said, because you're reading this, I'm interested in what you think."

Coleman never figured out the answer—and the rabbi didn't have one. But the search for understanding led Coleman to explore the text deeply, which left a lasting impression. That was the kind of experience he was hoping to provide for the students he was tutoring. And in fact, one of the kids offered a strikingly perceptive explanation.

"Well," the boy said, "when a plum dries up, there's a seed, so there's hope. When a raisin dries up, it's gone."

Decades later, when Coleman found himself in a position to help re-shape American education as one of the lead authors of the Common Core State Standards, both experiences—his own attempted exegesis of a biblical passage as a twelve-year-old, and the Hillhouse student's insight about the Hughes poem—deeply influenced his vision of how teachers and students should interact: bringing their powers of observation to a rich, complex text and engaging in a common effort, more or less as equals, to mine it for knowledge.

At the same time, Coleman understood that teachers need to *build* knowledge for students beginning in the early-elementary years, just as his own knowledge had been built by his environment and education since birth. By the time he began working on the Common Core literacy standards in 2008, he had read and admired Hirsch's work, which made that argument forcefully. Coleman saw no contradiction between the two imperatives of building knowledge and—as he would come to call the approach he had taken with the Hillhouse students—"close reading." As he saw it, close reading was an important *means* of building knowledge.

Eventually, some observers—including Hirsch himself—came to feel that the Common Core overemphasized close reading to the point that the message about building knowledge, which they believed was the key to unlocking complex text in the first place, got lost. But a more basic problem was that many Americans, including many of the nation's teachers, had no idea that the Common Core had anything to do with knowledge at all.

IN 2001, after the collapse of the National History Standards, reformers secured the enactment of No Child Left Behind, which required states to develop their own standards in reading, math, and science, along with annual tests to assess school performance. (Although the law has required some testing in science, its primary focus has been reading and math.) The vast majority, as we've seen, made their standards either so vague or so encyclopedic that they were meaningless. And predictably, they made their tests easy, so scores would look good.

By the mid-2000s, there was a growing feeling that NCLB wasn't working. The performance of American students as compared to their peers in developed countries remained mediocre. Government officials and business leaders continued to worry about US competitiveness in the global economy. Some were also concerned about the gap between the test scores of more- and less-advantaged groups of students—a gap that NCLB had done much to expose but nothing to narrow.

In 2005, Diane Ravitch—who as a federal official had been instrumental in funding the development of the National History Standards—pointed out in a *New York Times* op-ed that students looked far more accomplished on state tests than on a more reliable nationwide assessment. Alabama's own tests, for example, showed that 83 percent of its fourth-graders were proficient in reading, but on the national test, the figure was only 22 percent. The proverbial foxes had been put in charge of guarding the henhouses. "Americans must recognize," Ravitch wrote, "that we need national standards, national tests and a national curriculum."

Americans weren't ready for all that, but government officials and business leaders began to take some cautious steps. They had learned two lessons from the national standards fiasco: First, the federal government couldn't be perceived as leading the push. Second, the standards had to steer clear of content. The safest subjects would be math and reading, both of which—or so leaders of the initiative believed—consisted of a content-free set of skills students needed to acquire at prescribed levels.

Beginning in 2006, three groups undertook a bipartisan effort to come up with new "common"—not "national"—standards, which the states could adopt voluntarily. The following year, those leading that effort came across an intriguing paper coauthored by David Coleman. Since his undergraduate tutoring experience, Coleman had been keenly interested in education. After failing to get a job teaching high school, he had landed at a leading management consulting firm, specializing in education-related issues. In the late 1990s, he teamed up with Jason Zimba, a professor of physics, to launch a company that analyzed test scores for schools. They came to feel the tests themselves were flawed because the standards underlying them were "so vast and vague." Eventually, they collaborated on a paper arguing that math and science standards should be "fewer, clearer, and higher."

That was the paper spotted by leaders of the nascent common standards movement, who recruited Zimba to work on math and Coleman on English language arts. The Gates Foundation pledged funding that ultimately amounted to $240 million, and 135 experts were enlisted to help draft and review what would become the Common Core standards. The newly elected Obama administration announced plans to incentivize states to adopt the standards and help fund the development of rigorous tests based on them. The effort was moving ahead swiftly and smoothly, with what appeared to be nearly universal support.

In July 2009—while the Common Core was still embryonic and had not been publicly released—the first rumblings of criticism emerged. It came from an unexpected source: the Core Knowledge Foundation, founded by a man Coleman venerated, E. D. Hirsch. "Voluntary National Standards Dead on Arrival," read the headline of a post on the foundation's blog. The post argued that a draft of the literacy standards revealed they were just as skills-focused and content-free as the "dysfunctional state standards already in place."

Coleman—who had taken a lead role in creating the draft along with a team of about forty others—was stung. He wasn't sure Hirsch had written the unsigned screed (in fact, the author was Robert Pondiscio, then a vice president at the Core Knowledge Foundation), but the post must have reflected his views. Still, Coleman decided not to mount a counterattack.

"Rather than dismissing him," he says of Hirsch, "I said, let's really talk. Because you've got something."

Indeed, the draft was basically a list of skills students would need to be "college- and career-ready"—for example, supporting claims about a text by citing evidence from it, or summarizing a text and determining the main ideas. What texts? On what topics? The draft didn't say. While "common core" implies a shared pool of content, the phrase comes from a survey of high school standards in English language arts and math. The survey found that the states had independently reached a high degree of consensus on the "fundamental knowledge" that all students should acquire. But that formulation was misleading.

In math, there may be different ways to teach adding and subtracting fractions, but there's no separate "content." In language arts, though, the "knowledge" turned up by the survey consisted of skills that failed to identify specific content, like those listed in the draft Coleman had overseen. At the inception of what became the Common Core, there seems to have been little recognition that equating math and literacy standards was like equating apples and oranges—or apples and something really different, like fish.

This was the point E. D. Hirsch tried to impress upon Coleman when they met to discuss their differences. As Hirsch knew from painful experience, politics made it impossible to promulgate a national content-rich curriculum. But he did what he could. One change to the standards that came out of the discussion, according to Coleman, was requiring that students read a specific percentage of nonfiction—or "informational text"—not just in English class but in subjects like history and science as well. The final standards say that 50 percent of the texts young children are exposed to should be nonfiction, increasing to 70 percent by high school. Hirsch and Coleman saw this as a way of diversifying the steady diet of simple fiction fed to elementary students, which was unlikely to expand their store of knowledge.

Linda Bevilacqua, who heads the Core Knowledge Foundation, accompanied Hirsch to meet with Coleman. As Bevilacqua tells it, the men were deep into a hyperintellectual discussion of theories of literary interpretation when Coleman turned to her and asked, "Linda, what do you have to say?"

"And I'm pragmatic," Bevilacqua says. "I said, look, you have exemplar texts at each grade level that have nothing to do with each other. It gives the impression that all you care about is having kids read nonfiction text, but not *what* the text is. And he said, okay—can you fix that?"

Bevilacqua came up with a one-page example showing how, from kindergarten through fifth grade, schools could select a series of books on the same general topic—in her example, the human body—some of which were more complex and could be read aloud by a teacher. The official standards explain that this "is like giving children various pieces of a puzzle in each grade that, over time, will form one big picture."

Hirsch had one more suggestion for Coleman. The draft didn't even mention the word *curriculum*, which was something any state or school district would need to adopt if students were to be equipped to meet the new standards. Ultimately, this note on "range and content of student reading" was added:

> By reading texts in history/social studies, science, and other disciplines, students build a foundation of knowledge in these fields that will also give them the background to be better readers in all content areas. Students can only gain this foundation when the curriculum is intentionally and coherently structured to develop rich content knowledge within and across grades.

In 2010, when the Common Core standards were released, Hirsch was an enthusiastic booster. "The document has been criticized by many observers as offering little improvement over the broad and insubstantial individual state standards they would replace," he wrote in a *Washington Post* op-ed, echoing the criticism that his own foundation had lobbed the year before. But, he went on, "look closely." Pointing to the statements he'd had a hand in inserting, Hirsch argued that in fact, the Common Core represented an approach that would help narrow the "test-score gap, which is essentially a knowledge gap, between racial and ethnic groups."

The initiative appeared to be back on track. Coleman had obtained a seal of approval from the man whose ideas he considered to be at the heart of his work. Hirsch had reason to believe the Common Core would at last realize the vision of educational equity to which he had devoted twenty-five years of his life. And the standards themselves were sweeping the country. Within six months of their release, thirty-nine states had signed on; within three years, only four states were holdouts.

AT THE SAME TIME, fierce opposition was brewing. The first salvos came from the right, which saw the standards as an intrusion on the autonomy of states and localities. Led by members of the Tea Party and media personalities like Glenn Beck, the attackers discerned in the Common Core the very appearance of federal involvement in education its creators had taken pains to avoid. The right wing pointed to the massive amount of federal funding that was dangled before cash-strapped states to induce them to adopt the standards—a total of $4 billion. To many, that was coercion—and, even worse, coercion by the Obama administration. Beginning in 2011, the administration provided an additional powerful incentive in the form of waivers from the stringent requirements of No Child Left Behind, which were also used to encourage states to use test scores in teacher evaluations. Although the origins of the Common Core predate Obama's election, some started calling it "Obamacore."

Complaints from the left picked up when tests aligned with the standards began rolling out. Much of the opposition came from teachers who objected to being evaluated on the basis of scores on these harder tests—tests they said they hadn't been trained to prepare their students to take. Some English teachers mistakenly interpreted the required percentages of nonfiction as applying to their classes alone, rather than across all subjects, and warned that beloved or classic literature was being squeezed out. Early-childhood educators complained the standards overemphasized academics at an age when they felt priority should be given to social-emotional development and play.

Generally, those on the left felt the standards were unrealistic in their expectations and that teachers hadn't played enough of a role in their creation—despite the fact that both major teachers' unions said their members had participated in several review panels. Those who were already hostile to the Gates Foundation because of its support for test-based teacher evaluations and charter schools saw its heavy investment as part of a plot to "privatize" American education. By now, that group included Diane Ravitch, who had decided that her enthusiasm for "national standards, national tests and a national curriculum" had been a terrible mistake.

The last opponents to come forward were parents—mainly white, suburban, and relatively affluent—some of whom organized boycotts of

Common Core–aligned tests. They were influenced by their children's teachers, but many also objected to the length of the tests, which could take nine hours or more, and their difficulty. Some children suffered from test anxiety and feelings of failure, with one mother reporting that her nine-year-old had attempted to hang himself, and some pediatricians saw an uptick in stress-related illnesses. Educators complained that children were crying during or after the tests, while others vomited or lost control of their bowels or bladders. In New York, one of the first states to start giving Common Core tests, parental opposition was strong enough that by 2015, 20 percent of students in grades three through eight had opted out.

By early 2017, twenty-one of the forty-six states that had adopted the standards were in the process of revising them, although most were not making substantial changes, while another eight had repealed or withdrawn them. The plan had been that states would use tests created by two Common Core testing consortia, and at one point forty-five states had signed on. But now, just twenty states and the District of Columbia were using one of the common tests. Pundits began to debate whether the Common Core would soon go the way of other efforts at reform, although others predicted that the changes sparked by the standards would be hard to reverse.

Perhaps the most widespread misconception about the Common Core is that it requires specific content—a misconception fueled by the oft-quoted official formulation of the standards as defining what "students should *know* and be able to do." In light of Hirsch's objections, this charge is painfully ironic. Even more painful is the fact that very few are aware of the language added at Hirsch's behest, which doesn't appear in the standards themselves but rather in voluminous supplementary material that is rarely read.

The same is true of explanatory language known among Common Core aficionados as "the three shifts." The first shift is that students need regular practice reading complex text; the second is that they need to be able to ground their claims in evidence from the text; and the third is that students must have "extensive opportunities to build knowledge" through "content-rich nonfiction."

When I first sat down with Gaby Arredondo, the first-grade teacher whose class I followed during the fall of 2016, I discovered she'd never heard of the three shifts. When I listed the first two, she nodded; the standards made those points clear. But when I mentioned "building knowledge," she was suddenly confused.

"Wait," she said. "But *that's* not in the standards."

Ms. Arredondo is far from alone. David Liben, a former elementary educator who helped write the literacy standards, says he has spoken to perhaps ten thousand teachers about them. He routinely projects a slide showing the paragraph from the Common Core document that says building knowledge is like giving children "pieces of a puzzle" that will eventually form one big picture. Then he asks the audience to raise their hands if they've ever seen that language.

"And do you know how many people raise their hands?" he says, his voice rising in frustration. "Zero."

MANY TEACHERS AND administrators *have* gotten the message that the Common Core requires students to read more nonfiction and more complex text, even in elementary school. But many have assumed, despite Linda Bevilacqua's human body example, that it doesn't matter what topics kids are reading about as long as they're developing transferable skills.

Skills that appear to work with simple fiction, however, don't necessarily transfer to nonfiction. One lesson plan available online on "making inferences" focuses on the story *Too Many Tamales*, in which a young girl becomes convinced that she's lost her mother's diamond ring in a batch of tamales. Maria and her mother are working together in the kitchen, and the mother has placed her ring on the counter. Maria admires how it sparkles. The mother leaves to answer the phone. "Maria couldn't help herself," the text says. "She wiped her hands on the apron and looked back at the door."

The lesson plan advises the teacher to engage in the following think-aloud:

> The author says Maria loved how the ring sparkled. I know that if I love how something sparkles, I want to pick it up and look at it closely, so Maria probably wants to pick up the ring to look at it more closely.
>
> The author says Maria wiped her hands and then looked back at the door. I know that if my hands are dirty, I want to wipe them off before picking something up, and if I'm doing something I shouldn't do, I check the door to make sure no one will see me. I think she was going to try the ring on.

You could argue that this exercise is unnecessary—not only would most children be able to intuit that Maria is going to try on the ring, they'll also find that out when they turn the page. But at least they're being asked to make inferences based on something they're familiar with: typical human behavior. With nonfiction texts or historical fiction, it can be impossible to make an inference or draw a conclusion—or just understand the text—unless you have relevant knowledge.

Many educators have tried adding new Common Core "skills" to their students' repertoire: connecting claims to evidence, identifying nonfiction "text features" like glossaries, even the supposed skill of reading complex text. But if students can't understand the text, these skills are no more helpful than the old ones.

Some teachers have interpreted the Common Core to mean that it's good for students to grapple with *any* complex text, no matter how dry and boring. They may have been encouraged in this interpretation by some of the examples provided in an appendix to the standards: a treatise on recommended levels of insulation and an executive order on strengthening federal environment, energy, and transportation management.

No wonder many educators have denounced as cruel and unrealistic the directive that all students, including those who are far behind, engage with grade-level complex text. That's certainly true if teachers approach it in the standard way: teaching a ten-or-fifteen-minute "mini-lesson" on a "skill" and then sending students off with some complex nonfiction text to practice on—regardless of whether students know anything about the subject.

In 2016, I was visiting a first-grade classroom at a high-poverty charter school. A teacher was sitting at a desk in the corner, going over student work, while the students were busy filling out worksheets. I noticed one small girl, seated near the teacher, drawing on a piece of paper. Ten minutes later she was still drawing. She had sketched a string of human stick figures and was busy coloring them yellow.

I knelt next to her and asked, "What are you drawing?"

"Clowns," she answered confidently.

"Why are you drawing clowns?"

"Because it says right here, 'Draw clowns,'" she explained.

Running down the left side of the paper was a list of reading comprehension skills. The words the girl was pointing to were "Draw conclusions." It turned out that this first-grader was supposed to be making inferences and drawing conclusions about a dense text on Brazil, which was lying facedown on her desk. Not only was she unaware that the article was there until I turned it over, she had never even heard of Brazil and was unable to read the word.

This example may be egregious, but it reflects an assumption on the part of at least some teachers that the directive to have students read complex text means they should put impenetrable text in front of them and let them struggle. Or, perhaps, draw clowns.

At the same time, most teachers continue to use leveled readers as their primary means of instruction: in 2016, more than two-thirds of elementary teachers reported using them in some way, and they were the most commonly used type of English language arts material among both elementary and secondary ELA teachers. Perhaps some of these teachers are also giving their students complex, grade-level text and helping them navigate through it—or better yet, building their knowledge so they have a chance of understanding it independently. At this point, it's hard to say.

DAVID COLEMAN AND his coauthors didn't intend all this, nor did they envision that students would spend *all* their time engaged in close reading of complex text, as some critics have charged. That's not the way to build a base of knowledge or turn kids into avid readers. But they didn't want students locked into their individual "levels," either. The idea was for teachers to guide students through short, meaty texts as a group exercise, asking carefully crafted questions that would lead them to analyze the passage without giving away the answers.

In an attempt to help teachers understand what "close reading" looked like, the earnest, bespectacled Coleman became the unlikely star of a couple of internet videos that went viral. His objective was to reverse what he and others saw as a damaging tendency to focus students' attention on everything but the text itself. Under the balanced-literacy approach, teachers may spend more time previewing the text than actually reading it: summarizing what it says, explaining the context along with unfamiliar words and concepts, asking students to make text-to-self connections and predictions about what will happen.

In a video featuring the Gettysburg Address, Coleman warns against beginning with the historical context. Instead, he urges teachers to try asking students what word Lincoln uses most frequently. When they discover that it's *dedicate*, Coleman suggests, help them see how the meaning changes depending on the other words it's connected to: *conceive, consecrate, devotion*. Take your time, he advises; the lesson might take three to five days.

"Students can learn that the payoff of understanding one word can be deeper understandings of an entire text," Coleman says. "What's at stake here, in this kind of patient teaching, is letting kids of a very wide range of ability into the hard work of reading a text closely, carefully, and well."

The critics quickly piled on. One teacher complained that Coleman, by neglecting personal experience, was silencing student voices. Another said the technique "mimics the conditions of a standardized test" and "makes school wildly boring." Teachers characterized Coleman as a bumbling naïf who would be eaten alive if he tried to deliver one of those lessons to a classroom full of inner-city teenagers. And many bristled at his apparent exclusion of any kind of context.

"Imagine learning about the Gettysburg Address without a mention of the Civil War, the Battle of Gettysburg, or why President Abraham Lincoln had traveled to Pennsylvania to make the speech," fumed one anti–Common Core education columnist.

Coleman says he was only suggesting that teachers *start* by putting the text in front of kids. Once they've had a crack at making sense of it under the guidance of well-crafted questions, the teacher can fill in the gaps in their knowledge. If you start by trying to set the stage, Coleman argues, you may never get to the text itself. "If you're teaching the Gettysburg Address," he says, "and you ask kids first, let's talk about the Civil War, let's talk about slavery. . . . That conversation is an endless conversation."

Coleman is right that allowing kids to plunge into a rich text and see what they can make of it can have the surprising effect of leveling the playing field. Often, teachers who have tried the technique tell me, it's the struggling students—the English language learners, the kids with learning disabilities—who come up with the keenest insights. It's also true that all students need a chance to grapple directly with more challenging syntax, vocabulary, and grammar. It's important for students to learn that it's possible to wrest meaning from text that looks intimidating if they persevere. But in his zeal to discourage teachers from interposing pre-reading activities between the students and the text, Coleman unintentionally helped obscure the idea that building knowledge is an essential underpinning of the Common Core.

WHILE CLOSE READING has gotten far more attention, Coleman insists he has devoted just as much time and effort to spreading the message about knowledge. In one particularly well-turned phrase, Coleman has called for "restoring elementary school teachers to their rightful place as guides to the world." So why has that message been largely ignored?

Coleman's theory is that when he modeled close reading in the videos, he "crossed a red line" by "stepping into the shoes of an actual teacher." That invited attacks from teachers who resented his presumption. He may also have underestimated how loud and clear the knowledge message needed to be, given how radically it departs from current practice and how skills-focused the standards are. And, of course, it's hard for teachers to single-handedly build knowledge in the absence of a content-focused curriculum. Even if teachers hear that message, there may not be much they can do with it.

It doesn't help that many influential figures, like Lucy Calkins, have generally ignored the Common Core's message about the need to build knowledge. In a document aimed at textbook publishers, Coleman and another lead author of the standards made it clear the Common Core was taking aim at Calkins's balanced-literacy approach, cautioning that teachers should avoid "cookie-cutter" questions like "What is the main idea?" But in *Pathways to the Common Core*, Calkins manages to interpret the standards to require little change in existing balanced-literacy practice.

If there's one clear demand at the heart of the Common Core, it's that all students spend at least some time grappling with grade-level text rather than text presumed to be on their own level. But Calkins argues the standards put that decision "squarely into the hands of teachers and school leaders." Her recommendation would be familiar to any balanced-literacy practitioner: "Move students up levels of text complexity by providing them with lots of just-right high-interest texts and the time to read them."

Calkins isn't single-handedly responsible for the widespread misinterpretations among teachers—and the general public—of the Common Core. But her influence shouldn't be underestimated. After Ms. Arredondo expressed surprise that building knowledge was one of the shifts required, I asked what she had read in her training about the standards.

She could only remember being assigned one book on the subject: Lucy Calkins's *Pathways to the Common Core.*

STUDENTS MAY NOT have been acquiring much knowledge from simple fiction, but at least they had a good chance of understanding what they were reading. If they're asked to practice their "skills" on a nonfiction text that assumes a great deal of background knowledge and vocabulary they don't possess, it's liable to be a complete waste of time, and the Common Core could just end up making a bad situation worse.

That is the fear that has haunted E. D. Hirsch since he read the early draft of the literacy standards. The addition of his suggested language about the need for content-rich curriculum and building knowledge, while better than nothing, could only paper over the standards' original sin: the false equivalence between literacy and math skills. It also ignored a fundamental difference between Hirsch and Coleman. For Hirsch, whose focus is on the elementary years, it's critical to give kids as much knowledge as possible as quickly and efficiently as possible. The critics who accused him, back in the 1980s and 1990s, of taking a Trivial Pursuit approach weren't completely wrong. Depth of knowledge or aesthetic appreciation of literature isn't what he's after. He's said, for example, that he would be happy to have students read a CliffsNotes version of *Romeo and Juliet* rather than the play itself. His objective is to enable students to recognize allusions and concepts taken for granted by the cultural elite, so they'll be able to assimilate new material and join literate society. Rather than sharing Coleman's perspective that close reading is a way of building knowledge, Hirsch sees it as diverting precious attention away from a text's meaning and toward its surface features. If students who have already acquired broad knowledge choose to attend a liberal arts college and engage in close reading of lyric poetry— the kind of milieu where Hirsch thinks close reading belongs—that's fine with him. But it's not his main concern.

For Coleman, on the other hand, it's imperative that all students engage in the effort to mine complex text for nuggets of insight. While he acknowledges the need to provide students with some measure of broad knowledge, that's not the kind of knowledge he feels will stay with them and have meaning. "I think the biggest threat to reading, particularly in later grades," he says, "is walking away from a document with nothing but the most basic gist or summary. Kids don't really read it, they try to overhear, what's the bottom line from this, and they then repeat that to one another. And poorly done, the knowledge-based approach—you see the problem with literature especially. What's *Romeo and Juliet* about? Young love betrayed. Well, why read it now, because we've learned what we can know from it?"

Hirsch and Coleman are like the blind men in the parable with their hands on different parts of the elephant. Hirsch's hands are on elementary school, where it's important to acquaint children with lots of information so they can acquire deeper understanding later on. Coleman's hands are mostly on high school, by which time (he assumes, perhaps inaccurately) students will have acquired the foundational knowledge they need to take a closer look.

Coleman acknowledges that insisting students should look only within "the four corners of the text" underplays the amount of background knowledge required to understand *any* text. Even the student he was tutoring at Hillhouse High School had to know that plums have seeds and raisins do not. (Not to mention the knowledge of vocabulary and syntax that allowed him to interpret the phrase "a dream deferred.") Coleman says he perhaps overstated the case for excluding extraneous information in order to counter the emphasis in most classrooms on pre-reading activities.

Hirsch's vision and Coleman's aren't necessarily incompatible. It's both possible and desirable to build knowledge through a coherent curriculum *and* have students spend time carefully reading rich text. But eventually Hirsch could no longer stifle his doubts about the skills-based nature of the standards. In a book published in 2016, *Why Knowledge Matters*, he openly declared his disillusionment.

Still, some educators have managed to embrace both perspectives— and to recognize that it's impossible to satisfy the Common Core's demand that all students read complex text without systematically building their knowledge. While that community constitutes only a small fraction of the nation's three-million-plus teachers, it's likely at a high-water mark in American history. And for all the flaws in the Common Core literacy standards, we almost certainly wouldn't have reached that point without them.

MARCH 2017

At last I've found a replacement for Ms. Arredondo: Aasiya Townsell. Like Ms. Arredondo, she's young—in her third year of teaching—and she teaches first grade at a D.C. charter school that serves a predominantly low-income and African American population. Like Star Academy, Ms. Townsell's school—Excel Academy—uses a skills-focused basal reader. In fact, it's the same one: *Journeys.*

There are differences as well. Excel Academy, which goes from prekindergarten to eighth grade, is all girls. That's no guarantee of calm and order, but it helps. And Ms. Townsell is acutely aware that something is missing from her school's curriculum. A former art major with a warm and sunny disposition, Ms. Townsell would prefer to teach by engaging her girls in creative projects on substantive topics.

Excel calls for students to get forty-five minutes of social studies or science every day, and unlike some of her colleagues, Ms. Townsell ensures that her girls get it. Last month was Black History Month, and the school allowed teachers additional time to focus on topics relating to that theme. Ms. Townsell spent every morning on slavery, a topic her students voted for after a trip to the National Museum of African American History and Culture on the National Mall. She put together a curriculum on her own and taught about Harriet Tubman, Sojourner Truth, slave ships, and slave cabins. The girls were particularly excited about "slave food" after one group brought in cornbread, rice, and beans.

But the science and social studies "curricula" at Excel are largely haphazard and superficial. The lesson plans Ms. Townsell uses are put together by another first-grade teacher who relies on online resources and pages excerpted from a textbook that Ms. Townsell has never seen and doesn't know the name of. Lessons are often delivered at the last minute. One topic was simply "culture." Ms. Townsell says the lesson was "so random," dealing with "cultures in Paris, cultures in Japan. It was simply talking about the difference of like when they eat dinner," as well as differences in how people greet one another or what they wear. A lesson on climate that I observed ran into trouble when Ms. Townsell realized that a color-coded map had been printed out in black and white.

The lessons Ms. Townsell creates herself can also go in unexpected directions because of the priority she places on student choice. She decided the class would do a project for Women's History Month, but the girls aren't learning much about women's history. They voted for a project that would enable them to perform, so Ms. Townsell wrote new lyrics to a song called "Me Too," by Meghan Trainor, that the girls could dance to. While the original words talk about being sexy and never paying for drinks, Ms. Townsell's lyrics center on why it's important for girls "to read and to be smart and focus and learn." The girls also read aloud essays they wrote about how much they appreciate their mothers. "They unanimously decided, we want to talk about our mothers," she says, laughing. "So well, okay, that's your choice."

In any event, Ms. Townsell hasn't been able to engage the girls in projects as much as she'd like. The school is threatened with closure if test scores don't improve this year, and teachers are being required to stick closely to the scripts in *Journeys* in hopes that will do the trick.

On the day of my first visit, the class is rotating through centers while Ms. Townsell leads small groups in guided reading. One group focuses on the skill of recognizing character traits, using a simple story about a skunk who is cooking soup for her friends. Ms. Townsell tries to coax the girls to come up with precise adjectives to describe the skunk—not just *nice*, but *helpful* and *caring*. The next, more advanced group practices finding the main idea. Ms. Townsell has chosen a book on a topic close to her heart: Venus and Serena Williams, the black tennis stars she idolized as an African American girl. But she's surprised to find her students have never heard of them. After the girls read the book, she asks them to explain the main idea.

"Tennis?" one girl guesses.

That's a *detail*, Ms. Townsell informs her. She's pleased when another girl identifies the main idea as "loving sisters" and points to the sentence "Venus likes to help her sister" as evidence.

The other students are rotating through a variety of activities. One group is working on the *Journeys* skill of the week, comparing and contrasting. Ms. Townsell has provided a choice of topics that draw on everyday information: cats and dogs, apples and oranges, vegetables and fruits. The most popular topic is cats and dogs, and despite the efforts of the teacher's aide, Ms. Fletcher, to focus on comparing and contrasting, the conversation mostly revolves around personal anecdotes. One girl describes how her cat meows when someone rings the doorbell, another shows off her ability to make dog and cat sounds, and a third volunteers that cats are scared of cucumbers—a fact gleaned from a popular series of YouTube videos. Later, when I ask Ms. Townsell whether this exercise helped students with the activity in *Journeys*, she says not really. They were supposed to contrast a fictional text about art—a story called "The Dot"—with a nonfiction text about three different artists. But the nonfiction text contained so little information that there was nothing much to compare.

At another center, students are practicing creating past and present tense verbs by tacking on *ed* or *ing*. In the library corner, girls are reading books at their levels. The fourth center is a bank of computers programmed with software intended to boost reading skills by giving students passages to read on random topics and asking them comprehension questions.

A tiny girl named Keisha is surveying a screen of pictures with labels like *Diwali*, *Fast Food*, *Crayons*, and *Barack Obama*. She chooses Barack Obama and puts on headphones. The computer starts showing her screens with photographs of the former president and accompanying text that seems pretty challenging for a first-grader. But Keisha tells me she's not reading—she's just listening. When the program asks how many years Obama was president, she chooses the number ten. Later, I find out that Keisha had neglected to submit her "pre-test," so the program gave her access to a level that was far too advanced.

I also find out that a few years ago, Excel Academy used the Core Knowledge curriculum. At that time, Ms. Townsell tells me, the school was known for getting good results on reading tests and poor ones in math. Core Knowledge got dropped during a period of administrative turnover, and curricula that were supposedly better aligned to the Common Core were adopted on the advice of a consulting firm. Now the situation is the opposite, she says: math scores are rising, and reading scores are the problem.

Unlike the *Journeys* basal, the new math curriculum, called Eureka Math, does seem to be aligned to the Common Core. Once she got used to it, Ms. Townsell became convinced of the value of a good curriculum. In the past, she says, she "wasn't the best math teacher." But this year, "I'm like, oh my goodness, I love math! We could do it all day." And while the school as a whole is improving in math, Ms. Townsell's class is outpacing all the others.

As Ms. Townsell's students did last month, Ms. Masi's second-graders have been learning about slavery. A classroom poster describes a journey on the Underground Railroad, complete with stick figures representing "passengers" and a "conductor," who is saying, "Follow me!" There's also a chart about the Lincoln–Douglas debates of 1858, outlining the position each man held on slavery. Today's topic is the beginning of the Civil War.

Leading the class is Ms. Washington, the teacher-in-training who has been working alongside Ms. Masi. This is one of the first Core Knowledge lessons that Ms. Washington has planned on her own, and she's feeling a little overwhelmed. She's taken courses on how to do a read-aloud, how to build vocabulary, and how to do guided reading. But her teacher-training program hasn't prepared her to teach anything this substantive, and she isn't exactly an expert on the material. Still, the face she presents to the students is calm and confident.

During the read-aloud, Ms. Washington pauses periodically to ask questions that keep the students engaged: Who's going to fire the first shot at the Battle of Bull Run? Will the war end quickly? Who do you think is going to win, the Union or the Confederacy?

One student says he thinks the Confederates will fire the first shot, because they fired the first shot at Fort Sumter. Another predicts the war isn't going to end quickly because the Confederates have more soldiers than the Union thinks they do. A third predicts the Union will win: "That's why we don't have no more slavery in this century."

It helps that the students are fascinated by the subject matter. They've been especially struck by the story of Harriet Tubman and the harsh conditions of slave life. The Spanish-speaking mother of one girl told me her daughter used the word *pobrecitos*—poor little things—to describe the plight of the slaves. Many students are keen admirers of Abraham Lincoln.

Ms. Washington has some things to learn. When one girl volunteers that the Confederacy "was fighting for slavery to expand," and Ms. Washington accepts the answer, Ms. Masi interrupts, pointing out that the objective was for states to have the right to *choose* whether or not to have slavery. Ms. Masi is a stickler for precision. Later, when Ms. Washington reads about Lincoln's plan to end the war quickly by capturing Richmond, the capital of the Confederacy, Ms. Masi speaks up again, hoping to coach the kids into making a connection to their previous lessons. She says the plan reminds her of something that happened in the War of 1812, prompting Yolanda to recall that the British also wanted to capture a capital—Washington, D.C.

But those few missteps aside, Ms. Washington has been able to conduct a successful lesson despite her inexperience. That's largely because the curriculum provided engaging material for her to work with. Yes, she had to figure out how best to *present* it—what questions to ask, when to pause for clarification, how to keep the kids interested. But she didn't need to figure out *what* to teach, as so many inexperienced teachers do.

CHAPTER 10

No More Jackpot Standards

IN THE EARLY spring of 2011, a year after the release of the Common Core, Aaron Grossman was surfing the internet in his cubicle at the Washoe County School District's central office in Reno, Nevada, trying to figure out what it all meant. The more he read, the more puzzled he became. It seemed that he and pretty much everyone else in Washoe—and across the country—had been getting it all wrong.

Grossman, a former elementary teacher, had been working in the central office for a couple of years, recruited there because he'd managed to devise a foolproof way to boost scores on Nevada's state tests. The tests were supposed to be tied to the state standards, but, like most, Nevada's were ridiculously voluminous. One researcher has estimated that if teachers tried to cover all the standards they're supposed to, schools would need to go up through grade twenty-one or twenty-two. But Grossman had figured out that only about 18 percent of those standards showed up on the state tests—the same 18 percent, year after year. All teachers had to do was teach that 18 percent and they could forget about the rest.

For example, in any given year the third-grade tests would have a question on similes. Knowing that, third-grade teachers could be sure to cover similes. That didn't necessarily mean getting kids to appreciate the power or beauty of a literary device. More likely, it would mean just teaching them how to identify a simile so they could pick the correct multiple-choice answer. In some places, the standards that were tested were referred to as "power standards." This being Nevada, teachers called them "jackpot standards."

The focus on skills fit in with the district's overall approach. On Mondays, teachers gave students a pre-test focusing on the basal's skill of the week and then taught it for the next four days—with the principal popping in periodically to make sure they had the appropriate "I can" statement written on the board, as in "I can identify a simile." On Friday, the teachers would test kids again and work more intensively with those whose scores indicated they hadn't mastered it.

Then Nevada adopted the Common Core. National literacy experts and textbook publishers were sending out the message that the switch was no big deal. A skill that used to be taught in one grade might now be taught in another: homonyms used to be taught in fourth grade; now they're in third. Grossman was supposed to alert teachers to these minor differences—to create a "crosswalk" between the old standards and the new ones, in education-speak—so they could continue to use his jackpot-standards framework.

But now Grossman had come across a recording of someone named David Coleman talking about the "instructional shifts" required by the Common Core. This was before Coleman had been anointed as one of *Time* magazine's "100 Most Influential People," before YouTube commenters started castigating him as "the devil" and "a crook," before nearly every educator in America had a strong opinion about him. All Grossman knew was that Coleman seemed to have written the Common Core. It wasn't just about moving skills around, according to Coleman. It was about fundamentally changing instruction to focus on content, have students read more complex text and nonfiction, and build the kind of vocabulary that cropped up repeatedly in academic writing—words like *consequential, subsequent, hypothesis*. What Coleman was saying not only undermined Grossman's approach; it meant that Washoe was going in absolutely the wrong direction.

"I went to my director and I said, there's this guy David Coleman," Grossman recalls. "And the response was, who's David Coleman?" The chief performance officer and the director of assessment also evinced a lack of interest. But Grossman kept following one link after another and finding more and more information from Coleman and others who had created the Common Core. None of it squared with what his superiors were telling him—or with the advice of the literacy experts who sold expensive programs to school districts, or with the textbooks that now had "Common Core" stickers on their covers but were otherwise largely unchanged.

Then, in the summer of 2011, there was massive turnover in the central office. Grossman was told that his job functions were no longer needed, because the state standards he'd been working on had been replaced by the Common Core. He continued to get a paycheck, but he no longer had a job title or a sense of what he was supposed to do.

"And there are meetings going on about Common Core," Grossman says, "but nobody invites me to any of them, because I don't actually have a title at this point. So I feel like Kramer in *Seinfeld*, where he keeps showing up for a job that he's actually not employed to do. But everybody's too polite to say, why is he still here?"

One of the new faces in the office was a woman named Torrey Palmer, who had been hired as the English language arts coordinator for kindergarten through sixth grade. One day, Palmer spied Grossman over the low walls of the office cubicles. "What do you know about the Common Core?" she asked casually.

Grossman spent the next thirty minutes unloading the fruits of his ramblings in cyberspace. He sent Palmer links he'd found to audios and videos of Coleman and others. Palmer was amazed, not only at how much Grossman knew but at how different it was from what everyone else was saying. And it all resonated. She'd been going from school to school, introducing teachers to the Common Core framework that Grossman had created—the "crosswalk" that just moved skills around among grade levels. But something seemed off.

"I vividly remember looking at Standard 10 and saying, well, what do we do with this one?" Palmer recalls, "It didn't have a clear connection with the standards; it wasn't clearly present in the crosswalk documents. It just kind of didn't exist."

Standard 10 says that each year, students must read increasingly complex text at their grade level or above, rather than being restricted to their individual level. As Palmer would later realize, Standard 10 was the heart of the Common Core.

Why, she wanted to know, hadn't Grossman been at any of the meetings the district had been having on the new standards? You're coming with me to the next one, she said. By then, there had been so much turnover that people at the meeting were relatively receptive. The folks on the math side were skeptical about aspects of the Common Core's approach to math, and those in the secondary education division didn't buy Grossman's interpretation of the literacy standards. But that still left elementary literacy—Palmer's bailiwick.

The district needed a way to provide professional development that was aligned to the Common Core, and Grossman and Palmer were offering a simple one: they could play the recordings Grossman had found online for teachers and instructional coaches, who could then discuss what they'd heard. Participants could go back to their classrooms and try out a sample lesson that used close reading and then talk about how it had gone. The lesson had been created by Student Achievement Partners, an organization Coleman had co-founded and that Grossman had managed to Google his way to. And because the materials were available for free, it wouldn't even cost much.

OCTOBER 2011 saw the birth of the Washoe County Core Task Project—a name Grossman and Palmer came up with when they had to fill out a form. They emailed the district's sixty-three elementary school principals, asking if they'd like to participate in a pilot project, and ended up with eighteen educators from sixteen schools.

Not all the teachers and coaches who came to the meeting were enthusiastic about the Common Core—or what they knew of it. Linnea

Wolters, a fifth-grade teacher at a low-income school called Cannan, didn't like the idea of standards, period. Wolters had considered the old Nevada standards to be "like shackles," constraining her freedom to exercise her judgment about what her students needed. National standards, she figured, could only be worse. And there was nothing in the standards that specifically addressed the kind of students she taught: low-income Hispanic kids, many still learning English. Wolters came to the meeting only because she believed you should know your enemy. She wanted to find out what the Common Core was all about so she could figure out how to work around it.

Grossman and Palmer—joined by Cathy Schmidt, a teacher trainer who would become the third leader of the Core Task Project—played several videos, including one of David Coleman. "What really changes as kids grow as readers," Coleman says in the video, "is not that they suddenly learn how to find the main idea. It is that they can do so with much more complex text." If teachers' questions focused just on skills or personal experiences—as Coleman said 80 percent did—students were never going to learn to extract meaning from complex text. To advance students up the ladder of text complexity, teachers were going to have to show them how to "read like a detective and write like an investigative reporter." The clip was only thirteen minutes, but because they kept pausing for discussion, it took forty-five minutes to get through. Wolters wasn't exactly bowled over, but she "didn't hate it."

Grossman says the idea of focusing on evidence in the text rather than skills "immediately made sense" to those at the meeting. Teachers weren't necessarily fans of the skills-focused approach; they just accepted it. Palmer says she had certainly questioned the common wisdom about how to teach literacy. Working on a single skill at a time "just didn't make sense. You were just not seeing those lightbulbs go off with kids." But, she adds, "you were constantly told that these were the practices that we should be employing with our at-risk kids."

Then they unveiled the lesson they wanted teachers to try: a close reading of an essay by the physicist Richard Feynman about how his father taught him to view the world like a scientist. Rather than giving background information, asking kids about their own experiences, or "previewing" the article, teachers were to start by just having kids read it. Then they would pose questions about what it meant. If students weren't able to provide an answer, the lesson plan cautioned, teachers shouldn't just reveal it; instead, they should reread aloud the passage that provided the evidence to give students another chance to come up with one themselves.

Virtually all the teachers at the meeting said, "this is way too hard for our kids, our kids can't do this," recalls Schmidt. They understood that all students need to learn to read complex text, but they feared that just putting it in front of kids who were struggling would cause them to shut down. "This idea of throwing kids into the deep end, putting them in frustration," says Grossman, "that was pretty counterintuitive and counter to how a lot of people had been trained."

But the organizers of the Core Task Project said: Just try it. We don't know if it will work either, but this is what the Common Core expects kids to be able to do. If it turns out to be too hard, we'll try to figure out what to do together.

Three weeks later the teachers came back to report that, much to their surprise, the lesson had gone very well. Yes, it was challenging, but their kids had been so engaged. And it turned out they *could* answer the questions.

"They said they were shocked at how well the kids did," Schmidt recalls. "There was a big feeling that—a realization that—they had been underestimating their kids. And," she adds, laughing, "they said they wanted to do it *again*."

Grossman, Palmer, and Schmidt wanted to respond to the requests for another round, but some in the central office remained unconvinced—especially those in charge of instruction for English language learners, or "ELLs." While the sprawling Washoe district includes affluent areas like Lake Tahoe, it also serves many low-income students, primarily from Spanish-speaking families. The prevailing approach to teaching ELLs was to provide "sheltered instruction," giving these students texts that covered the same content other students were getting but with simplified language.

As with leveled reading in general, this may sound like it makes sense. In practice, though, simplifying a text can change its meaning significantly. One Washoe high school teacher gives the example of a textbook that had multiple versions of the same information: higher-level students read about "the founders of our nation," while lower-level ones were told—inaccurately—that "Ben Franklin started the nation." The sheltered approach also meant that lower-level readers would never have the opportunity to encounter complex text, except on standardized tests. Besides, as the teachers who participated in the first round of the Core Task Project had found, kids who were still learning English were not only capable of attacking complex text, they enjoyed it.

By this time, the three leaders of the project had gotten to know some people at Student Achievement Partners, thanks to Grossman's dogged pursuit of information about the Common Core. Prominent among them were the husband-and-wife team of David and Meredith Liben, former elementary educators who had helped develop the literacy standards and were leading the effort to get publishers, school districts, and teachers to implement them as intended.

When the Libens heard that Washoe was trying to shut down the Core Task Project, they were aghast. They flew to Reno and gave a two-hour presentation to a roomful of principals and other educators, explaining that Grossman was not only right about the Common Core, he was ahead of the pack.

"You don't know what's going on right under your nose," David Liben told the principals, according to Cathy Schmidt.

Afterward, says Kindra Fox, Washoe's director of curriculum and instruction, 75 to 80 percent of those who attended the meeting were on board with the Core Task Project.

Grossman says the Libens' visit didn't reduce the pushback, but it did give the project enough credibility that it could keep going *despite* the pushback. Even though, he points out, he still didn't have a job title.

THE SECOND ROUND finally got off the ground in February 2012, and by that time word had spread. Because the videos shown at the October meeting were freely available online, people had been passing along the links like virtual samizdat. The Coleman video proved particularly powerful.

"I would run into a friend at a school," Grossman says, "and they would say, hey, have you seen the David Coleman thing? And I was like, I was the one who *found* the David Coleman thing."

This time, all sixty-three elementary schools sent at least one educator to the meeting. The trio at the helm had come up with a new close reading lesson to try out. And while there may have been reservations about the difficulty of the Richard Feynman text, those were nothing compared to the reservations they heard about this one: "The New Colossus," the poem by Emma Lazarus inscribed on the Statue of Liberty. The Feynman piece had at least contained most of the information kids would need to make sense of it, and it had been written for children. But "The New Colossus," written in 1883, is studded with complex syntax and obscure references:

> Not like the brazen giant of Greek fame,
> With conquering limbs astride from land to land;
> Here at our sea-washed, sunset gates shall stand
> A mighty woman with a torch, whose flame
> Is the imprisoned lightning, and her name
> Mother of Exiles. From her beacon-hand
> Glows world-wide welcome; her mild eyes command
> The air-bridged harbor that twin cities frame.
> "Keep ancient lands, your storied pomp!" cries she
> With silent lips. "Give me your tired, your poor,

Your huddled masses yearning to breathe free,
The wretched refuse of your teeming shore.
Send these, the homeless, tempest-tost to me,
I lift my lamp beside the golden door!"

"You gotta be freaking kidding me," Linnea Wolters said to herself. She didn't know many *adults* who would be able to understand the poem. Who would know that the "brazen giant of Greek fame" was a reference to the Colossus of Rhodes, the statue of a Greek god that straddled an ancient harbor? Who would care? But, despite her "extreme" skepticism and anxiety, she and the other teachers at the meeting agreed to give it a try.

As the lesson plan suggested, Wolters first had the kids try to read the poem on their own before reading it aloud. The next step was for them to figure out the rhyme scheme—a task she viewed as unrealistic for fifth-graders. But she distributed highlighters and told the kids to use As, Bs, Cs, and Ds for the different rhymes. At first, the kids floundered. But then a student—a girl who had been diagnosed with a learning disability—called out, "It's a pattern!"

They had more trouble with the poem's meaning. At one point, the room was silent except for the sound of crickets in the classroom lizard cage. Wolters waited. If she'd been using her usual approach, she might have asked, "What was the author's purpose in writing this poem?" With a lot of "scaffolding" and support, she would have aimed to get them to say, "Oh, the author is comparing two statues." And that would have been the end of the lesson. But this plan told her to *give* students that basic information, so they could try to figure out what the author was *saying* about the statues. Could they do that? It didn't seem likely.

Then two boys who had been working together—kids who didn't speak English at home and were struggling readers—raised their hands.

"It's about the Statue of Liberty," they announced.

The class didn't buy it. Wolters asked the two boys if they could find any evidence to support their idea.

"It says it's a woman with a torch," they responded, pointing to the line.

The other kids still weren't sure, so Wolters asked the class if they could find more evidence about the statue's identity.

"All of a sudden I've got kids popping off with, 'She's in a harbor!' and 'There's two cities!'" Wolters recalled later. "They're giving me all this information."

Wolters was not only amazed by what the kids were able to glean on their own, she was also struck by how engaged they were. That didn't happen often.

At the next Core Task Project meeting, she found other teachers had similar experiences. As in Wolters's class, it was often the students who were English language learners or struggling readers who worked hardest and came up with answers. The higher-achieving kids, the ones who were used to having things come easily, were sometimes *less* engaged. Their attitude, one teacher says in a video made shortly afterward, was: "What do you want me to do? Just tell me what you want me to do."

They were shocked to realize they had been vastly underestimating what their students were capable of. In the video, Wolters says she came to see that the anxiety she'd felt had been about her own beliefs. She'd assumed that because her students lacked background knowledge and vocabulary, she needed to protect them from the frustrations they would encounter in trying to extract meaning from a sophisticated text. Now, she realized, those struggles were necessary if they were going to learn.

"We've been underselling our kids, at all levels," she said, "for a really long time."

THESE EXPERIENCES SEEM to vindicate David Coleman's vision of close reading as a way of leveling the playing field and enabling all students to mine complex text for insights. On the other hand, you could argue, as E. D. Hirsch would, that additional context would have enabled Washoe students to get even *more* out of "The New Colossus"—if they'd read it as part of a unit on immigration, for example, rather than as an isolated "complex text." True, to everyone's surprise, the kids knew enough to be able to figure out that one of the statues was the Statue of Liberty. But wouldn't some awareness of what was going on in the world when the poem was written have made it easier for them to focus on the overall point?

Eventually, many in Washoe County came to embrace that view, but it wasn't where they started. Despite Grossman's careful study of the standards, despite repeated viewings of Coleman's videos, no one got the message about the need for a content-focused curriculum. Besides, teachers were eager to see what Common Core instruction would look like in the classroom; it wasn't clear how to show them what building knowledge was going to look like.

The message started coming through only after the Core Task Project's first year, when Grossman was still trolling the internet, looking for videos to share. He and Palmer were being asked to hold more and more meetings at schools in the district, and, Grossman says, "You can only play the David Coleman video so many times." (Grossman's eight-year-old son tagged along to so many trainings that he was able to perform a spot-on David Coleman impression.)

During the summer of 2012, Grossman came across a video of Robert Pondiscio talking about the Common Core. Pondiscio was the Core Knowledge Foundation official who had attacked an early draft of the standards as "dead on arrival." But like Hirsch, he changed his mind after the addition of language about the importance of a knowledge-building curriculum, language that Pondiscio has since called "the 57 most important words in education reform." In the video, Pondiscio reads that language aloud and describes the famous baseball experiment conducted by Recht and Leslie in the 1980s—the one that showed that when the text was about baseball, "poor" readers who knew a lot about baseball outdid "good" readers who didn't. "The authors of the Common Core Standards," he says, "totally get this." He also mentions cognitive scientist Daniel Willingham and his work on the importance of knowledge in reading comprehension.

"He's brilliant," Pondiscio says. "If you don't know his work, you should."

Eventually, both Pondiscio and Willingham traveled to Washoe County and made presentations in person.

The following school year saw two significant developments. In the fall, the Core Task Project evolved into the Core Task Implementation Project—CTIP, as people started calling it. It became a yearlong professional development project, with a syllabus built around the topics teachers said they needed help with: making vocabulary stick, getting students to write using evidence from texts, orchestrating content-focused discussions, and, of course, close reading of complex text.

While the structure was more formal, CTIP retained what its founders considered the basic strength of the Core Task Project: the cycle of having teachers learn about a topic, collaboratively plan a lesson, go back to their classrooms to try it out, come back to reflect on how it went, and repeat. This structure was fundamentally different from the "drive-by" professional development that teachers normally get, disconnected from specifics and likely to be soon forgotten.

The other significant development was that—as a result of Grossman's discovery of the Pondiscio and Willingham videos—the district started a pilot project focused on content-rich curriculum. One school tried the Core Knowledge Language Arts curriculum, which had been developed by Hirsch's Core Knowledge Foundation, in kindergarten through second grade.

"Initially," says Grossman, "it was a train wreck." Some topics were "really dry." The kids didn't always have the stamina to listen to the read-alouds, and the teachers didn't necessarily have enough familiarity with the subject matter to deliver the lessons in an engaging way. No one had been trained in how to use the curriculum, because, says Grossman, "naively, we thought we could put it together ourselves."

But because the Core Knowledge curriculum was freely available online, teachers at other schools—teachers who had been at the CTIP meetings and seen the Pondiscio and Willingham videos—started trying it out on their own. "They'd say, you've got to come into my classroom; you've got to see what's happening," Grossman recalls.

After a while, teachers got comfortable with the curriculum. It turned out kids really liked it. And parents *loved* it. Suddenly, they were having amazing conversations with their kids about what they'd learned in school.

The following year, the number of Core Knowledge pilot schools went up to eight. CTIP set up monthly meetings, where they would show videos they'd made of Core Knowledge classes in the district. Teachers started getting ideas from one another and realized they didn't have to stick to the script, as long as the kids were getting the information and vocabulary. The next year—2014–15—there were twenty-three Core Knowledge schools in the district. Teachers began to see that students were retaining the information and making connections between topics. They began to appreciate the way Core Knowledge is structured to build knowledge gradually and logically, so that new information has something familiar to attach itself to.

By 2017, when I visited Washoe, there were lots of stories circulating about kids like the third-grader whose babysitter, an eleventh-grader, was writing a paper on Greek mythology. The third-grader challenged her babysitter's facts. When they resorted to Google to settle the dispute, it turned out the third-grader was right.

LINNEA WOLTERS'S SCHOOL, Cannan Elementary, adopted Core Knowledge in 2013. The first year was the hardest, she says, with some teachers resisting the focus on facts. Even now, Wolters still has to remind teachers it's important to provide kids with what she calls "free information."

"It's very hard for them to remember that knowing stuff makes you a better reader," she says. "And so I try to put it into those simple terms all the time: knowing stuff makes you a better reader."

The most powerful way of getting that message across is for teachers to see the evidence themselves. Wolters recounts the story of a second-grade student at another school who "struggled like crazy." His teacher noticed there was a text in her reading test kit that dealt with Westward Expansion—the topic that the class had just covered in Core Knowledge. The text was classified as being at a fourth-grade level, but, out of curiosity, the teacher had the boy try it.

"And he read it with 98 percent accuracy and 100 percent comprehension," Wolters says.

At Cannan, it was recess that really changed teachers' minds. Recess there tended to be a free-form affair, with no regard to rules even during games like soccer. But then the teachers noticed that their second-graders were playing Greek gods and goddesses—with rules.

"So they are forming themselves in clusters," Wolters says, "telling this little girl, well you can't be *our* Athena, but *they* need an Athena, but if you want to be Artemis then we're good to go, because we don't have one yet."

The second-graders also used a large map of the United States in the playground to recap the tall tales and legends they were learning. A kid would stand inside the outline of, say, Minnesota, and tell the story of Paul Bunyan and his blue ox. The same thing happened with the kindergarteners: during their unit on rocks, they devoted recess to that subject for almost two weeks, ignoring the swings.

"All they wanted to do was dig around," says Wolters, "because they were rock-hounding all day every day, trying to talk to each other about the things they found and the things they didn't, about the things they were encountering." Core Knowledge "changed the structures and the thinking of our students, and their orientation toward *play*. And never have I seen in my entire life academic content feed over into *recess*." Neither had the other teachers. "When they started seeing that, they got on board."

Still, a high-poverty school like Cannan has its challenges. Core Knowledge is in place from kindergarten through fifth grade, but beyond third grade, read-alouds are no longer provided in the curriculum. Kids are expected to take in the information they need by reading solo. For some, those texts are simply too difficult or too dry. Wolters advises teachers to resort to other ways to deliver the same knowledge—maybe a ten-minute YouTube video "that they can watch twice, with a good set of guiding questions that develop the same vocabulary, the same knowledge base, and offers them the same sort of support that they're used to having" from the read-alouds. While this might sound like another version of sheltered instruction, it doesn't limit kids' knowledge to text they can read themselves. But an even better solution might be to continue to read the texts aloud at those grade levels or provide audio recordings, while giving students copies so they can follow along.

"We think of reading as a knowledge delivery system all throughout school," Wolters says. "And it *can't* be. *There is no way*—I would argue—through the fifth and sixth grade. For an adult, reading is the most efficient way to gain new knowledge. For a child who is gaining the skills of literacy, it is a completely inefficient way for them to gain knowledge and vocabulary."

At the same time, Wolters tries to get across the message that Core Knowledge is about "exposure, not mastery." In other words, it's okay if students don't absorb every detail presented in the dense "domains." What's important is that they absorb the big ideas, which they'll be exposed to in multiple ways.

For example, Core Knowledge touches repeatedly on the attributes of ancient civilizations: in first grade, students learn about Mesopotamia; in second grade, they learn about ancient Chinese and Indian civilizations as well as ancient Greece—and so on. What students need to retain is the idea that these civilizations existed, that they appeared in a certain chronological order, and that they had common attributes. Whether they remember what cuneiform is or who Hammurabi was is less important—although some will. But it's the basic historical concepts that are crucial. Students who haven't been exposed to them early on, Wolters says, have a much harder time grasping them later.

Wolters feels confident that the focus on knowledge is helping equip Cannan's students to succeed, although she would like more minutes in the school day. Proficiency rates on standardized tests are still significantly lower than those at more affluent local schools. But in 2015–16, Wolters says, Cannan's fourth-graders—the first group with two years of Core Knowledge before being tested—significantly outpaced the average growth rate in the district.

Given where they ended up, it might seem that teachers in Washoe approached this way of teaching from the wrong end: instead of starting by building knowledge, they simply handed kids complex text—just as David Coleman had urged. But that may also have been the key to CTIP's strength. Thanks to those experiments, teachers realized that it was their own assumptions that had been holding their students back. They came to understand, more or less viscerally, that what their students lacked was not ability but information. So when the same message eventually came through from the experts, they were primed to receive it.

MANY OF THE WASHOE SCHOOLS using Core Knowledge are not high-poverty like Cannan. Their experience has been somewhat different, but no less impressive. One school called Westergard, which serves a largely white and affluent population, has a number of lower-performing students, including some who are low-income and learning English. Teachers said both higher- and lower-achieving children have benefited from participating in the same activities.

Every year, Chris Hayes asks her second-graders to write about Civil War–era leaders they've studied, choosing the three they think are bravest and providing supporting evidence. A few years ago, two girls—Abril and Mia—were scribbling away. Abril, who spoke Spanish at home and struggled with reading, drew on earlier read-alouds to write about Ulysses S. Grant, describing him as "a civil war general" and "a really brave man." Mia wrote almost twice as much, using complex sentences and grilling her teacher for more information. While their writing may have been at different levels, they both had absorbed the same substance. As Hayes explained to a reporter, if Abril had been in a typical elementary classroom, where students are limited to texts they can read themselves, she would have been reading about topics like "Pat's favorite cat" while her classmates learned about the Civil War.

"There's no discussion there," Hayes said of the leveled texts. "There's no deeper-level questioning. She needs to be exposed to that questioning, that discussion, which cannot be done with the text she's able to access on her own right now."

Westergard's experience suggests that adopting content-rich curricula could address a long-standing and seemingly intractable problem: educational segregation. Research has shown that all kids benefit from attending diverse schools, and many white and affluent parents like the idea of having their kids educated alongside peers of different races and socioeconomic groups. But high-poverty schools that serve many struggling readers have focused nearly all their time on the basics, and parents whose children are reading just fine are likely to want them to learn about history and science rather than spend every day practicing "skills." A curriculum that teaches all children about ancient Greece or the human digestive system could bring different types of families into the same schools, reversing a disturbing trend toward increased segregation.

Wolters's own kids have gone through Core Knowledge, and she—like other Core Knowledge teachers I spoke with who are also Core Knowledge parents—has been thrilled with the results. During Cannan's first year of using the curriculum, Wolters says, educators from other schools would visit to see what it was like, and "they were like, oh my God, I want *my* kid to have this." Still—as at Center City in D.C.—the school hasn't seen an increase in the diversity of students' backgrounds.

While a knowledge-focused curriculum has the potential to serve as a tool for integration, it will take work and time to make it happen. Meanwhile, parents with lower levels of education shouldn't have to shoulder the burden of advocating for content. Schools, districts, and states must make sure it reaches the kids who need it most.

GIVEN WHAT I'D HEARD about the success of CTIP, I was surprised to learn that the project had come to an end in 2015. That year, both Cathy Schmidt and Torrey Palmer left the school district to work with national organizations promoting content-focused curriculum and teaching.

That left Aaron Grossman to shoulder the work on his own: eight different cohorts going through the yearlong professional development cycle, a menu of classes for teachers, training sessions for school personnel, state-level meetings. It was too much. Not to mention that he *still* didn't have a job title.

Ultimately, Grossman decided to go back to the classroom. Not only did he miss teaching, there was continuing pushback from others in the district. Keeping CTIP going felt like a game of whack-a-mole: one constituency would be placated, but then another would pop up with objections. One reason, Grossman speculates, is that many educators are personally invested in the skills-and-leveled-reading status quo. If you did your dissertation on that system or have published articles endorsing it, the Common Core's demand for grade-level reading could feel like a threat.

Palmer and Schmidt say that while there certainly was resistance, the problem was more that the district kept undertaking new initiatives, some of which seemed to be working at cross-purposes, and those initiatives took precedence over CTIP. And CTIP's goals—implementing the instructional shifts—can seem vague. Nor were its results immediately evident in terms of test scores. School districts want to see quick, quantifiable progress.

"Building knowledge takes *years*," Schmidt says. "It'll be three, four, five years before we start to see the payoff of teaching Core Knowledge in Washoe, in fourth- or fifth-grade test scores."

If then. Officially, the district still requires a basal reader. And although half the district's elementary schools had adopted Core Knowledge to some extent by 2016, Cannan was the only one using it schoolwide. Elsewhere, only one or two teachers might be using Core Knowledge, or teachers might pick and choose which domains to cover, usually favoring science over history. That piecemeal approach saps it of much of its strength, since it's the cumulative nature of the curriculum that helps kids retain knowledge and vocabulary. Even if the district were tracking students who have been exposed to Core Knowledge, which it's not, it would be hard to tell under these conditions if it's actually "working."

CORE KNOWLEDGE IS still spreading to some schools in Washoe. But at others it's fading out as teachers leave or retire. As with so much in education, a lot depends on leadership. If a principal who supports a content focus leaves, it can become impossible to keep it going.

That's what happened at Maree G. Farring Elementary/Middle School in Baltimore. When I visited in 2016, a veteran teacher, Jean Choma, told me that years earlier, long before the Common Core was a twinkle in David Coleman's eye, Farring had been a Core Knowledge school. A new principal, Thom Stroschein, introduced a curriculum based on the Core Knowledge Sequence, and everyone loved it: teachers, students, parents.

"And test scores went like this—*zhoom*," Choma said, raising her hand from waist level to high above her head.

In 2005, after the curriculum had been in place for several years, Farring was recognized as one of forty "distinguished" high-poverty schools in the nation. The award goes to a school that has narrowed test-score gaps between different subgroups of students, including those in special education. Just a few years before, the performance of the school's special education students had been so abysmal it was operating under a consent decree.

But eventually, Stroschein left for another job, and the next principal replaced Core Knowledge with a basal program she had used before. Scores fell to their previous levels. By the time I visited, Farring had yet another principal, who had never heard of Core Knowledge. Choma showed me a walk-in supply closet stacked floor-to-ceiling with forgotten books and materials, some still in their plastic wrappers.

What happened at Farring—and what is happening now in Washoe County—illustrates how fragile the switch can be when it isn't strongly supported by the district. Because of its scale, CTIP may have a more lasting impact on Washoe than Core Knowledge did on Farring. By the time it ended, CTIP had touched more than a thousand elementary teachers—half the district. Still, says Torrey Palmer, unless key personnel get on board, "we are probably never going to see district-wide implementation" of a content-focused approach.

CTIP's strength—its grassroots nature—was also its weakness. While its leaders were from the central office, they invited teachers to partner with them in a common quest and thus short-circuited the skepticism that teachers often bring to yet another approach they're told to try—without necessarily being told *why*. CTIP worked, Aaron Grossman says, "because we genuinely had no clue." At the same time, the fact that there was little support from the central office may have doomed it. When CTIP's leaders left, it died. And while the district still includes teachers who were profoundly affected, they're powerless to engineer the kind of systemic changes needed to implement it more widely.

The trick is to combine the power of a grassroots movement like CTIP with the sustainability of a district-supported initiative—and to scale up that effort fast enough to turn around the *Titanic* that is our education system before it founders on the iceberg of skills-focused elementary instruction. Is that possible? Some are betting the answer is yes.

APRIL 2017

Seventeen first-grade girls are lying alongside one another on their stomachs, pretending to be bodies of water—*silent* bodies of water, Ms. Townsell reminds the giggly students as she lies beside them: lakes, rivers, oceans. They can decide.

Then the water begins the process of *evaporation*: slowly they rise from the rug, as the sun shines hard on them, turning them into vapor. Now they're standing and their hands are in the air, transforming back into a liquid.

"We are now doing *what*?" Ms. Townsell asks.

"We are now . . ." The girls' voices peter out in confusion. But someone says a word, and then the rest follow: "Conservation!" Unfortunately, it's the wrong word. Ms. Townsell was hoping for *condensation*.

All morning, the girls have been confusing the two words, prompting her to come up with the idea of having them act out the water cycle. Their confusion is understandable. For the past two days they've been learning about *conservation*. This morning, they wrote paragraphs on what they could do to conserve water, like turning off the faucet while brushing their teeth. And now all of a sudden there's this other word—*condensation*—that sounds a lot like *conservation* and also has something to do with water.

None of this is in *Journeys*. It's not even in the school's rudimentary science and social studies curriculum. This was just supposed to be a simple exercise to help administrators assess students' writing skills: write a short composition answering the question "What can *you* do to save water?" Currently, teachers take bits and pieces from three different writing curricula, and the school is searching for a new approach.

Ms. Townsell was supposed to simply show her students a video about conservation and read them a brief text, but she felt they would need more information. So she developed a four-day lesson that will ultimately include taping Ziploc bags of blue water to the windows to see what happens after they're exposed to the sun. Despite the confusion over vocabulary, the additional activities she's led so far have helped. But the writing her students produce shows that these first-graders—like first-graders anywhere—don't understand how to compose sentences or organize paragraphs.

Later, when the elementary teachers meet with their principal, they enumerate the skills the school needs to target: conjunctions, complete sentences, listing reasons in support of claims, transitions, creating some sort of closing. Ms. Townsell says she found the discussion far more helpful than most of the "professional development" provided by the school. But if Excel Academy wants to improve student writing, it will first need to ensure students are studying topics in some depth. As Center City's experience shows, giving students information on a topic doesn't guarantee they'll be able to write about it coherently, but it's a necessary first step.

"WHY ARE NUTRIENTS an essential part of staying healthy?" reads the question on today's chart, displayed at the front of Ms. Masi's classroom.

The second-graders are in the midst of Core Knowledge's Domain 10, titled "The Human Body: Building Blocks and Nutrition," and evidence of what they've been learning is scattered throughout the classroom, interspersed with posters and charts relating to the history topics the third-graders are studying in the same room. At Ms. Masi's left, beneath illustrations of the human body, is a chart headed, "What led to the establishment (building) of English colonies in North America?"

There's also the chart Ms. Masi and her second-graders filled in yesterday about the excretory system, brimming with information about sweat and urine in red, green, and black marker. The day before that, they focused on the digestive system and excretion of solid waste. Core Knowledge doesn't mince words.

"Feces are stored in the rectum, the final section of the large intestine," explains one read-aloud, "until another muscular gate, or sphincter, opens and allows the feces to pass through the anus, the body's exit point for solid waste."

Of all the systems of the human body to choose for second-graders! Ms. Masi thought. Kids that age revel in pee and poop jokes. A few months ago, Amir—who has trouble controlling his behavior and is often relegated to a desk while other students gather on the rug—repeatedly called out "poop" during a discussion of the invention of plumbing by the ancient Romans. What would these kids do with two whole days of lessons focused on feces and urine?

Ms. Masi decided she would address the issue head-on. She reminded the kids how much they had been learning about the human body and said the digestive and excretory systems were part of that. She was sure they were mature enough to handle this and take it seriously, she lied. Amazingly enough, they did. When she reached the part of yesterday's read-aloud that said urine is actually cleaner than saliva, Amir—Amir, of all people!—asked thoughtfully if that meant you could drink urine. Yes, Ms. Masi explained, sometimes people have to do that when they have no access to water and they need liquid to survive. The kids were fascinated.

Today, not so much. Ms. Masi has to struggle to keep the kids' attention focused on the four types of nutrients and the function they serve. They also have some trouble with the vocabulary.

"Water, protein, fats, and then . . . ," one boy recites. After a pause, he ventures, "Categories?"

Ms. Masi's students have a science class several times a week that provides them with hands-on activities. In contrast, Core Knowledge is supposed to familiarize students with the science concepts and vocabulary they need to become fully literate. But compared to the history narratives that feature characters, action, and suspense, the read-aloud on nutrients is a bit of a slog. While the kids enjoyed learning about the insect life cycle, Ms. Masi tells me, the science domains have generally been more repetitive and less engaging. There's definitely a way to enliven science through the power of storytelling, but Core Knowledge hasn't managed to do that consistently.

Ms. Masi had planned to supplement the science read-alouds with hands-on projects and field trips, but given all that she's been juggling, it just didn't happen.

CHAPTER 11

————

Don't Forget to Write

ONE DAY IN THE LATE 1970S, Judith Hochman found herself at a workshop in Hoboken, New Jersey, that focused on teaching writing to a rapidly growing segment of the state's population: Hispanic students who were still learning English. Hochman isn't sure why she signed up for the workshop. She didn't teach English language learners. She didn't even teach in New Jersey.

She had started her career, some twenty years before, as a classroom teacher in public schools. Now she was the curriculum coordinator at the Windward School, an independent school for students with language-based learning disabilities in a New York City suburb. The focus at Windward was on reading—and more specifically on decoding. Most schools in the 1970s were encouraging children to guess at and memorize words rather than systematically teaching them how to sound them out. Windward, like other schools for kids with learning disabilities, drew its students from the large numbers for whom that approach didn't work. Instead, they used systematic phonics instruction, which worked well. The school tackled comprehension in the usual way: students read short, disconnected passages in a basal reader and answered questions. But writing? Windward wasn't doing much with that.

Neither was anyone else. Writing instruction in elementary school consisted of teaching spelling and grammar rules and sentence structure: a noun is a person, place, or thing; a verb is an action word; a sentence contains a noun and a verb and expresses a complete thought. In later grades, students would learn about the structure of paragraphs and compositions and be expected to produce them. That kind of abstract, rules-focused instruction didn't work for many students—including those at Windward.

Hochman suspected that writing could be important in helping her students compensate for their disabilities and reenter mainstream schools, which was the goal. Despite her undergraduate and graduate degrees in education, she had never been trained in how to teach writing, just when to *assign* it. When confronted with disappointing writing, she—like most teachers—simply gave her students vague injunctions to go over what they'd written and "make it better." While she must have felt she could learn something from the Hoboken workshop, she had no idea it would change her life.

The presenters talked about how Hispanic kids managed to pick up spoken English well enough, as immigrant kids have for generations. But writing, they said, needed to be taught explicitly and sequentially, beginning with how to construct a sentence in English. Instead of grammar rules, the presenters offered strategies. Oh my God, Hochman realized: this was what her Windward kids needed too. They could *speak* English well enough, but they tried to write the way they spoke.

"My sense was *we* had to teach English as a second language," Hochman says. "Because written English *is* a second language."

In the decades following Hochman's epiphany, elementary classrooms would come to be dominated by a freewheeling approach to writing instruction that rejected the emphasis on grammar rules. But for many children, it worked no better than the old one. By the first decade of the twenty-first century, it was clear that most students—especially those who were black, Hispanic, and low-income—were struggling to write coherently.

As with reading, the Common Core standards released in 2010

would demand that students' writing abilities improve dramatically. But those standards would fail to explain how teachers were supposed to engineer that change. Like Hochman, the vast majority of teachers never learn anything about teaching writing during their training. And writing, it turns out, is even harder to teach than reading.

Meanwhile, Hochman and her colleagues at Windward were gradually figuring out a system that worked—not just for the kids at Windward but for all students, including English language learners and those from less-educated families. Eventually, Hochman thought back to the many students she'd taught earlier in her career who hadn't been diagnosed with learning disabilities but faced the same difficulties with writing.

"I realized I did a big disservice to these kids," Hochman says now. "That was not easy for me to deal with."

Hochman discovered that writing, reading comprehension, and analytical ability were all connected—and that writing was the key to unlocking the other two. If you wanted to enable students to understand what they were reading, convert information into long-lasting knowledge, and learn to think critically, teaching them to write was about the best thing you could do.

THE WRITING STRATEGIES Hochman saw in Hoboken were rudimentary. She tried to find academic studies on writing instruction, but there weren't many. So she started to experiment. Her initial goal was simply to get students to provide more information in their writing. If a student wrote, for example, "My dog hid," Hochman would coax, "Tell me *when* that happened." Then she might ask *where*, and then *why*. The student would note down his responses to these "question words" and combine them to create a sentence that both conveyed more information and used a structure that was common in written but not spoken English. "During the storm," he might write, "my dog hid under the bed because he was scared."

The Windward teachers tried other approaches too, like giving students the beginning of a sentence—a "stem"—and asking them to finish it using *because*. A student might get the stem, "The teacher was happy *because* _____," and add, "we raised our hands." Later on, teachers added other conjunctions: *but, so.*

When students got comfortable, teachers racheted things up a notch by giving them the beginnings of sentences with subordinating conjunctions: "*Although* the teacher was happy, _____." These sentence stems familiarized students with types of sentences beyond the simple declarative and focused their attention on a specific task; if the conjunction was *but* or *although*, they had to come up with information that went in a different direction. Hochman incorporated practice in using appositives—phrases that describe nouns and provide more information—and combining short sentences into longer ones.

Windward teachers began to notice that as students learned to construct complex sentences, they became better able to understand them when they encountered them in their reading. They also began to use more complex sentences and provide more information in classroom discussions.

Then Hochman had a second epiphany: these strategies would work even better if they were "embedded in content." Instead of asking students to practice writing on topics that didn't require any particular knowledge—like what makes a teacher happy—she asked them to write about what they were learning. This worked especially well in history and social studies. If students were learning about the American Revolution, the teacher could give them a bare-bones sentence like "They rebelled" and ask the kids to expand it: *Who* rebelled? *When*? *Why*?

The faculty soon realized there wasn't enough information in social studies textbooks to enable students to write meaningfully about the topics they covered. So teachers started providing additional material. Once the kids had enough information to draw on, their writing became richer and more interesting. And their understanding increased, because they *had* to figure out the meaning of what they were reading in order to write about it.

Students moved on to writing paragraphs and compositions, always creating an outline first to organize their thoughts, but Hochman came to believe they should keep practicing sentence-level activities. That went against the traditional sequence: first students learned to write sentences, and once they had "mastered" them, they moved on.

But writing a sentence can be just as challenging, and just as much of a lever for deepening understanding, in high school as in elementary school—as long as it's embedded in content. Like reading comprehension, writing isn't a freestanding set of skills that can be learned once and then applied anywhere. Whether you can write a meaningful sentence depends on your knowledge of the particular topic; if the content is complex, so is the activity. There's nothing simple about completing the following sentence stem: "Immanuel Kant believed that space and time are subjective forms of human sensibility, but _____."

As Hochman came to understand, writing is a lot harder than most people realize. It's commonly assumed that if kids read a lot, they'll simply pick up the techniques of good writing. But for many that's not the case. Writing is far more difficult than reading—just as speaking a foreign language is more difficult than understanding it—because it's expressive rather than receptive. Excellent readers can still struggle with writing. The same goes for speaking ability. As Hochman intuited, written English is like a second language, with different demands and conventions.

When we speak, we often use fragments rather than full sentences. We don't always clarify what our pronouns refer to, and we tend not to use words and phrases like *although* and *in addition*. Nor do we usually plan out what we're going to say during a conversation. Generally, we know something about how much our listeners already understand and how much we need to explain. We can use gestures, facial expressions, and intonation to help get our meaning across. And if listeners are confused, they can always ask, "Wait—what do you mean?"

With writing, those aids to communication aren't available. We need to be precise about our meaning, using full sentences, imposing organization on our thoughts, signaling when we're making transitions—and, perhaps most difficult of all, putting ourselves in the shoes of hypothetical readers and figuring out what they need to know. When we make mistakes in writing, they don't just evaporate, as they do in conversation. They sit right there, concrete representations of our shortcomings.

Writing also places huge demands on working memory—the aspect of cognition that might be called consciousness. Inexperienced writers are trying to juggle all sorts of things within the boundaries of working memory: penmanship or keyboarding, spelling, word choice, sentence structure, paragraph structure, essay structure. Students who are trying to deal with these factors simultaneously are likely to become anxious and stressed, decreasing their cognitive power. And they need that cognitive power to understand and explain the content they're trying to write about. As important as background knowledge is to reading, it's far more critical to writing. It may be tough to *read* about a topic you don't know well, but it can be done. If you're asked to write about it, you'll struggle to produce anything coherent.

But when all of that is in place—when the mechanics aren't too burdensome and the writer has sufficient information to work with—writing may be the most powerful teaching tool we have. Writing assignments quickly alert students and their teachers to information students have missed or failed to understand, enabling them to fill in gaps or correct errors before it's too late. If students have absorbed the right information, writing about it forces them to retrieve it in a way that lodges it in their long-term memories, where it can be drawn on in the future. Cognitive scientists call this *retrieval practice*. Writing also provides the kinds of benefits referred to as the *protégé effect*: when people try to teach material to others, or simply plan to, their own understanding gets a powerful boost.

Writing may also be the best way to develop old-fashioned skills like finding the main idea, metacognitive skills like asking questions about one's own understanding, and the highly prized "twenty-first-century" skills of analytical or critical thinking. Skills-focused teachers haven't been wrong to want students to acquire those abilities. They've just been mistaken in their assumption that they can be taught directly, isolated from content.

That mistake is much harder to make when it comes to writing. When teachers demonstrate a skill like finding the main idea in the context of reading and send students off to practice with their leveled readers, it may *look* like students have taken it in. But if students are asked to *write* about a text's main idea, they won't be able to produce anything that makes sense unless they've acquired a fair amount of related factual information. And as the Windward faculty discovered, asking students to write can even reveal the shallowness and inadequacy of the teaching materials themselves.

Writing may also be the best way to guard against what progressive educators have feared will result from a focus on content: rote memorization and the regurgitation of disconnected facts. While educators' fears have been overblown, it can happen. But when students write in response to a well-crafted prompt, they have no choice but to analyze how facts are related, which ones are truly important, and how best to communicate them to an unknown reader. In short, teaching writing is not only inseparable from teaching content, it can also be tantamount to teaching students how to think critically.

Having students write about what they're learning can yield greater benefits than the techniques currently favored by teachers: discussion, projects, and group work. While there's a role for each in the classroom, they also have disadvantages. Class discussion is not only less rigorous than writing, it's often dominated by the same few kids. Similarly, the details—and fun—of creating a project can easily obscure the learning objectives. As Daniel Willingham has observed, if students bake biscuits as part of a lesson on what slaves ate on the Underground Railroad, they're likely to remember more about baking biscuits than about the Underground Railroad. Group work, which has become almost mandatory at all grade levels, often devolves into students chatting about whatever strikes their fancies, with the more conscientious group members doing all the work. "When I die," goes one internet meme, "I want my group project members to lower me into my grave so they can let me down one last time." If each student is also writing in a focused way, group activities are likely to become more productive and valuable for everyone.

It's important to bear in mind that the benefits of writing will accrue only if the mechanics aren't overwhelming. Just as with reading, the best way to prevent working memory from becoming overwhelmed is to ensure that some parts of the process are stored in long-term memory. In writing, what needs to be stored are not only spelling and background knowledge but also things like the ways to vary sentence structure or begin a paragraph. When inexperienced writers try to compose longer pieces of writing, they need a written plan to follow so their working memory isn't constantly trying to figure out what to do next, interrupting their train of thought.

All of this means that simply writing, and possibly making the same mistakes over and over, isn't likely to help struggling students. Teachers need to break down the components of the process into manageable chunks and guide students through practicing those chunks in a logical sequence while providing prompt feedback. Psychologists have called this approach *deliberate practice*, and it's crucial to developing mastery and expertise.

Much of this research hadn't yet been done when Hochman was developing her method through trial and error. And more research is still needed on writing, which has attracted far less interest from academics than reading. But what she came up with conforms remarkably well to what the research indicates will work.

In the 1980s and 1990s, news of Hochman's work began to spread within the special-education community. At the same time, a different approach was taking hold in regular elementary classrooms. Commonly known as "writers' workshop," it's a key component of the balanced-literacy movement. In fact, the educator with whom it is most closely associated is Lucy Calkins. Calkins got her start as a writing guru, and that's where her influence is greatest. Schools across the country—including many elite private schools—use her Units of Study in writing and send their teachers to her writing institutes.

Generally, balanced literacy disdains instruction in mechanics and prioritizes student choice. When it comes to writing, that means de-emphasizing conventions like punctuation and capitalization, instead encouraging children to freely express themselves about whatever they choose—as long as it relates to their own experience.

Hochman and writers' workshop theorists both believe that schools have paid too little attention to writing, treating it as a product when it's really a process. In traditional classrooms, students get assignments back with their mistakes circled in red ink, possibly without further explanation, and then move on to the next assignment. Hochman and Calkins want students to engage in planning, drafting, revising, and editing a piece of writing, receiving targeted feedback along the way to help them improve it. Both also recognize that teaching rules of grammar in isolation doesn't work for most students—even though many members of the public insist that the reason students can't write today is that teachers don't spend enough time on things like sentence diagramming. (Studies going back a century show that kind of instruction has no positive impact on student writing, and some have actually shown a small negative effect.) And both Hochman and Calkins understand that students can only write about subjects they know well.

Despite the similarities in their starting points, their approaches are radically different. Calkins urges students to "flash draft," writing at a furious pace without overthinking, and then go back and revise repeatedly. If kids don't write everything down in one fell swoop, she warns, their writing will be wooden. And if they labor over a draft, they'll be less willing to revise it later. As for the skills necessary to create interesting, complex sentences, she trusts children will pick those up largely by studying "mentor texts."

For Hochman, the place to start is the sentence. If students don't yet know how to write a good sentence, they'll never write good paragraphs, let alone good essays. And Hochman places as much emphasis on planning, by means of a clear, linear outline, as she does on revising.

As for grammar, proponents of writers' workshop trust that students will naturally develop a sense of the conventions if they write enough about subjects that matter to them. Focusing on mistakes, they believe, will inhibit children's ability to express themselves and prevent them from developing fluency. If a student uses run-on sentences, for example, Calkins cautions against explaining that "writers use periods at the ends of sentences, at the end of a complete thought. . . . The truth is that deciding where a sentence ends is one of the more complicated decisions a writer makes, and this writer is on her way toward figuring it out. She needs to be supported, encouraged, and guided rather than corrected and reprimanded." Calkins anticipates that students will get whatever feedback on mechanics they need after completing their drafts. But confronted with page after page of error-filled writing, teachers often feel overwhelmed. One second-grade teacher showed me a student's indecipherable two-page journal entry; he was supposed to "respond" to writing like this, but he couldn't tell what the student was trying to communicate. Others who have tried Calkins's approach with struggling writers have found it to be a disaster.

The result is that students who don't naturally pick up the conventions of written language—of whom there are many—*never* manage to master them. Studies may have shown that it doesn't work to teach rules of grammar in isolation, but they've also shown that most children do not in fact acquire writing skill by osmosis; they need to have mistakes corrected in the context of their own writing. If teachers begin instruction at the sentence level, as Hochman recommends, that is a far more manageable task.

Lastly, Calkins's understanding that writers need to know their subject well has led her to limit children primarily to their interests and experiences—"small moments" in their lives, which they can stretch and "explode" with sensory details. Kids may not know much about the larger world, but they're experts on their own lives. They might choose to write about a scary ride on a roller coaster, a visit from their grandparents, or perhaps something as big as the death of a parent. Calkins began to develop this approach in the late 1970s while doing research in a third-grade classroom. One day the teacher, Mrs. Howard, asked her students to write about "lost dolphins," a topic in the basal reader. The resulting paragraphs, Calkins reports, were dull, lifeless, and virtually indistinguishable—because the children "knew little, if anything, about dolphins." Mrs. Howard concluded that the assignment had been "stupid." She wondered aloud if it would be better to let the students choose their own topics. "I wanted to hug her," Calkins writes.

Another alternative, of course, would have been to *teach* the kids about dolphins, supplementing the textbook with more in-depth material—as Hochman did at Windward—and only then ask them to write. By restricting students to their own experiences, the writers' workshop model squanders the enormous potential of writing as a tool for teaching content and skills simultaneously. It also fails to equip students for writing about "domains" beyond their lives, in genres other than personal narrative. Even when students do write about material beyond their own experience, balanced literacy's bias in favor of choice can impede their learning. If everyone chooses a different topic, it's impossible for the teacher to know enough about each to ensure students are acquiring both accurate knowledge and the writing skills that can only develop in tandem with it.

A fourth-grade teacher in a high-poverty school in Ohio told me that writing is "a perfect example of why choice isn't always the best thing." She recently switched from a system in which students chose their own topics for a social studies composition to one in which their choices were restricted. Under the old system, she said, she wasn't able to help many of them, because she couldn't be an expert on all their topics. "It becomes an independent study," she said. "That can be fun, but it's not productive."

But the writers' workshop ethos holds that a teacher shouldn't assume a position of authority, handing out assignments and giving students information she has access to and they don't—becoming the "sage on the stage" rather than the "guide on the side." The model is the fulfill-ment of the progressive educator's dream: a classroom where the teacher and her students are equals—or, to borrow from the title of Calkins's first book, *Lessons from a Child*, where the students *are* the teachers. While it's designed to enable students to pursue their own interests and develop their writerly voices, this well-intentioned approach ends up leaving many of them unaware of topics that might fascinate them—and rendering them effectively voiceless.

IN MOST ELEMENTARY CLASSROOMS, the obstacle to writing instruc-tion is a lack of content. But in the few that use a content-rich curricu-lum, there's often a different problem: students whose writing skills are still developing can easily become overwhelmed, both by the abundance of information and the open-ended nature of the assignments.

One second-grade classroom I visited in Reno was in the middle of the Core Knowledge unit on the Civil War. That day, the teacher gave each student a blank sheet of paper and asked them to write down "everything you've learned about slavery over the last two days." In response to students' requests, she wrote certain spellings on the board: *Harriet Tubman, African American, kidnap, passengers, conductors, sta-tion*. Even so, the children struggled to articulate their knowledge coher-ently on paper. "Harriet Tubman's a slavery," one began. Remember how Abril and her classmate Mia were each writing about Civil War–era he-roes but Mia was able to craft more complex, information-rich sentences? If their teacher (who happens to have been the same teacher who handed out the slavery assignment) had been using an explicit method of writing instruction, Abril could not only have accessed the same content as Mia but also acquired similar writing skills.

In a fourth-grade classroom at the same school, students were writ-ing up a research project on an ancient Native American mummy. They seemed engaged, but much of their writing consisted largely of verbatim quotations copied from the texts they had read. If they had been explic-itly taught to paraphrase in their own words, they would have had a better chance of understanding and remembering the material. And they could have simultaneously learned how to make their writing smoother and more coherent. (The Common Core's demand that students cite evidence for their claims, while well-intentioned, has led to writing that consists largely of undigested quotes.)

If students don't learn these skills in elementary school, they're unlikely to acquire them in middle or high school. Teachers at that level don't see teaching writing as part of their job—and they, like most elementary teachers, haven't been trained to do it. High school teachers confronted by classes full of struggling writers are likely to assign very little writing, thereby continuing to deprive students of an essential means of learning material in depth and developing analytical skills. As with reading, students from more-educated families have a better chance of absorbing the basics of writing at home, leaving others to flounder.

In her book *Other People's Children*, published in 1995, African American educator Lisa Delpit quotes a friend named Cathy, also African American, a teacher at an alternative high school in Philadelphia. "These people keep pushing this fluency thing," Cathy says, referring to middle-class white literacy gurus who focus on simply getting students comfortable putting pen to paper without expecting them to conform to conventional standards of written English. "Our kids *are* fluent. What they need are the skills that will get them into college. . . . This is just another one of those racist ploys to keep our kids out. White kids learn how to write a decent sentence. Even if they don't teach them in school, their parents make sure they get what they need. But what about our kids? They don't get it at home and they spend all their time in school learning to be *fluent*. I'm sick of this liberal nonsense."

Even some teachers who are fervent advocates of writers' workshop have told me their students never manage to produce work that's as well written as the writing samples Calkins includes in her books. But Calkins rejects the suggestion that her approach might not work for all students. The problem, she maintains, lies with the teachers.

"Sometimes teachers will say to me," Calkins said during a

teacher-training session I attended, "I look at the student work that you give us to study, and I just look at that work, and my kids can't do that. And then I say to those teachers, you know, I think you're right." She paused for dramatic effect. "I think your kids *can't* do that. Because your expectations are their ceiling. And they will *never* do more than you expect."

Calkins is right that teachers need to have high expectations. But even astronomical expectations won't do any good unless children get the explicit instruction they need to meet them. Without that, it's unfair to blame teachers—or students. As Lisa Delpit has observed, writing-process advocates sometimes "create situations in which students ultimately find themselves held accountable for knowing a set of rules about which no one has ever directly informed them."

THE COMMON CORE was designed to shine a spotlight on writing, which had been largely ignored during the reading-and-math-obsessed era of No Child Left Behind. And just as the reading standards were aimed at changing many of the practices associated with balanced literacy, the writing standards were designed in large part to uproot the writers' workshop emphasis on personal narrative.

In another infamous Common Core video, David Coleman tells an audience of educators that the "two most popular forms of writing in the American high school today" are personal opinion and personal narrative. "The only problem with those two forms of writing," he continues, "is that as you grow up in this world, you realize that people really don't give a shit about what you feel or what you think." In a similar vein, Coleman has remarked that it would be rare for a supervisor to tell an employee, "Johnson, I need a market analysis by Friday, but before that I need a compelling account of your childhood."

These colorful observations sparked outrage among many teachers: How dare Coleman, who wasn't even an educator, be so dismissive of students' experiences, thoughts, and feelings? Clearly, critics charged, all he cared about was creating worker bees who had no ability to think creatively or appreciate literature.

What got lost in the outcry was Coleman's point: students need to be taught how to write in forms in *addition* to the relatively straightforward one of narrative—and they need to learn to write about topics other than their own lives and experiences. They need to be able to explain processes or events clearly and construct coherent arguments supported with evidence. That's the kind of writing expected in college and the workplace, and it's also the kind most likely to develop the abilities to understand complex text and think analytically.

But while the standards set forth worthy goals, they don't provide teachers with anything like a road map. Examples of student work in an appendix begin with a brief "argument" piece by a kindergartener, reproduced in a five-year-old's imperfect scrawl. "My fabit book is do you want to be my friend," it begins. Toward the end there are smoothly written essays by twelfth-graders on topics like the 1918 influenza epidemic and the nuances of the distinction between fiction and nonfiction. How students are supposed to move from one end of this spectrum to the other is unexplained. The standards assume the basics will somehow be acquired, advising eleventh- and twelfth-grade teachers to ensure their students "use appropriate and varied transitions to link the major sections of the text, create cohesion, and clarify the relationships among complex ideas and concepts"—whether or not they know how to construct a sentence.

Unfortunately, the Common Core also endorses Calkins's position that students should write at length beginning in kindergarten and, like her, defines goals in terms of the number of pages: fourth-graders need to be able to produce a minimum of one typed page in a sitting, fifth-graders two pages, and sixth-graders three. Teachers might easily misinterpret these guidelines to mean the quality of the writing is beside the point.

Calkins has tried to adapt her approach to align with other requirements of the Common Core, expanding her units of study beyond personal narrative and producing new ones on informative and argumentative writing. But as with reading, she's retained her fundamental philosophy, and it's incompatible with the standards' demands for increased rigor. Her updated units, for example, continue to insist on flash-drafting rather than first creating a linear outline. Given the cognitive demands imposed by writing, the wisdom of having inexperienced writers take that approach is dubious even for personal narrative. For the more demanding genres of informational and argumentative writing, it can easily lead to incoherent results. Even accomplished writers often need to spend a good deal of time planning before they plunge in.

Beyond that, Calkins has continued to treat writing—like reading—as a free-floating collection of skills. Content can and should be taught elsewhere, she says: "But when I'm teaching people to write, I'm teaching them a method—I'm teaching them how to do something." She is sufficiently aware of the connection between writing and knowledge that she has grounded her units in specific topics: the American Revolution for fourth grade, the pros and cons of chocolate milk for fifth. But the idea is that other topics could easily be substituted, so the approach is still generic.

In a fifth-grade unit on Westward Expansion, for example, teachers aren't supposed to tell kids, "The question we're going to write about today is how the opening of the Erie Canal in 1825 led to settlers moving west." Instead, they're advised to say, "Historians write about relationships between events because the past will always have an impact on what unfolds in the future." Students are encouraged to consider generalities like "what historians might care about that is special to history." It's difficult enough for many kids to understand Westward Expansion without also having to think about what historians "might care about"—a directive that is so broad as to be almost meaningless.

Still, Calkins's approach is preferable to many of the "Common Core–aligned" writing programs that have sprung up in response to cries for help from teachers and administrators. She at least has students spend several weeks on the same topic—whatever it may be—giving them a chance to absorb some actual knowledge. Most programs provide no more than a jumble of disconnected subjects for students to write about. One shows students how to make an outline by giving them a paragraph about Arches National Park, followed by an example of informative writing about how bats use sound to fly in the dark. Students are then invited to write an informative paragraph by choosing *any* topic, before being shown a model paragraph on the Battle of Yorktown. To teach them how to plan and organize, they get a paragraph on yet another subject: "How Crocodiles and Alligators Are Different."

EVEN BEFORE THE Common Core arrived on the scene in 2010, the Hochman Method was beginning to spread beyond the special-education world. When Windward students reentered the mainstream schools they had come from, usually after two or three years, their writing ability attracted attention.

"Occasionally, we'd have a student attend Windward," the head of a nearby elite private school, Rye Country Day School, told a journalist. "And they'd come back and we'd find that that student had writing *down*."

Public and private schools began sending faculty members to the teacher-training institute Windward had established. Hochman—who headed Windward for eleven years before stepping down in 1999—also started working directly with schools and school districts. In 2009, the principal of a low-performing high school on Staten Island called New Dorp enlisted Hochman's help in a last-ditch effort to stave off closure. Nothing else had worked to improve the performance of the school's largely poor and working-class students, many of whom were still learning English. The faculty had concluded that a large part of the problem was students' inability to express themselves well in writing.

When the principal, Deirdre DeAngelis, and a group of New Dorp teachers visited Windward, they were amazed to see writing samples from learning-disabled sixth- and seventh-graders that were clearer and better organized than the writing some of their seniors were able to produce. The next day, the teachers told DeAngelis, "We *have* to do this."

After a few years of school-wide implementation, starting with social studies and eventually including English, math, science, and even PE, New Dorp saw dramatic results. In 2009, the teacher of an Advanced Placement US history class had only two of her twenty-three students do well enough on the final exam to qualify for college credit, squeaking by with the minimum qualifying score of three out of a possible five. After three years of the Hochman Method, twenty-six of the teacher's twenty-eight students passed with a score of four or five. Pass rates on the New York State Regents exams were also climbing, as were graduation rates. No longer in danger of being shut down, New Dorp was now attracting educators from across the country who wanted to replicate its success.

Then, in 2012, as anxiety about the Common Core's writing requirements was rising, an article about New Dorp appeared in the *Atlantic*. The result was a veritable tsunami of interest, which led Hochman to establish a nonprofit that took its name from the *Atlantic* article: The Writing Revolution.

I was one of the many who read the article and came away impressed. I had been trying to tutor low-income high school students in writing and, despite what I thought were realistic expectations, I'd been shocked that most couldn't even distinguish a complete sentence from a sentence fragment. Nor—for reasons I didn't yet grasp—had they acquired enough knowledge of the world in their ten years of schooling to understand the fairly straightforward texts I was asking them to write about. A method that started at the sentence level and taught content at the same time as skills sounded like just what they needed.

Officials within the D.C. Public School system, having also read the article, launched a pilot to bring the method to D.C. Several years later, preliminary data collected by the district showed improvement at all the Hochman schools on measures of literacy growth and attendance. One of those schools is the high school where I tutored, which has had phenomenal success with a writing-heavy college-level program called the International Baccalaureate. Educators at several others, including some serving many English language learners, have expressed amazement at the transformation they've seen not only in their students' writing but also in their speaking, reading, and thinking. (I ended up coauthoring a book on the method with Judith Hochman and chairing the board of the nonprofit she founded.)

But DCPS's plans to disseminate the method system-wide have run into obstacles, raising questions about how quickly an approach like Hochman's can be scaled up. Other district initiatives have taken precedence, and so far, few teachers outside the schools Hochman worked with directly have been trained in her method. The district was supposed to embed her writing strategies in the content-focused curriculum it has been creating over the last several years, but many assignments ask students to write at length without regard to whether they have mastered sentence-level skills, even in the early grades.

The DCPS official in charge of literacy, Corinne Colgan, says one problem has been pushback from teachers and school leaders who believe inexperienced writers shouldn't be limited to sentence-level work. "Lots of people feel very strongly about kids building up writing stamina," she told me, "or needing more than a sentence to get all the information out."

Even if they or their schools don't embrace Hochman's entire philosophy, individual teachers can use sentence-level strategies to boost students' comprehension and enable them to retain and critique material they're learning. They can show students how to create linear outlines before they write to help them organize their thoughts and lighten their cognitive load.

But that piecemeal approach probably won't be enough to fully unlock the power of writing instruction to develop students' abilities to express themselves coherently and with sophistication, understand complex text, and think about that text critically. For that to happen, school leaders will need to commit to ensuring students are exposed to the same strategies throughout the curriculum, ideally on a daily basis and perhaps for years. While it's crucial for a school district to ensure the new approach is sustained despite teacher and administrative turn-over, it's unlikely to work if imposed from the top down. As in Washoe County, teachers need to understand *why* a radical shift makes sense and have an opportunity to see it in action at pilot schools that choose to adopt it.

Beyond all that, teachers will need to ignore the Common Core's implication that success should be measured in quantity rather than quality. And if writing instruction is to begin in elementary school, as it should, the elementary curriculum will need a hefty injection of content.

MAY 2017

It's been almost a month since my last visit, but Ms. Townsell's first-grade girls greet me like an old friend, with smiles and waves. One even remembers my name. "Hi, Ms. Wexler!" she chirps.

The class is going through its usual morning literacy routine—more or less. Today, the first-graders don't have computers to work on because they're all being used for testing. All public schools in D.C., both traditional and charter, administer the Common Core–aligned test called PARCC in the spring, and there are signs on the front door and throughout the school that read: "Quiet—Testing!"

And even though first-graders don't have to take PARCC, their lives aren't free from testing. They take a widely used test called Measures of Academic Progress, or MAP, three times a year: once in the fall to register their baseline ability, and again midyear and in the spring to measure growth. The midyear exam—which first-graders took several times, in hopes scores would improve—showed there were problems with foundational skills like phonemic awareness and phonics. The administration has decreed that teachers need to focus on those skills intensively before the spring testing in just a few weeks.

So instead of this week's *Journeys* unit, Ms. Townsell has been directed to do a "close read" of a poem called "Ready for the Rain." Whether the poem is the kind of layered and stylistically complex text for which close reading is intended is debatable. Its unnamed narrators smell rain in the air and get excited about splashing in puddles. There are a few words and phrases that Ms. Townsell's students are unfamiliar with—*rain gear* and *refreshing*—and some words are challenging to decode, like *tongue*. But how the poem will help with phonemic awareness and phonics isn't clear.

To Ms. Townsell's mind, it's too late to do much before the MAP test anyway; there simply hasn't been enough time devoted to reading. Last year, when she taught kindergarten, the literacy block was two and a half hours. This year, it's only ninety minutes—if that, because kids often trickle in late, and she doesn't want to start until everyone is there.

That gets to an even more fundamental problem: the school's lax attitude toward attendance. Ms. Townsell's sense is that the administration doesn't want to come down hard on parents for fear of losing more of them—something that could hurt the school's chances of getting its charter renewed. The lack of progress on test scores is another looming threat, and tensions are running high.

Ms. Townsell has toyed with the idea of moving to another school that does a better job with both culture and instruction, but she isn't yet ready to give up on her vision of Excel as a place where African American girls learn about sisterhood and pride. She's decided to stay but in a new role as the elementary art teacher. Not only was art her original career plan, now she won't have to worry about reading and math tests. She's looking forward to having more freedom to teach as she wants—and possibly boosting students' literacy skills at the same time. The model lesson she taught as part of her application, for example, focused on the concepts of "juxtaposition" and "contrast," teaching vocabulary through art. It's not ideal, but it will work for now.

There's another glimmer of hope on the horizon: Tara Warrington, the elementary principal—who has been just as frustrated with the *Journeys* basal as Ms. Townsell—tells me she's gotten approval to try a content-focused curriculum called Wit & Wisdom with next year's third grade.

But Ms. Warrington ends up moving to another state. Then, in January 2018 comes the news that everyone at Excel has feared: over impassioned objections from administrators, parents, and students, D.C.'s Public Charter School Board votes to revoke the school's charter, citing declining reading and math scores and low attendance in its decision.

IT'S TESTING SEASON at Center City too. On the walls outside Ms. Masi's fourth-floor classroom, motivational posters have taken the place of the student work usually on display. Large sheets of red and yellow construction paper feature handwritten notes from students and teachers: "TRY HARD . . . We can do anything! . . . No fear!! . . . Believe! . . . I know that I am going to do good." A colorful paper chain is poignantly labeled the "3rd grade PARCC worry chain." A note reads: "We are leaving our fears outside and *refuse* to take them into the test! . . . Each link is something we worry about but together we can tackle it all!"

Ms. Masi's second-graders, being exempt from state testing until next year, are in the thick of their next-to-last Core Knowledge domain. It's one that has particular resonance for many: immigration. In previous lessons, students read about a four-foot-tall German immigrant who made important scientific discoveries; an Irish family fleeing the potato blight; and Chinese immigrants who came to America hoping to find gold. Yesterday's read-aloud was about a Scandinavian family who moved to the Midwest in search of farmland.

Today's lesson is a more general discussion of the various "push" and "pull" factors that brought different groups to the United States. Ms. Masi's chart has blanks for each factor as applied to immigrants from England, Scotland, Ireland, China—and "Today." This lesson could easily be taken over by text-to-self connections, and Ms. Masi addresses that possibility head-on. First she reveals that her own ancestors were immigrants from Italy, and then she asks kids to raise their hands if a parent is an immigrant. About half the hands go up. Most of the rest go up when she asks about grandparents and great-grandparents. But Ms. Masi is determined to keep the class focused on the read-aloud. She wants the kids to connect the material not just to their own lives but to what they've already learned.

When she reads that for many years "the people of Europe did not know that the Americas existed," she pauses and asks the kids what connection they can make. It takes a while, but eventually some get it: Christopher Columbus and other explorers stumbled across America in their search for a route to Asia. Ms. Masi pauses again after a reference to "the Pilgrims." Where did they come from? Why did they leave? After each correct answer from one student who has raised a hand, there are disappointed rumblings from the others.

"If you already knew that," Ms. Masi responds calmly, "give yourself a pat on the back."

When she's almost finished with the read-aloud, a boy named Dawi raises his hand and volunteers, apropos of nothing, "In Ethiopia, the government was very bad, and they just hurt the people for no reason!"

"That seems like it would be a push factor, if the government is not running in a way that people feel safe," Ms. Masi observes. But there's hubbub brewing.

"And Barack Obama don't do nothing about it!" Dawi continues.

Ms. Masi tries to point out that Dawi's sentence has some grammatical problems, but the din is growing louder. Exactly what the kids are grumbling about, she's not sure.

"I do want to talk more about the connections you're making," Ms. Masi says firmly, "but we are absolutely not going to do it if side conversations start, and if opinions are being expressed in a disrespectful way." She promises that later on, the class will talk more about students' personal connections to immigration. And when "center" time begins, she makes a spur-of-the-moment decision: the kids can choose to write about their experiences, explaining the push and pull factors for their own families.

But now the students seem uncertain: What if you don't know the push and pull factors? What if your parents only told you a little bit?

Then just write a little bit, Ms. Masi reassures them. There's no right or wrong answer.

In the end, only three students take Ms. Masi up on her invitation, and they don't say much that connects their own families to past immigrants. While Ms. Masi didn't dismiss or stifle her students' desire to talk about their lives, she didn't allow it to dominate the lesson either. Yes, it's important for kids to relate their own experiences to what they're learning. But in order to do that, they need to learn something first.

Ms. Masi has gotten positive feedback from Center City for her ability to teach Core Knowledge, but as the year draws to a close, her frustrations are coming to the fore. She values what the curriculum has done for these kids, but it isn't her natural teaching style. The school's policy of having students write daily notes and exit tickets—written responses at the end of a lesson—seems "robotic." Like Ms. Townsell, she would prefer a more creative, project-based approach, along the lines of the end-of-year "capstone project," when students collectively write and perform skits on the theme of gender equality. Perhaps if she were to continue with Core Knowledge, she could come up with more creative ways of teaching it—as Ms. Williams did with her first-grade time-travel expedition to Mesopotamia. And perhaps the administration would give her the flexibility to try them.

But that is not to be. Ms. Masi decides to leave Center City for a first-grade classroom at one of D.C.'s elite private schools, where she feels she'll have more freedom to teach in a way that feels natural. Also, like Ms. Townsell—and many other talented teachers—she's fed up with testing, and private schools don't have to administer standardized tests.

Ms. Masi has seen the effects of high-stakes testing on her third-graders. Two months before PARCC, they started taking practice tests and filling out exit tickets framed to mimic test questions: What is the meaning of this word in the context of this sentence? What evidence from the text supports your answer from part A, which then justifies your answer in part B? "*My* mind is blown sometimes when I have to answer questions like that," Ms. Masi says. Even her second-graders have been affected. Like the first-graders at Excel, they take the MAP test three times a year. And they're close enough to third grade to feel the pressure. At the end of the year, when each class visits the class above, the only thing the second-graders want to ask the third-graders about is PARCC: How long is it? Were you scared?

"And I was just like, hey, let's think about some other things that third-graders have to do," Ms. Masi says. "Like that's the only message we sent to them all year."

When I spoke to Center City's CEO, Russ Williams, many months before, he told me he advises teachers not to worry about tests—if they pay attention to the curriculum the tests will take care of themselves. But the signs posted in the hallway outside Ms. Masi's classroom, and her experience, show that's not so easy to do.

After a few months at the private school, Ms. Masi is surprised to discover she misses the structure and coherence of Core Knowledge. At her new school, she tells me, not much thought is given to ensuring that the curriculum builds across grade levels, or even within grades. Teachers have assembled the first-grade curriculum over the years, and the social studies units feel "disconnected." Reflecting the usual assumptions about the interests and capabilities of young children, the first six weeks of the school year are spent on a unit called "All About Me." Some time on that topic would be fine, Ms. Masi says, but *six weeks*? "Some students are so smart and ready to learn new things," she says, "and it seems we're not building them up to their capacity."

She knows this school would never adopt Core Knowledge, but she's hoping that eventually she'll be able to introduce some of its underlying concepts. Perhaps she would start with history. "I think about how much history *I* learned at Center City," she says, "and how I saw kids making connections." She'd also like to try teaching some vocabulary words, which she's sure these highly verbal children would pick up quickly. But when she suggested choosing three words as "words of the week" during the "All About Me" unit, her co-teacher—a veteran at the school—said "Oh, no, these kids already know that stuff—we don't need to do that."

"And I wanted to say, the kids at Center City were also smart," Ms. Masi remembers. "The kids may be smart, but that doesn't mean we don't need to teach them anymore."

CHAPTER 12

Scaling Up: Can It Be Done?

I N THE FALL OF 2009, two men arrived in Albany, New York, to take over the state's education system at a critical juncture. The Obama administration had recently announced it would be distributing a jackpot of federal grant money—$4 billion—to state education authorities through a competition called Race to the Top.

New York's potential winnings were sizable, but the application was complex and demanding, with nineteen categories scored on a five-hundred-point scale. And it was due just a few months after the men took up their posts. One was David Steiner, the former dean of the Hunter College School of Education in New York City. The second was his deputy, John B. King Jr., who had been managing a network of high-performing charter schools. Their hope was to use Race to the Top money to bring about fundamental improvements in the state's mammoth, and largely underperforming, education system.

New York didn't win. But the competition would have a second round. Steiner and King got to work on an improved proposal.

Race to the Top dangled a humongous carrot to get states to adopt the kinds of changes favored by the Obama administration and education reformers generally, including the expansion of charter schools and teacher evaluation systems based partly on growth in student test scores. New York had a cap on charters and didn't require districts to factor scores into evaluations. King and Steiner knew that to make their second application viable, the legislature would need to change both of these positions. And the state's teachers' union was intent on keeping them in place.

They undertook a tension-filled, months-long effort to find a compromise. Just days before the deadline, legislators managed to reach an agreement that seemed to satisfy the Race to the Top demands. Steiner and King went to the Assembly Hall together at 3:00 a.m. to watch the vote.

"It was an extraordinary moment," Steiner later recalled. "I had tears in my eyes."

New York won almost $700 million.

Lost in the intense lobbying, fevered negotiations, and lavish press coverage was a detail in the state's application that would turn out to have a significant impact, not just in New York but across the United States. New York proposed to use a fraction of the money, about $23 million, to develop its own kindergarten-through-twelfth-grade literacy and math curriculum, aligned to the new Common Core standards. In the case of English language arts, that would mean putting the focus squarely on building knowledge, especially in the crucial early-elementary grades. By 2017, the curriculum would become among the most commonly used materials for English language arts and math in the United States.

Before New York's offering appeared, there was no readily available content-focused early-elementary curriculum in this country. Within a few years, it would be joined by several others—most, like New York's, freely available online. This was a necessary first step in giving all children similar access to knowledge of the world. But it was only the first step, and in some ways it was the easiest. Making the shift to knowledge is as much about changing teachers' beliefs and daily practice as about changing the materials they're supposed to use. If the American education system is to provide all students with a meaningful education and act as an engine of social mobility, the gut-level transformation that has begun to happen in places like Washoe County and the Center City charter network needs to spread to fourteen thousand school districts and more than three million teachers.

Even in New York, it's still not clear how many teachers have embraced either the curriculum or the approach needed to implement it. Some remain outright hostile. While the reasons are complex, much of the opposition is rooted in another feature of New York's Race to the Top bargain: its pledge to link teachers' evaluations to students' test scores.

NEW YORK'S CURRICULUM almost didn't happen. Some at the top of the state's education bureaucracy worried that proposing it in the Race to the Top application would jinx the entire project. The very idea of a state creating its own curriculum was unusual, to say the least. Even more alarming, the proposal was to create this curriculum with federal funds, stirring memories of the National History Standards debacle in the 1990s.

The idea originated with David Steiner. He had grown up in England, where it was accepted as a matter of course that *what* got taught was supremely important. The British national education system is based on high-school-level essay exams that cover a range of subjects and texts. Schools and students choose a subset to focus on, and those choices largely determine what students study, beginning at the age of eleven or twelve.

Steiner's concern was less the absence of content in the American elementary curriculum than the overabundance of it in later grades—the encyclopedic textbooks that allow for only superficial treatment of a dizzying range of topics. His own experience had been to dive deeply into a few classic texts and historical periods. At the same time, as someone who was familiar with the ideas of E. D. Hirsch, he was aware of the problems of skills-focused elementary education. And as a former education school dean, Steiner was also exasperated by the challenge of training teachers, as he puts it, to "teach nothing in particular." His background, Steiner says, "came together in a very simple question: How can we launch brand-new standards and not offer teachers the curriculum through which to teach those standards?"

Steiner's deputy, John King, wasn't among those who feared the curriculum proposal would torpedo the state's application. Nor did he need to be convinced of the importance of content. He had a different concern, shaped by his own background—specifically by the experiences of his parents, both of whom had been educators in the New York City public school system. King's father was the first African American principal in Brooklyn. His mother, a native of Puerto Rico, was a middle school guidance counselor. Teachers, he knew, saw detailed, district-mandated curriculum as low-quality, dusty, and burdensome.

"People didn't feel ownership of them, and they weren't organic," King says. "They felt like Central telling you what you should be doing."

Having a local district try to impose a curriculum was bad enough. Having staff at the state department of education try to come up with materials that would work across the state's seven hundred districts could only be worse. But King and Steiner managed to craft a plan the two of them—and the state's Board of Regents—could endorse. The state would enlist outside experts to develop the curriculum with the participation of New York teachers. No one would be required to use it.

One other wrinkle came later. At the time, there was no such thing as a free, online curriculum. But some officials were aware that instructional materials, usually lesson plans created by individual teachers, were being posted on the internet for anyone to use. Often these so-called *open educational resources* were posted under licenses that avoided traditional copyright restrictions. People might be allowed, for example, to use or adapt the materials with attribution but not to make money off them. Why not make New York's entire curriculum an open resource? If the curriculum were free, poor districts and schools would have the same access as wealthy ones, and users would be able to tweak and improve it.

As the curriculum was rolled out, King's fears began to subside. At the thirty or so "institutes" the education department held over the five years it spent developing the curriculum—meetings of hundreds of educators representing districts around the state—the enthusiasm was palpable. There was something about the way it was constructed, "the flexibility that people had to change it, to do their own piecing around it, the voluntariness of it, that just made it a different thing from the mandated curricula of the past." Groups of teachers would talk about what did and didn't make sense. "It would be: 'does this timing work, who's confident about this?'" says Kate Gerson, who oversaw the development of the curriculum and ran the institutes. "'I've never tried this before. . . . I *have* tried this before!' And then, coming back together, talking about how did it go." They were having the same trial-and-error, collaborative experience as teachers who had experimented with Common Core lessons at the Washoe County Core Task Project.

It seemed the curriculum was living up to its name: EngageNY. And it wasn't just New York that was getting engaged. One day, a friend of King's sent him a link. You should see these great materials that this district in California is using, the friend urged. King doesn't remember the name of the district, but it wasn't one he had heard of.

"And I clicked on it," King recalls, delighted at the memory, "and it was EngageNY stuff. But they had taken out EngageNY and they had put their district logo on it."

By late 2014, the EngageNY website had received more than fifteen million visits, an average of twenty-six thousand per week. By the following spring, its materials had been downloaded nearly twenty million times. In September 2016 alone, there were more than a million visits. One survey that year showed that about 30 percent of math teachers across the country were using EngageNY, along with a little more than 25 percent of ELA teachers.

EngageNY triggered something like a movement. By 2018, most states were sharing instructional materials online to some extent, and at least twelve (including Washington, D.C.) were engaged in developing their own open curricula in one or more subject areas. Louisiana and D.C. were developing content-focused elementary literacy curricula, as were a number of small nongovernmental organizations.

Meanwhile, the textbook publishing industry—traditionally the chief source of curriculum for districts—has been undergoing an upheaval. The few behemoths that used to dominate the field have been losing market share as teachers, schools, and districts have gravitated to start-ups that are better able to take advantage of new technology and better aligned to the Common Core.

At the same time, a large plurality of districts are now using something other than a major textbook *or* an open educational resource for their elementary curriculum. What they're using isn't clear, but—desperate for ways to supplement or replace outdated textbooks—teachers across the country are regularly resorting to Google to find materials or downloading them from places like Pinterest or a site called Teachers Pay Teachers, where educators pay modest fees for lesson plans their peers have created. Just as it did before EngageNY, the term *open educational resources* still often means fragmentary materials of uneven quality rather than a coherent curriculum—and in the area of literacy, many still focus on skills.

The advent of open educational resources has the potential to introduce vast numbers of educators to a new way of teaching. But, given the free-for-all nature of the internet, it could just as easily lead to a perpetuation of the status quo—or possibly something worse.

Perhaps New York's most radical move was choosing the Core Knowledge Foundation to develop a literacy curriculum for kindergarten through second grade. That portion of Core Knowledge Language Arts is now available to anyone through EngageNY, and a version that goes from preschool through fifth grade is freely available on the foundation's website. (In addition, there's a version that can be purchased from a publisher, for those who don't want to print out all the materials.)

Core Knowledge exposes children to massive amounts of information and probably does the best job of giving them a sense of history. And yet, because it looks so different from what elementary teachers are used to, it can be a tough sell. Instead of relying on "authentic," commercially available books, Core Knowledge has created its own texts for teachers and students. That makes it much easier to bring back concepts and vocabulary throughout the school year and across grades, so they'll lodge in children's long-term memories. But teachers have come to love certain works of children's literature, and they know their students will love them too. Many associate any texts written specifically for the classroom with the basal readers that they would prefer to avoid.

Another obstacle is the lingering impression on the part of some educators that Core Knowledge's intellectual godfather, E. D. Hirsch, is politically reactionary and that the curriculum is overly Eurocentric. But as part of the EngageNY development process, the foundation worked with New York teachers and others to ensure the materials reflect a diversity of viewpoints, particularly with regard to subjects like slavery and the arrival of Columbus in the New World.

Still, there are now other content-rich choices that use authentic texts and will appeal to different constituencies. A left-leaning district that wants a focus on science might gravitate toward EL Education. Formerly called Expeditionary Learning, the nonprofit helped develop the EngageNY literacy curriculum for grades three through eight and has its own free version that covers kindergarten through fifth grade. EL immerses children in project-like "expeditions" focused on specific content areas, with lots of hands-on activities. Kindergarteners spend months learning about trees; first-graders dive deeply into birds. By fourth and fifth grade, social justice comes to the fore, with units on women's struggle to win the vote and athletes as leaders of social change. One unit includes an excerpt from the United Nations' Universal Declaration of Human Rights.

Those who prefer a heavier dose of history and art could choose to pay for Wit & Wisdom, which is not an open resource. A kindergarten unit focuses on "America Then and Now" and offers Emanuel Leutze's famous painting *Washington Crossing the Delaware* for analysis. A first-grade unit on animals includes Albrecht Dürer's detailed painting of a young hare. Second-graders delve into the American West with help from Albert Bierstadt's majestic depiction of the Sierra Nevada. One of Wit & Wisdom's slogans is "books not basals."

American Reading Company is the closest to balanced literacy, offering sets of authentic texts. But the books are grouped by topic as well as reading level, and schools can pick and choose themes in literature, science, and social studies. A curriculum called Bookworms is distinctive in that it includes read-alouds of complex text through the upper elementary grades, which boosts both reading fluency and knowledge-building. As compared to the traditional guided reading, leveled-text approach, both American Reading Company and Bookworms can significantly increase reading comprehension after only one year.

It's a massive undertaking to create a comprehensive curriculum from scratch, as New York did—and given the existence of ready-made options, it's no longer necessary. But several years ago, when those options weren't yet available, Louisiana and D.C. each undertook the creation of their own literacy curricula, using a combination of authentic texts and online resources. Louisiana's is freely available to anyone, and at least parts of D.C.'s will be eventually.

While many resources have sprung up to satisfy the demands of the Common Core, there's no guarantee that just because something is free and online it will meet that objective any better than a traditional textbook—even if it's a complete curriculum. Michigan's social studies curriculum, freely available, adopts the standard expanding-environments approach: kindergarten is entirely devoted to "Myself and Others," first grade to "Families and Schools," and second grade to "Community Studies." The texts are simple and superficial, and to the extent that history makes an appearance, the objective is more to get kids to understand that history has something to do with the past than to provide engaging narratives or content. To help educators choose wisely, some states and other entities have started rating literacy curricula or providing rubrics for doing so, with knowledge-building being one criterion. Generally, traditional basal readers like *Journeys* get low ratings and newer content-focused options like Core Knowledge get high ones.

The number of districts and schools that have adopted content-rich curricula remains small, but the good news is that it's growing, including in high-poverty areas where it's desperately needed: Detroit recently adopted EL Education, for example, and Baltimore chose Wit & Wisdom. There are signs that a movement toward knowledge is spreading across the country, with organizations of teachers and even education school deans calling for a greater focus on content. But it's still not clear how many teachers are changing their approach.

EVEN IF A STATE or district endorses a content-rich curriculum, ensuring principals and teachers embrace it is another matter. D.C. public schools are theoretically required to use the district-created literacy curriculum, but it's clear some don't—like Reeves Elementary, where Ms. Bauer teaches, which, like other schools in affluent neighborhoods, has been exempted. Some schools serving low-income populations also don't use the curriculum, and the district has done little or nothing to address the situation.

To those outside the education world, the solution might seem simple: just tell teachers what to teach and how to teach it. In practice, however, that rarely works. Teachers appreciate guidance and support, especially if they're new to the profession—as many in high-poverty schools are. At the same time, most deeply value their freedom to provide the kind of instruction they believe their students need. And even if education authorities *say* it's content that counts, if the tests they require appear to focus on skills, that's what most teachers will put in the foreground—especially if that's how they're used to teaching.

In New York State, some teachers are so outraged at having their performance evaluated on the basis of tests they feel are unfair that they reject anything to do with the Common Core, including New York's curriculum. When the state introduced rigorous Common Core–aligned tests in 2013 and scores plummeted, many erupted in anger at John King, who had replaced David Steiner as commissioner of education. At a series of public forums, audiences of parents and teachers booed and mocked him. Tempers ran particularly high in places like Syracuse, where 40 percent of teachers had been rated less than effective, partly because their students failed to show "growth" on the new, harder tests.

In the face of these verbal assaults, King, a soft-spoken man with a calm manner, maintained a composure that only seemed to further infuriate his detractors. In the spring of 2014, the New York state teachers' union, representing more than six hundred thousand members, called for his resignation.

Today, King downplays the conflict, saying that while Common Core opponents garnered media attention, huge numbers of teachers in New York have quietly embraced EngageNY. And a nationwide study found that 65 percent of downloads of the literacy curriculum came from computers within the state. Still, anger over test scores, combined with deeply held convictions about the superiority of balanced literacy in places like New York City, has impeded the spread of the curriculum and the changes in teaching practice that would make it work. In 2015, a task force appointed by the governor reported "widespread belief that the curriculum does not allow for local district input, lacks breadth, and is too one-size-fits-all." It also found that EngageNY was "complicated and difficult to use." While teachers who attended the state's institutes may have developed a sense of ownership, that clearly hasn't always been the case for the vast majority who didn't.

Recently, Louisiana rather than New York has become the model for getting teachers to understand and implement the Common Core shifts. Like New York—and unlike D.C.—Louisiana doesn't require districts and schools to use its curriculum. It even ranks other literacy curricula for their alignment to the Common Core—and engages teachers in that process, a practice that has helped them grasp the need to build knowledge. The state has made it easier for districts to buy curricula that get its highest rating, with the result that at least 70 percent were using them in 2016, up from only 20 percent four years before. Recognizing that teachers often respond better to peers than administrators, the state created a cadre of five thousand "teacher-leaders," with a presence in every school, who convene several times a year to get information and training and then act as ambassadors and advocates. This collaborative approach has helped Louisiana teachers gain a relatively accurate understanding of the Common Core. In most states that have adopted the standards or something like them, about three-quarters of all teachers believe incorrectly that they call for giving students texts on their individual reading levels and prioritizing skills over content. In Louisiana, just under half hold those views.

That understanding appears to have carried over into classroom practice. In 2017, a group of education leaders from other states toured elementary classrooms in Louisiana that were using Core Knowledge Language Arts—one of the curricula that received a high rating from the state—and were bowled over. "It was one of the most powerful visits I've ever taken," said an official from Wisconsin. With philanthropic support, some education leaders are now embarking on a collective effort to determine whether they can make their own education systems look more like Louisiana's.

But in all the coverage of Louisiana's success, which has been ample, one fact has been largely overlooked: Louisiana suspended the practice of tying teacher evaluations to test scores when it adopted the Common Core in 2012, only resuming it four years later. That moratorium may have enabled teachers to put test scores out of their minds long enough to embrace a new way of teaching. Some education reformers—including John King—fear that abandoning test-based teacher evaluation will only trigger a return to the days when the lower achievement of disadvantaged students was invisible. When the Every Student Succeeds Act replaced No Child Left Behind in 2015, it gave states the freedom to measure teacher quality any way they wanted, and reformers worried that states would eliminate test scores as a factor. But—for better or worse—two years after ESSA was enacted, only four states had done so.

ESSA also allows states to count factors other than reading and math scores as 49 percent of a school's overall rating. As secretary of education in the Obama administration—a job he took after stepping down as New York's commissioner—King saw that as an opportunity for states "to broaden their definition of educational excellence to include providing students strong learning experiences in science, social studies, world languages, and the arts." Unfortunately, few states have followed that path, instead choosing criteria like a decline in absenteeism, an increase in the number of advanced high school courses, or the results of student surveys. The Trump administration, which has the responsibility for approving state plans, has even discouraged states from emphasizing scores in subjects like social studies and science.

But here again, Louisiana may be leading the way. Instead of removing reading and math scores from teacher evaluations or proposing criteria in addition to them, the state has received federal approval to experiment with an innovative kind of *reading* test—one that draws on the content of the state's own English and social studies curricula. Echoing the writings of Daniel Willingham, Louisiana's superintendent of education, John White, observed that "by not requiring knowledge of any specific book or facts, reading tests have contributed to the false impression that reading is mainly about having skills such as being able to summarize, and not about background knowledge." Instead of keeping the topics on the test a closely guarded secret, Louisiana will announce in advance what content and books are covered. White noted that teachers will "have good reason to focus on the hard and inspiring lessons of history and books."

The plan is to start small, with twenty high schools, putting off the development of similar tests for lower grade levels to the indefinite future. Still, it's hard to believe it took so long for someone in a position of authority in the United States to propose that students be tested on what they've actually been taught rather than what they just happen to know. If this revolutionary idea gains traction, it may be our best hope of paving the way for a large-scale shift in teacher practice.

EVEN IF STANDARDIZED READING tests disappeared tomorrow—or if all states followed Louisiana's lead—teachers would still need help shifting their approach. And given that the tests are unlikely to vanish or change anytime soon, it's essential to inform the general public, parents, and especially teachers about what the tests really measure—and what students need.

As John King realized when he saw teachers tweaking EngageNY, technology has enabled every teacher to become a curriculum hacker. Teachers have always put their own spin on textbooks and other materials, but the internet has dramatically expanded the possibilities for adding or substituting lesson plans and classroom activities. Whether they're trying to supplement inadequate textbooks or further enrich a content-focused curriculum, teachers' efforts will bear fruit only if they understand what to look for. Especially if they're desperately trying to plan a lesson the night before they need to deliver it, they can easily find activities that waste students' time. And many online materials are searchable only by the skills they supposedly develop—including Common Core "skills" like close reading—rather than by their content.

It can also be hard to change deeply engrained habits, even for teachers who grasp the importance of building knowledge. Rather than asking students generic questions, they have to decide what larger understanding they want students to reach and pose questions that lead there. They also need to develop a sense of when to provide information and when to allow students to engage in productive struggle. That can be particularly difficult when students are significantly below grade level. And some curricula are more difficult to implement well than others—for example, those that, like EL Education, rely heavily on project-based learning.

"Even teachers who had drunk the knowledge Kool-Aid were having trouble making the shifts in practice," says Silas Kulkarni, who spent many hours explaining the Common Core to teachers around the country as a staff member at Student Achievement Partners.

The key to getting people to embrace change is enabling them to understand its value at a visceral level, through experience. What that means for teachers, essentially, is professional development—but not the usual drive-by kind. Instead, they need the cyclical, trial-and-error, collaborative PD, grounded in specific content, that teachers in Washoe County got through the Core Task Project and teachers in New York

State got through the EngageNY institutes. They need to meet with colleagues to hear about a fresh idea, try it out, and reconvene to talk about how it went—and then do it again.

Officials in both D.C. and Louisiana are trying to adopt this approach. DCPS brings educators together in weekly sessions, organized by subject or grade level, to learn from one another—although some teachers complain the agendas are too prescribed. Louisiana has created incentives for districts to hire PD providers whose training is connected to curricula the state has endorsed. Meanwhile, some entrepreneurs—including Kulkarni—are trying to bring Washoe-style PD to teachers across the country, with the support of school districts and states like Louisiana.

Districts need to be willing to pay for this kind of PD, and that's where open educational resources could change the landscape. Administrators are used to getting PD for free from publishers once they adopt a textbook. But, says former textbook company executive Larry Singer, it's generally worthless, consisting of little more than "trainers" who walk teachers through tables of contents. He has a different idea: instead of having districts pay a lot of money for low-quality textbooks and get low-quality PD for free, why not *give* them high-quality curriculum and let them use the money they save to pay for high-quality PD? Singer helped found an organization called Open Up Resources to offer just that, and many are eager to try it. Even before Open Up Resources announced its first literacy curriculum in 2017, Singer says he had heard from more than 180 districts.

But the number of people knowledgeable enough to train others in using the new curricula is tiny relative to the number of teachers who need training. That could be the biggest obstacle to the spread of content-focused teaching, at least in the short term. Singer favors creating a cadre of trainers who may or may not have a teaching background. But curriculum developers can be reluctant to hand over training to third parties who might not fully understand their framework. And teachers are generally wary of taking pedagogical advice from those who don't have classroom experience.

On the other hand, Kulkarni—a former teacher—says a "light touch" works best. Like Aaron Grossman in Washoe, he gives teachers information and minimal guidance and allows them to collectively hash things out. There are also unknown numbers of teachers out there who have yearned to embrace content but haven't had the right materials and support. For them, it may not be necessary to provide much training at all.

DURING THE 2016–17 SCHOOL YEAR, Sarah Webb tried an experiment with her fourth-grade class in a low-income, largely white school district outside of Dayton, Ohio. Her district's test scores have always been among the lowest in the Dayton suburbs, and, Webb says, many students have limited aspirations. Her students had always done relatively well on state assessments, but when Ohio switched to a Common Core–aligned test, their scores plummeted along with everyone else's. Webb was ready for something different, and when she found out that the district was planning to pilot a content-focused curriculum for kindergarten through eighth grade called Wit & Wisdom, she volunteered to participate.

At Webb's school, teachers for each grade level had collectively decided what and how they taught. Most chose a version of balanced literacy, while one grade used a basal reader. But the skills focus never made much sense to Webb. She and the other fourth-grade teachers tried to organize the curriculum around themes—"text structure," or "drama, poetry, and folktales"—but they never had enough time to develop the lessons. There would be some carefully chosen texts, she says, "and then it was like, here's these random articles from Scholastic News." Wit & Wisdom provided Webb with thematic sets of books, both fiction and nonfiction. Built into the curriculum were activities that had kids not only talking but also writing about what they've learned.

There were skeptics. Kindergarten teachers thought the approach was developmentally inappropriate, and teachers of kids with special needs worried their students wouldn't be able to handle it. Some were dubious they would have time to get through everything in a given lesson or feared children would lose motivation if they couldn't choose what to read. Would they have enough time to practice reading on their individual level? That, Webb says, was the biggest concern.

Webb didn't have those reservations, but the adjustment wasn't easy for her either—especially because she never got the required training before the school year began. (She did get some in the spring.) She had to spend a lot of time preparing for class, and her twenty-four students struggled to participate in the "Socratic Seminars" that were part of the curriculum. But it got easier. This was the way she'd always wanted to teach; she had just never had the time to make it happen. And her students were enthralled. They wanted to know more about certain topics and read more by authors featured in the curriculum, so Webb took books out from the public library to satisfy their curiosity. After the module on "What Makes a Great Heart?" one girl, Webb said, "talked about plasma all year long." Students were also retaining information and making connections. They brought up the concept of a figurative "great heart" in subsequent modules, when they read a novel about a boy who survives a plane crash and again when they learned about the American Revolution.

The high achievers were flourishing—Webb saw them realize "way more growth than ever before." But so were the struggling students. The fact that they were studying the same content as their peers gave them confidence. And the slower pace—looking closely at one text or one work of art—gave them an opportunity to contribute to the discussion.

The concerns other teachers had expressed turned out to be groundless. Kids still had thirty minutes every day to read whatever they wanted. And, says Webb, "I have seen these kids—especially the low ones—getting way more motivated by this [curriculum] than by reading *Captain Underpants.*"

Webb says she'll always remember one student in particular. Matt was a sweet, blond kid from a military family who had been in a different school every year since kindergarten. At the beginning of the year, Matt's mother took Webb aside and confessed she was worried about his reading. He was one of those kids, Webb says, who thought he was "in the dumb group." But it turned out that Matt was keenly interested in everything the class was studying. During the "great heart" module, Matt wrote an entire paragraph about Clara Barton—more than he'd ever written before—which he proudly read to his parents. He soon became a leader, participating eagerly in discussions. Webb found him delightful, and his mother said she'd never seen him so enthusiastic about school. At the end of the year, Matt wrote Webb a thank-you note telling her reading was "not a struggle anymore."

How much of that, I ask her, was because of you as a teacher, and how much was because of the curriculum?

"Some of it was me," she admits. "I love reading. But for him, it was also the exciting topics, the challenging books, being pushed to do all this thinking. Instead of just, 'You're a level L.'"

Webb's district decided to require all elementary and middle school teachers to use Wit & Wisdom beginning the following year. Webb predicted the transition wouldn't be easy. Still, a report from the first year of district-wide implementation shows teachers were thrilled to see all students benefiting, especially those who struggled most. One said the curriculum had made her "see how I teach and why I teach in a very different way."

"I could never go back to what we did before," said another.

That kind of change won't happen on a broad scale overnight. But state by state, district by district, school by school, and teacher by teacher, the transformation from a focus on comprehension skills and reading levels to one on content and knowledge is beginning to take hold.

And for the millions of kids across the country like Matt, who are only waiting for someone to actually teach them something in order to unlock their potential, it's about time.

EPILOGUE

'D LOVE TO point to a school district, or even a single school, and say: *This* is how it should be done. Here is a model that proves education can enable all children to achieve their full potential and serve as the engine of social mobility we assume it to be—and that the kind of education that maximizes their chances of success is also the kind they enjoy the most.

Unfortunately, I have yet to see an American school that consistently combines a focus on content with an instructional method that fully exploits the potential of writing to build knowledge and critical thinking abilities for every child. Still, as I hope this book makes clear, extraordinary things are transpiring across the country, and I'm optimistic proof points will emerge. I recently read about a network of twelve districts in Tennessee that is piloting content-rich curricula—some using Core Knowledge Language Arts, others Wit & Wisdom—in kindergarten through second grade. In one of the districts, adults were amazed at the response of a first-grader who was asked to sit down on his behind: "You mean," he queried, "on my gluteus maximus?" Overwhelming majorities of teachers are delighted with the new materials, saying they feel more supported and that their students are clearly benefiting.

From what I can tell, this network, LIFT, is changing instruction in a way that could lead to long-term success. While the effort is being led by superintendents, it hasn't simply been imposed. Instead, the superintendents worked to build the knowledge of classroom teachers and school leaders about why the changes are important. They also began by experimenting with a few schools where educators wanted to try out the approach, which can serve as models for others. To sustain progress, of course, the districts will need to ensure students continue to get content-focused instruction beyond second grade. But they're laying the groundwork.

That sort of patient, collaborative shift is also in progress in one entire state, Louisiana, with several others considering following suit. For those in a hurry to improve outcomes for children—and who is not?—it's tempting to simply mandate changes. But teachers need to be provided with the reasoning behind them and given an opportunity to try them out if they're going to have a chance to take hold.

One huge question is what to do about our system of high-stakes testing. That well-intentioned regime is not only narrowing the curriculum to reading and math and reinforcing the assumption that reading comprehension is just a collection of skills; it's also contributing to the departure of gifted, dedicated teachers—like Ms. Masi and Ms. Townsell—from classrooms that need them. Testing has been seen as the means of ensuring that all children get a high-quality education, but in many ways it's been just the opposite.

We do need some reasonably objective way of determining whether schools are serving all students. But there are alternatives that don't cause the same damaging consequences as the system we have now. For lower grade levels, we need to put a priority on testing pure decoding skills, as is currently being done in the UK. For the sake of clarity about what is actually being tested, I would advocate abolishing any other so-called reading, English language arts, or literacy tests, and substitute tests that openly state they're assessing knowledge of topics in history or social studies, science, and literature. Even a change of name—"general knowledge tests" instead of "reading tests"—could help dispel the erroneous and dangerous impression that the entire realm of learning can be divided into reading and math, and the equally dangerous idea that reading should be taught as a "subject." (One scientist has gone so far as to suggest that we redefine the word *reading* to mean "word recognition," which he argues would free teachers to teach decoding through systematic phonics and build comprehension in the only way possible—through subjects like history, science, and literature.)

Alternatively, states can follow Louisiana's lead and continue to give "reading tests," but ensure they draw on knowledge students have acquired in school—and not just in English class. Even states that don't recommend specific content-rich curricula could go that route. Test designers could announce in advance a list of topics, some of which will be covered. For example, they could let it be known that the fourth-grade reading test might include questions assuming knowledge of Westward Expansion and the human digestive system, among other possibilities. Teachers would then know what content to focus on to equip their students to understand the passages.

That sort of change would dovetail nicely with a shift to a greater role for writing. At higher grade levels, let's add the kind of well-constructed essay questions that many other countries employ. While the two major Common Core tests purport to test writing, they attempt to do so in isolation from content. If content areas were announced in advance, teachers could ensure that students have both the knowledge that would enable them to craft coherent responses and the writing skills that can only develop alongside that knowledge. Written answers could also reliably test the analytical skills that Common Core exams attempt to get at through convoluted multipart questions that even many adults find confusing. At lower grade levels, when students' writing skills are still emerging, some multiple-choice questions are inevitable. But children could also be asked to compose discrete sentences or complete sentence stems based on topics they've studied in school.

Some may object that it's not feasible to grade millions of essays—and not just for their grammatical correctness but also for their level of analysis and coherence. It's true that would be far more labor-intensive than grading multiple-choice tests, and it would require human graders, not computers, who are familiar with the topics being addressed. But if other countries have managed to do it, why can't we? We could also adopt a system of school inspections, as other countries have, assuming the inspectors understand what they need to look for.

There's no one right way to provide a high-quality education, and this country is too big and varied for one-size-fits-all prescriptions. But if we're equipped with a basic scientific understanding about which methods are most effective—and most likely to provide an engaging experience for kids—we should all be able to distinguish between approaches that are likely to produce the outcomes we want and those that will only lead to a heartbreaking waste of precious time.

We'll need to simultaneously pursue many other reform efforts, of course, including improving teacher training, ensuring that students living in poverty get the mental health and support services they need, and engaging families in their children's learning. But if we don't also give students access to knowledge of the world during elementary school, we'll never achieve the result we want: a system that equips all students to lead productive and fulfilling lives and carry out their responsibilities as members of a democratic society.

ACKNOWLEDGMENTS

A mere five years ago, I knew nothing about the subject of this book—even though I thought I knew quite a bit about education. My first inkling came from Judy Hochman, a veteran educator whom I had come to know through her work on writing instruction. I had a hard time understanding what she was trying to convey.

"What do you mean?" I said when she told me that most elementary schools weren't even trying to teach anything of substance. "They're *schools*, aren't they?" She began to explain. Shortly thereafter, Lynne Munson—who heads the organization that developed the Wit & Wisdom curriculum—unwittingly planted a seed when I overheard her remark that someone should write a book about "this whole curriculum thing."

"Maybe *I* should do that," I murmured, half to myself. And Judy—who happened to be sitting next to me—immediately began encouraging me. She hasn't stopped since, and I am deeply grateful for her support, her friendship, and for all that I have learned from her.

I began to realize that for all the time I'd spent in elementary classrooms, I hadn't understood what I was looking at—and neither did many others. I soon sought out a few individuals who did understand, in depth, and who had devoted a great deal of effort to addressing the situation: Lisa Hansel, Silas Kulkarni, David and Meredith Liben (who graciously allowed me to invade their home in rural Vermont for a crash course), Robert Pondiscio, Kate Walsh, and Ruth Wattenberg. They took time from often hectic schedules to patiently answer my many questions and help me grope my way toward clarity.

Once I had begun to grasp the enormity of the problem, I was aided by the remarkable young education journalist Elizabeth Green, who I first met years ago when I was assigned to be her college alumni interviewer. I doubt that any other college interview has resulted in such benefits for the interviewer, as opposed to the interviewee. (Elizabeth did get into Harvard, but I'm sure that had more to do with her own qualifications than my enthusiastic endorsement.) Not only did Elizabeth connect me with Rachel Dry at the *New York Times*—who accepted an op-ed I wrote—she also put me in touch with her agent Alia Hanna Habib, who would become my agent (more about her later).

The most challenging part of researching this book was finding teachers brave enough to allow a stranger to observe their classrooms and then go off and write about the experience, warts and all. I couldn't have begun to locate candidates without the help of several people at the Urban Teachers teacher-prep program, especially Jacqueline Greer and Tricia Peterson. My heartfelt thanks go to the talented, hardworking teachers who generously opened their classroom doors to me, especially Liz Masi at Center City, Aasiya Townsell at Excel, and the teachers I have called Gaby Arredondo and Abby Bauer.

At Center City, Adrienne Williams first showed me what extraordinary content-focused teaching could look like and, after she took a job supporting other teachers, continued to share her wisdom and expertise. Amanda Pecsi spent hours describing her journey from skills-focused teacher to content-focused curriculum developer; I'm only sorry there wasn't room for that fascinating story in the final draft. Others at Center City who helped make this book possible include Robin Chait, Alexis Fields, Samantha Flaherty, Rachel Tomelleo, Lenee Washington, and Russ Williams.

At Excel Academy, elementary principal Tara Warrington embraced the idea of this project with enthusiasm, and chief executive officer

Deborah Lockhart welcomed me even though the school was at a delicate juncture in its history.

Other D.C. teachers shared their experiences and reflections and sometimes opened their classrooms to me. They include Liz Braganza, Athena Burkett, Claire DeMarco, Greg Dwyre, Laura Fuchs, Matt Kennedy, Kayla Larkin, Jeanne Liu, Brittany Perna, Nona Ransom, Kim Stalnaker, Kerry Sylvia, and David Tansey.

I am indebted to Brian Pick, Corinne Colgan, and Scott Abbott in the DCPS central office for explaining the challenges of designing and implementing a content-focused curriculum in a major urban district. I also had illuminating conversations with educators in D.C.'s charter sector, including Katie Severn at D.C. Prep and Liz Striebel and Susan Toth at KIPP DC. Several D.C. parents were generous enough to share their sometimes frustrating experiences, including Joe Weedon and Andrea Tucker.

In Reno, Aaron Grossman, Torrey Palmer, and Cathy Schmidt patiently led me through the story of the Washoe County Core Task Project and set up an itinerary for a visit that deepened my understanding of the changes that occurred there. I benefited enormously from conversations with and observations of many teachers, including Angela Bibby, Kitty Gillette, Cathy Hayes, Allie Hughes, Kim Price, and Linnea Wolters, as well as interviews with administrators Diana Bowles and Kindra Fox.

In Baltimore, I got an illuminating tour of two schools that are part of the Baltimore Curriculum Project, led by Laura Doherty—including a class co-taught by veteran teacher Georgie Smith, whom I have known since the fourth grade. I am grateful to Ben Crandall and Allison Gregory for facilitating my visit to another Baltimore school, Maree G. Farring, where I learned much from observing and speaking with teachers—especially Jean Choma. She pointed me toward former principal Thom Stroschein, who described his remarkable experience with the Core Knowledge curriculum there years before.

Katharine Birbalsingh at the Michaela Community School in London and Katie Megrian at Brooke Charter Schools in Boston shared their perspectives and made it possible for me to visit classrooms. I am also grateful to Whitney Whealdon of the Louisiana Department of

Education, who described the state's effort to create a content-focused literacy curriculum and generally promote a new approach to teaching.

I have relied heavily on the writings of scholars and authors who have gone before me. Chief among them are E. D. Hirsch Jr., Daniel Willingham, and Diane Ravitch, whose work on the history of American education was invaluable. Mark Seidenberg's *Language at the Speed of Sight* helped me understand the process of decoding. And without Peg Tyre's excellent 2012 *Atlantic* article, "The Writing Revolution," I might never have heard of Judy Hochman.

I knew from the beginning that to bring this complex and rather abstract topic to life, I would need to find engaging narratives to tell. And to do that, I needed to convince certain key figures to share their stories. I couldn't have written this book without the generous cooperation of Lucy Calkins, David Coleman, E. D. Hirsch Jr., Judy Hochman, John B. King Jr., Joel Klein, Doug Lemov, David Steiner, and Daniel Willingham. I am also indebted to Linda Bevilacqua, Kelly Butler, Colleen Driggs, Deb Glaser, Rachel Leifer, Larry Singer, Stephanie Tatel, Ken Wagner, and Sarah Webb.

Others who gave generously of their time and expertise include Lisa Bernstein, Katherine Bradley, Steve Bumbaugh, Kate Gerson, David Grissmer, David Harrington, Joan Kelley, Maura Marino, Arthur McKee, Amy O'Leary, Benjamin Riley, Jon Rybka, Jason Sachs, Liz Whisnant, Sarah Woodard, and Judy Wurtzel.

I cannot adequately express my gratitude to my agent, Alia Hanna Habib, and editor, Megan Newman. They immediately recognized the importance of this story and trusted that I would be able to tell it. Along with Nina Shield, they then deployed their formidable wisdom to steer me away from potential pitfalls and toward a narrative that would convey my message as clearly and effectively as possible; any errors or shortcomings are my responsibility, not theirs. Thanks as well to Hannah Steigmeyer for her help in keeping the publishing process on track.

I'm also grateful to the friends, relatives, and mentors who read early drafts and gave me thoughtful comments: Ann Cumming, Barbara Davidson, Sam Feldman, Sue LeBeaux, David and Meredith Liben, Susan

Matchett, Dale Russakoff, and Ruth Wattenberg. Each brought a distinct perspective that was hugely helpful. Nancy Heneson not only critiqued parts of the manuscript but also offered a sympathetic ear and asked perceptive questions over the years I was working on the book; she has been the person I turn to for writing advice (and many other things) since we met at the age of fifteen. Numerous other friends and acquaintances spurred me on in less formal ways—often simply by saying they couldn't wait to read the finished product.

In addition to providing me with unflagging support, my children Sam and Sophie have enriched my perspective on this subject—as they have immeasurably enriched my life in general. My memories of their successful journeys to literacy many years ago provided me with firsthand insight into what the process involves.

My husband, Jim Feldman, enthusiastically shouldered the task of being the first reader of every chapter, offering encouragement when I needed it and astute criticism even when I thought I didn't (although I often eventually realized that I did). He has witnessed countless iterations of my "elevator speech," never succumbing to the temptation to zone out (well, *hardly* ever) and frequently giving me pointers on how to improve it. He has comforted me when things haven't gone well—as happens inevitably with any writing project—and rejoiced with me when they have. For his wisdom, his love, his support, and his sense of humor I am eternally grateful. Quite simply, I don't know where I would be without him.

NOTES

Chapter 1: The Water They've Been Swimming In

6 **early-elementary teachers were spending more than twice as much time on reading as on science and social studies combined:** Iris R. Weiss, "Report of the 1985–86 National Survey of Science and Mathematics Education," Center for Educational Studies, Research Triangle Institute, Durham, NC (November 1987), Table 2.

7 **widely recognized as impossible to meet:** Amit R. Paley, "'No Child' Target Is Called Out of Reach," *Washington Post*, March 14, 2007, http://www.washingtonpost.com/wp-dyn/content/article/2007/03/13/AR2007031301781.html.

7 **particularly social studies:** Paul G. Fitchett, Tina L. Heafner, and Phillip VanFossen, "An Analysis of Time Prioritization for Social Studies in Elementary School Classrooms," *Journal of Curriculum and Instruction* 8, no. 2 (December 2014): 7–35, doi:10.3776/joci.2014.v8n2p7-35; Diane S. Rentner et al., "From the Capital to the Classroom: Year 4 of the No Child Left Behind Act," Center on Education Policy, March 2006, xi, http://www.cep-dc.org/displayDocument.cfm?DocumentID=301.

7 **correspondingly decreased:** Jennifer McMurrer, *Choices, Changes, and Challenges: Curriculum and Instruction in the NCLB Era* (Washington, DC: Center on Education Policy, 2007), 1–2. In a 2007 survey of 349 school districts, 62 percent reported increasing time for English language arts and/or math in elementary schools since NCLB's enactment five years before. The average increase in minutes per week was 47 percent for English language arts and 37 percent for math. As a result, 44 percent of districts cut time from one or more other subjects, including social studies, science, and art or music, with the average decrease across all subjects amounting to 145 minutes per week.

7 **an average of only sixteen minutes a day on social studies and nineteen on science:** Ruth Wattenberg, "Complex Texts Require Complex Knowledge: Will the New English Standards Get the Content Curriculum They Need?" in *Knowledge at the Core: Don Hirsch, Core Knowledge, and the Future of the Common Core*, ed. Chester E. Finn Jr. and Michael J. Petrilli (Washington, D.C.: Thomas B. Fordham Institute, 2014), 31–47, http://edex.s3-us-west-2.amazonaws.com/publication/pdfs/EDHirsch-Report-Papers-Final.pdf.

7 **they're often pulled from social studies and science to get extra help:** Farkas Duffett Research Group, "Learning Less: Public School Teachers Describe a Narrowing Curriculum" (Washington, D.C.: Common Core, 2012), 1, http://greatminds.net/maps/documents/reports/cc-learning-less-mar12.pdf.

7 **Up to a quarter of the school year:** Anya Kamenetz, *The Test: Why Schools Are Obsessed with Standardized Testing—But You Don't Have to Be* (New York: Public Affairs, 2015), 15–16.

8 **many parents joined an "opt-out" movement:** "The Opt-Out Movement," in Bellwether Education Partners, *The Learning Landscape: A Broad View of the U.S. Public School System*, last updated June 21, 2016, http://www.thelearning landscape.org/the-opt-out-movement. In New York State, for example, 20 percent of eligible students in grades three through eight didn't take the tests during the 2014–15 school year.

8 **acknowledged that the situation had gotten out of hand:** Arne Duncan, "Improving American Education Is Not Optional," *Washington Post*, January 16, 2015, https://www.washingtonpost.com/opinions/arne-duncan-a-quality-education-is -not-optional/2015/01/16/ac8ad214-9ce6-11e4-bcfb-059ec7a93ddc_story.html.

8 **four times less likely to graduate from high school:** Donald J. Hernandez, "Double Jeopardy: How Third-Grade Reading Skills and Poverty Influence High School Graduation" (Baltimore: The Annie E. Casey Foundation, 2012), 4, http:// gradelevelreading.net/wp-content/uploads/2012/01/Double-Jeopardy-Report -030812-for-web1.pdf.

8 **an overwhelming majority of teachers deplore:** "Learning Less," 1–2.

9 **have shown little improvement:** Mark Seidenberg, *Language at the Speed of Sight: How We Read, Why So Many Can't, and What Can Be Done About It* (New York: Basic Books, 2017), 219–22. These results are from the National Assessment of Educational Progress, a series of tests that are generally considered impossible to game or manipulate.

9 **Writing scores are even worse:** National Center for Education Statistics, "The Nation's Report Card: Writing 2011: National Assessment of Educational Progress at Grades 8 and 12," 1, https://nces.ed.gov/nationsreportcard/pdf/main2011 /2012470.pdf.

9 **literacy levels are falling:** Sarah D. Sparks, "Global Reading Scores Are Rising, But Not for U.S. Students," *Education Week*, December 5, 2017, https://www.edweek .org/ew/articles/2017/12/05/global-reading-scores-are-rising-but-not.html; Marilyn Jager Adams, "Advancing Our Students' Language and Literacy: The Challenge of Complex Texts," *American Educator* 34, no. 4 (Winter 2010–2011): 3–4.

9 **"There is a lot to be concerned about":** Sparks, "Global Reading Scores Are Rising." The official quoted is Peggy Carr, the acting commissioner of the National Center for Education Statistics, which oversees the US administration of a reading test given to fourth-graders in fifty-eight countries.

9 **only 18 percent scored proficient or above in US history:** National Center for Education Statistics, "The Nation's Report Card: 2014 U.S. History, Geography, and Civics at Grade 8," April 29, 2015, https://nces.ed.gov/pubsearch/pubsinfo .asp?pubid=2015112; Fitchett et al., "An Analysis of Time Prioritization," 8.

9 **were unable to answer questions:** Linton Weeks, "Who Won the Civil War? Tough Question," *NPR*, November 18, 2014, http://www.npr.org/sections/the protojournal ist/2014/11/18/364675234/who-won-the-civil-war-tough-question. In a more scientific study conducted in 1999, 81 percent of seniors from fifty-five top colleges and universities flunked a test composed of questions drawn from "a basic high school curriculum." "Losing America's Memory Executive Summary," American Council of Trustees and Alumni, February 2000, accessed July 28, 2018, https://www.goacta .org/executivesummary/losing_americas_memory_executive_summary.

9 **One survey of American adults:** "Americans Are Poorly Informed About Basic Constitutional Provisions," Annenberg Public Policy Center of the University of Pennsylvania, September 12, 2017, https://www.annenbergpublicpolicycenter .org/americans-are-poorly-informed-about-basic-constitutional-provisions.

9 **Another found that more than half of Americans:** George H. Gallup Jr., "How Many Americans Know U.S. History? Part 1," *Gallup News*, October 21, 2003, http:// news.gallup.com/poll/9526/how-many-americans-know-us-history-part.aspx.

10 **some commentators:** For example, Richard D. Kahlenberg and Clifford Janey, "Is Trump's Victory the Jump-Start Civics Education Needed?," *The Atlantic*, November 10, 2016, https://www.theatlantic.com/education/archive/2016/11/is -trumps-victory-the-jump-start-civics-education-needed/507293.

10 **were "shocked" by the poor results:** Camila Domonoske, "Students Have 'Dis-maying' Inability To Tell Fake News From Real, Study Finds," *NPR*, November 23, 2016, https://www.npr.org/sections/thetwo-way/2016/11/23/503129818/study-finds-students-have-dismaying-inability-to-tell-fake-news-from-real.

10 **beef up civics education:** Jennifer Kavanagh and Michael D. Rich, *Truth Decay: An Initial Exploration of the Diminishing Role of Facts and Analysis in American Public Life* (Santa Monica, CA: RAND Corporation, 2018); Robert Pondiscio and Andrew Tripodo, "Seizing the Moment to Improve Civics Education," *Flypaper* (blog), Thomas B. Fordham Institute, November 29, 2017, https://edexcellence.net/articles /seizing-the-moment-to-improve-civics-education; Alina Tugend, "In the Age of Trump, Civics Courses Make a Comeback," *New York Times*, June 5, 2018, https:// www.nytimes.com/2018/06/05/education/learning/schools-civics-trump.html.

10 **struggle to absorb and retain historical concepts:** Fitchett et al., "An Analysis of Time Prioritization," 8.

12 **Very few states even track:** Cory Koedel and Morgan Polikoff, "Big Bang for Just a Few Bucks: The Impact of Math Textbooks in California," *Evidence Speaks Reports* 2 no. 5 (January 2017), https://www.brookings.edu/research/big-bang-for -just-a-few-bucks-the-impact-of-math-textbooks-in-california.

12 **50 percent or more:** According to one source, 74 percent of schools and teachers use a basal reading program, at least to some extent. Peter Dewitz and Jennifer Jones, "Using Basal Readers: From Dutiful Fidelity to Intelligent Decision Making," *The Reading Teacher* 66, no. 5 (February 2013): 391–400. Some literacy experts I've spoken to, however, put the percentage much lower. Even if a school district or state has adopted or recommended a basal program, individual schools or teachers often feel free not to use it. And the distinction between teachers who use basal readers and those who don't is far from clear-cut. Teachers who rely on commercially available books are still usually guided by some published curriculum materials, and teachers who use a basal reader generally supplement it with commercially available books.

13 **generally canceled out:** Timothy Shanahan, "To Group or Not to Group—That Is the Question," *Shanahan on Literacy* (blog), *Reading Rockets*, June 3, 2015, http://www.readingrockets.org/blogs/shanahan-on-literacy/group-or-not-group-question.

14 **Reeves has some of the highest test scores:** In 2017, overall reading test scores at Reeves were about 70 percent proficient or above in reading and math, with

22 percent testing in the "advanced" category. Among the school's economically disadvantaged students, though, proficiency rates were 51 percent in reading and 45 percent in math. The proficiency rates for D.C. as a whole were about 32 percent in reading and 27 percent in math. At Star Academy, the proficiency rates were 19 percent in reading and 25 percent in math.

16 **subsumed into the literacy block:** Elizabeth R. Hinde, "The Theoretical Foundations of Curriculum Integration and Its Application in Social Studies Instruction," in *Becoming Integrated Thinkers: Case Studies in Elementary Social Studies*, ed. Linda Bennett and Elizabeth R. Hinde, National Council for the Social Studies, 2015, 25–26, https://www.socialstudies.org/sites/default/files/images/becoming _integrated_excerpts.pdf.

16 **broad themes:** Ohio Department of Education, *Ohio's New Learning Standards: Social Studies Standards*, adopted June 2010, 9 (theme for first grade), https:// education.ohio.gov/getattachment/Topics/Ohio-s-New-Learning-Standards /Social-Studies/SS-Standards.pdf.aspx.

16 **out of order and context:** Carol McDonald Connor et al., "Acquiring Science and Social Studies Knowledge in Kindergarten Through Fourth Grade: Conceptualization, Design, Implementation, and Efficacy Testing of Content-Area Literacy Instruction (CALI)," *Journal of Educational Psychology* 109, no. 3 (April 2017): 301–320, http://dx.doi.org/10.1037/edu0000128.

17 **One national survey found:** "Economic Issues Decline Among Public's Policy Priorities," Pew Research Center, January 25, 2018, http://www.people-press.org /2018/01/25/economic-issues-decline-among-publics-policy-priorities.

17 **Still, most public school parents:** "Grading the Public Schools," *Phi Delta Kappan*, September 2017, K26–K27, http://pdkpoll.org/assets/downloads/PDKnational _poll_2017.pdf.

17 **many parents are concerned:** pagrundy [Pamela Grundy], "Why More Standardized Tests Won't Improve Education," *Parents Across America* (blog), September 2, 2011, http://parentsacrossamerica.org/why-more-standardized-tests -wont-improve-education.

19 **far less likely to have positive feelings:** Logan Casey and Elizabeth Mann Levesque, "New Survey of Minorities Adds Dissenting View to Public Satisfaction with Schools," *Brown Center Chalkboard* (blog), January 11, 2018, https:// www.brookings.edu/blog/brown-center-chalkboard/2018/01/11/new-survey-of -minorities-adds-dissenting-view-to-public-satisfaction-with-schools.

19 **were "in an uproar":** Natalie Wexler, "The Inappropriate Focus on Math and Reading Hurts Students," *All Opinions Are Local* (blog), *Washington Post*, February 26, 2018, https://www.washingtonpost.com/blogs/all-opinions -are-local/wp/2018/02/26/the-inappropiate-focus-on-math-and-reading-hurts -students.

19 **prioritize reading and math:** "Learning Less," 6–7.

20 **terms that are generic and vague:** "Report on Classroom Observations: Curriculum 2.0, Montgomery Country Public Schools, Maryland," Student Achievement, Partners 2018, 10, https://www.montgomeryschoolsmd.org/uploadedFiles/cur riculum/integrated/MCPS_Learned%20and%20Taught%20Curriculum%20 Review_Classroom%20Observations%20and%20Student%20Work.pdf.

20 **take a narrower, more skills-focused approach:** Tim Walker, "The Testing Obsession and the Disappearing Curriculum," *NEA Today*, September 2, 2014, http://neatoday.org/2014/09/02/the-testing-obsession-and-the-disappearing-curriculum-2; Kamenetz, *The Test*, 7.

20 **a 2007 study:** Paul Tough, *Helping Children Succeed: What Works and Why* (Boston and New York: Houghton Mifflin Harcourt, 2016): 100–101.

20 **On nationwide reading tests:** The figures cited are from a Department of Education website that summarizes the results of the National Assessment of Educational Progress, also known as the Nation's Report Card. The specific percentages can be accessed at https://www.nationsreportcard.gov/reading_math_2015/#reading/acl?grade=4; https://www.nationsreportcard.gov/reading_math_2015/#reading/acl?grade=8; https://nces.ed.gov/nationsreportcard/pdf/main2011/2012470.pdf; and https://www.nationsreportcard.gov/hgc_2014/#history/achievement.

21 **hasn't changed:** Eric A. Hanushek, Paul E. Peterson, Laura M. Talpey, and Ludger Woessman, "The Achievement Gap Fails to Close," *Education Next* 19, no. 3 (Summer 2019).

21 **how low our lowest scores are:** Sparks, "Global Reading Scores Are Rising."

21 **"You have to start with":** Kerry Sylvia, former teacher at Cardozo Education Campus, Washington, D.C., conversation with author, July 12, 2016.

21 **was surprised by the term** *South America*: David Tansey, former teacher at Dunbar High School, Washington, D.C., conversation with author, April 30, 2016.

21 **she's even had a few students:** Kim Stalnaker, teacher at Eastern Senior High School, Washington, D.C., conversation with author, June 16, 2016.

22 **national graduation rate reached an all-time high:** Moriah Balingit, "U.S. High School Graduation Rates Rise to New High," *Washington Post*, December 4, 2017, https://www.washingtonpost.com/news/education/wp/2017/12/04/u-s-high-school-graduation-rates-rise-to-new-high/?utm_term=.e24ef2c39174.

22 **have turned to subterfuges:** Mark Dynarski, "Is the High School Graduation Rate Really Going Up?," *Brookings* (blog), May 3, 2018, https://www.brookings.edu/research/is-the-high-school-graduation-rate-really-going-up.

22 **hadn't met requirements:** Kate McGee, "In D.C., 34 Percent of Graduates Received a Diploma Against District Policy," *NPR*, January 29, 2018, https://www.npr.org/sections/ed/2018/01/29/581036306/in-d-c-thirty-four-percent-of-graduates-received-a-diploma-against-district-poli.

22 **Studies suggest:** Raj Chetty, John N. Friedman, and Jonah Rockoff, "Great Teaching," *Education Next* 12, no. 3 (Summer 2012), https://www.educationnext.org/great-teaching; Eric A. Hanushek et al., "Education and Economic Growth," *Education Next* 8, no. 2 (Spring 2008), http://educationnext.org/education-and-economic-growth.

22 **is on the rise:** Karen Grigsby Bates, "Report Updates Landmark 1968 Racism Study, Finds More Poverty and Segregation," *NPR*, February 27, 2018, https://www.npr.org/2018/02/27/589351779/report-updates-landmark-1968-racism-study-finds-more-poverty-more-segregation; Drew DeSilver, "U.S. Income Inequality, on Rise for Decades, Is Now Highest since 1928," *Fact Tank* (blog), Pew

Research Center, December 5, 2013, http://www.pewresearch.org/fact-tank/2013
/12/05/u-s-income-inequality-on-rise-for-decades-is-now-highest-since-1928;
Richard V. Reeves, *Dream Hoarders: How the American Upper Middle Class Is
Leaving Everyone Else in the Dust, Why That Is a Problem, and What to Do About
It* (Washington, D.C.: Brookings Institution Press, 2017).

22 **never manage to get that coveted degree:** David L. Kirp, "Ending the Curse of
Remedial Math," *New York Times*, June 10, 2017, https://www.nytimes.com
/2017/06/10/opinion/sunday/cuny-ending-the-curse-of-remedial-math.html.
More than two-thirds of community college students need to take remedial
math or English classes, which cost them money but don't earn them any credit.
Only 15 percent of these students get their degrees on time.

Chapter 2: A Problem Hiding in Plain Sight

26 **test scores began to rise:** Between 2016 and 2017, scores on the end-of-year state
reading tests for the Center City network as a whole grew by more than 5 percent,
whereas comparable scores for all D.C. students (about 25 percent of whom are
middle-class or affluent) rose only about 3 percent. At the Brightwood campus
specifically, scores grew by more than 9 percent. In 2017, the proficiency rate
there was 35 percent for math and 34 percent for reading. For D.C. as a whole, the
percentages were 27 percent and 31 percent, respectively.

28 **more capable of abstract thinking:** Daniel T. Willingham, "Unlocking the Science of How Kids Think," *Education Next* 18, no. 3 (Summer 2018), http://educa
tionnext.org/unlocking-science-how-kids-think-new-proposal-for-reforming
-teacher-education.

28 **"any subject can be taught effectively":** Jerome Bruner, *The Process of Education*
(Cambridge, MA: Harvard University Press, 1960), 33.

29 **constructed a miniature baseball field:** Laurence Holt, "The Baseball Experiment: How Two Wisconsin Researchers Discovered That the Comprehension
Gap Is a Knowledge Gap," *Amplify Blog*, accessed July 28, 2018, http://blog
.amplify.com/baseball-experiment.

29 **prior knowledge of baseball made a huge difference:** Donna R. Recht and Lauren Leslie, "Effect of Prior Knowledge on Good and Poor Readers' Memory of
Text," *Journal of Educational Psychology* 80, no. 1 (March 1988): 16–20.

30 **comprehension was essentially the same:** Tanya Kaefer, Susan B. Neuman, and
Ashley M. Pinkham, "Pre-existing Background Knowledge Influences Socioeconomic Differences in Preschoolers' Word Learning and Comprehension," *Reading Psychology* 36, no. 3 (2015): 203–231, https://doi.org/10.1080/02702711.2013
.843064.

30 **so they will stick:** Gina N. Cervetti, Tanya S. Wright, and HyeJin Hwang, "Conceptual Coherence, Comprehension, and Vocabulary Acquisition: A Knowledge
Effect?" *Reading and Writing* 29, no. 4 (April 2016): 761–779, https://doi.org
/10.1007/s11145-016-9628-x.

31 **"a knowledge party":** Michael Fordham, "The Knowledge Party in My Head,"
Clio et cetera (blog), November 21, 2016, https://clioetcetera.com/2016/11/21
/the-knowledge-party-in-my-head.

31 **little evidence to support that theory:** Timothy Shanahan, "Should We Teach Students at Their Reading Levels?," *Reading Today*, September/October 2014, 14–15, http://shanahanonliteracy.com/upload/publications/98/pdf/Shanahan—-Should-we-teach-at-reading-level.pdf; Douglas Fisher and Nancy Frey, "Scaffolded Reading Instruction of Content-Area Texts," *The Reading Teacher* 67, no. 5 (February 2014): 347–351. Shanahan, a leading academic researcher on reading, tracked down a supposed 1940s research study that has been relied on for years to justify leveled reading; he found that no such study had ever been done. Timothy Shanahan, "The Informal Reading Inventory and the Instructional Level: The Study That Never Took Place," in *Reading Research Revisited*, ed. Lance M. Gentile, Michael L. Kamil, and Jay S. Blanchard (Columbus, OH: Merrill, 1983), 577–580.

31 **difficulties begin to emerge in fourth grade:** Jeanne S. Chall and Vicki A. Jacobs, "The Classic Study on Poor Children's Fourth-Grade Slump," *American Educator* 27, no. 1 (Spring 2003): 14–15, https://www.aft.org/periodical/american-educator/spring-2003/classic-study-poor-childrens-fourth-grade-slump.

31 **they continue to be assigned texts at their individual levels:** V. Darleen Opfer, Julia H. Kaufman, and Lindsey E. Thompson, *Implementation of K–12 State Standards for Mathematics and English Language Arts and Literacy: Findings from the American Teacher Panel* (Santa Monica, CA: RAND Corporation, 2016), 34, 60. This can also be read online at https://www.rand.org/pubs/research_reports/RR1529-1.html. Teachers of English language arts at the secondary level estimated that students spend 34 percent of their time in class reading texts at their individual reading levels. Outside of class, the estimate was 47 percent.

32 **one reading expert has observed:** Alfred Tatum, quoted in Fisher and Frey, "Scaffolded Reading Instruction."

32 **unlikely to stick without reinforcement:** Daniel T. Willingham, *The Reading Mind: A Cognitive Approach to Understanding How the Mind Reads* (San Francisco: Jossey-Bass, 2017), 89.

32 **words that are used frequently in academic writing:** Isabel Beck, Margaret McKeown, and Linda Kucan, "Choosing Words to Teach," in *Bringing Words to Life: Robust Vocabulary Instruction* (New York: Guilford Press, 2002), 15–30, http://www.readingrockets.org/article/choosing-words-teach.

32 **children add eight words a day:** Seidenberg, *Language at the Speed of Sight*, 111–113; Cervetti, Wright, and Hwang, "Conceptual Coherence."

32 **an average score in the fifth percentile:** Louisa C. Moats, "Overcoming the Language Gap," *American Educator* 25, no. 2 (Summer 2001): 8–9, https://www.aft.org/periodical/american-educator/summer-2001/overcoming-language-gap-0.

33 **"we're not teaching them to be thinkers or readers":** Linnea Wolters, quoted in Emily Hanford, "Common Core Reading: 'The New Colossus,'" *NPR*, November 11, 2014, http://www.npr.org/sections/ed/2014/11/11/356357971/common-core-reading-the-new-colossus.

33 **are far more likely to suffer the consequences:** Nadine Burke Harris, *The Deepest Well: Healing the Long-Term Effects of Childhood Adversity* (New York:

Houghton Mifflin Harcourt, 2018); Mimi Kirk, "What Kids' Trauma Looks Like Across the U.S.," *The Atlantic*, February 27, 2018, https://www.theatlantic.com /education/archive/2018/02/the-complicated-map-of-trauma-in-the-us/554336/.

33 **better able to invest in their children:** Elizabeth Caucutt, "Why Do Poor Children Perform More Poorly Than Rich Ones?," *The Conversation*, April 23, 2015, http://theconversation.com/why-do-poor-children-perform-more-poorly-than -rich-ones-39281.

34 **were spending *nine* times as much:** Tavernise, "Education Gap Grows Between Rich and Poor."

34 **according to sociologist Annette Lareau:** Annette Lareau, *Unequal Childhoods: Class, Race, and Family Life* (Berkeley: University of California Press, 2003).

34 **Children whose parents read to them:** Maryanne Wolf, *Proust and the Squid: The Story and Science of the Reading Brain* (New York: HarperCollins, 2007), 85–90.

34 **children hear thirty million more words:** Betty Hart and Todd R Risley, *Meaningful Differences in the Everyday Experience of Young American Children* (Baltimore: Brookes Publishing, 1995).

34 **the number of "conversational turns":** Anne Trafton, "Back-and-Forth Exchanges Boost Children's Brain Response to Language," *MIT News*, February 13, 2018, http://news.mit.edu/2018/conversation-boost-childrens-brain-response -language-0214.

34 **the ubiquity of cell phones:** Erika Christakis, "The Dangers of Distracted Parenting," *The Atlantic*, July/August 2018, https://www.theatlantic.com/magazine /archive/2018/07/the-dangers-of-distracted-parenting/561752.

34 **"a double dose of disadvantage":** Susan B. Neuman, Tanya Kaefer, and Ashley M. Pinkham, "A Double Dose of Disadvantage: Language Experiences for Low-Income Children in Home and School," *Journal of Educational Psychology* 110, no. 1 (January 2018): 102–118. http://dx.doi.org/10.1037/edu0000201

35 **almost a year behind those of their peers:** Sara Bernstein, et al., "Kindergartners' Skills at School Entry: An Analysis of the ECLS-K," Mathematica Policy Research, July 15, 2014, 3, http://www.sesameworkshop.org/wp_install/wp -content/uploads/2014/07/Kindergarten-Skills-Report-2014.pdf.

35 **the gap only widens:** Chall and Jacobs, "The Classic Study on Poor Children's Fourth-Grade Slump." On nationwide reading tests, the gaps don't appear to increase much if you look only at standard deviations, which is the way the results are reported. But it takes far more work to make up one standard deviation at upper grade levels than at lower grade levels. In the early grades, a student might need to make up only one grade level to move up a standard deviation. By eighth grade, it would take three grade levels to move up one standard deviation—and far more at the high school level. David Grissmer, research professor, Curry School of Education, University of Virginia, conversation with author, April 27, 2016.

35 **"the Matthew effect":** Keith Stanovich, "Matthew Effects in Reading: Some Consequences of Individual Differences in the Acquisition of Literacy," *Reading Research Quarterly* 21, no. 4 (Fall 1986): 360-407.

35 **children need to *listen* to their teachers read:** Adams, "Advancing Our Students' Language and Literacy," 5; Susan L. Hall and Louisa C. Moats, "Why Reading to Children Is Important," *American Educator* 24, no. 1 (Spring 2000):

26–33. While class discussion is also important, teachers need to read aloud to children because virtually all written language uses more complex vocabulary and syntax than spoken language, with the only exception being expert witness testimony.

35 **can take in far more sophisticated content:** Douglas Fisher and Nancy Frey, "Speaking and Listening in Content Area Learning," *The Reading Teacher* 68, no. 1 (September 2014): 64–69, https://doi.org/10.1002/trtr.1296, accessed July 29, 2018, at http://www.readingrockets.org/article/speaking-and-listening-content -area-learning.

35 **middle school as well:** McMurrer, *Choice, Changes, and Challenges*, 1. In a 2007 survey of 349 school districts, more than 20 percent reported increasing time for English language arts and math at the expense of other subjects since the enactment of No Child Left Behind.

37 **according to the report:** James S. Coleman, et al., *Equality of Educational Opportunity* (Washington, D.C.: U.S. Government Printing Office, 1966), 325, quoted in David E. Bartz, "Revisiting James Coleman's Epic Study Entitled *Equality of Educational Opportunity*," *National Forum of Educational Administration and Supervision Journal* 34, no. 4 (2016): 1–2.

37 **more difficult to get their students through high school and college:** Greg Toppo, "Charter Schools' 'Thorny' Problem: Few Students Go on to Earn College Degrees," *USA Today*, March 14, 2017, https://www.usatoday.com/story /news/2017/03/14/charter-schools-college-degrees/99125468. Roughly 23 percent of charter school alumni earn college degrees. While that compares favorably to the overall college completion rate for low-income students, which is 9 percent, it's far below the rate for the most advantaged American students, which is 77 percent.

38 **its fastest-growing segment:** "English Language Learners: A Policy Research Brief," National Council of Teachers of English, 2008, 2, http://www.ncte.org /library/NCTEFiles/Resources/PolicyResearch/ELLResearchBrief.pdf.

38 **consider the example of France:** This discussion of the French education system and its inadvertent experiment in curriculum relies on E. D. Hirsch Jr., *Why Knowledge Matters: Rescuing Our Children from Failed Educational Theories* (Cambridge, MA: Harvard Education Press, 2016), 131–158.

39 **greatest among the neediest students:** "French Falling Behind in Maths Says Pisa Global Education Survey," *RFI*, March 12, 2013, http://en.rfi.fr/general/20131203 -french-falling-behind-maths-pisa-global-education-survey.

39 **American law prohibits that:** The U.S. Constitution doesn't authorize the federal government to regulate education, and various federal provisions have barred it from interfering in curriculum decisions. See, for example, Exec. Order No. 13,791, 82 Fed. Reg. 20427 (April 26, 2017), https://www.federalregister .gov/documents/2017/05/01/2017-08905/enforcing-statutory-prohibitions-on -federal-control-of-education; Prohibition against Federal Mandates, Direction, or Control, 20 U.S. Code § 7906a (2015), https://www.law.cornell.edu/uscode /text/20/7906a.

39 **and some others:** Notably the United Kingdom, Australia, and New Zealand— although the pendulum has begun to swing in favor of knowledge-focused instruction in those countries, especially the UK.

39 **can't be taught directly:** Paul A. Kirschner, John Sweller, and Richard E. Clark, "Why Minimal Guidance During Instruction Does Not Work: An Analysis of the Failure of Constructivist, Discovery, Problem-Based, Experiential, and Inquiry-Based Teaching," *Educational Psychologist* 41, no. 2 (2006): 75–86, http://www.cogtech.usc.edu/publications/kirschner_Sweller_Clark.pdf.

39 **evaluate the reliability of websites:** Sarah McGrew, et al., "The Challenge That's Bigger Than Fake News: Civic Reasoning in a Social Media Environment," *American Educator* 41, no. 3 (Fall 2017): 4–9, https://www.aft.org/ae/fall2017/mcgrew_ortega_breakstone_wineburg.

41 **less likely to be ready for school:** Julia B. Isaacs, "Starting School at a Disadvantage: The School Readiness of Poor Children," Center on Children and Families at Brookings, March 2012, 8, https://www.brookings.edu/wp-content/uploads/2016/06/0319_school_disadvantage_isaacs.pdf.

41 **considered "at risk":** The proportion of economically disadvantaged students—a broader category than "at risk"—was about 90 percent at Center City's Brightwood campus and 100 percent at Star Academy.

Chapter 3: Everything Was Surprising and Novel

46 **there's a huge gulf:** Willingham, "Unlocking the Science of How Kids Think."

47 **as many as 95 percent:** *Teaching Reading Is Rocket Science: What Expert Teachers of Reading Should Know and Be Able to Do* (Washington, D.C.: American Federation of Teachers, 1999), 8, http://www.aft.org/sites/default/files/reading_rocketscience_2004.pdf.

47 **diagnosed as dyslexic:** Emily Hanford, "Hard to Read: How American Schools Fail Kids with Dyslexia," *APM Reports*, September 11, 2017, https://www.apmreports.org/story/2017/09/11/hard-to-read; Seidenberg, *Language at the Speed of Sight*, 153–173; Emily Finn, "Dyslexia Independent of IQ," *MIT News*, September 23, 2011, http://news.mit.edu/2011/dyslexia-iq-0923. Children from low-income families who struggle with reading are less likely to be diagnosed as dyslexic than their more affluent counterparts, as are children with lower IQ generally. But data suggests that systematic instruction in phonics and other foundational skills can have the same beneficial effect for virtually all struggling readers, regardless of IQ.

47 **a limited amount of instruction in comprehension strategies:** Daniel T. Willingham, "The Usefulness of *Brief* Instruction in Reading Comprehension Strategies," *American Educator* 30, no. 4 (Winter 2006–07), 44, https://www.aft.org/sites/default/files/periodicals/CogSci.pdf; Willingham, "Infer This . . . ," *Science & Education* (blog), March 5, 2018, http://www.danielwillingham.com/daniel-willingham-science-and-education-blog/infer-this. Studies show students derive no more benefit from fifty sessions of strategy instruction than from ten.

47 **have come to exactly the opposite conclusions:** For this observation, I am indebted to Seidenberg, *Language at the Speed of Sight*, 271–274.

47 **many others have been taught:** Emily Hanford, "Hard Words: Why Aren't Our Kids Being Taught to Read?" *APM Reports*, September 10, 2018, https://www.apmreports.org/story/2018/09/10/hard-words-why-american-kids-arent-being

-taught-to-read. A 2015 survey found that many professors of reading instruction struggle with basic concepts of phonics themselves. Daniel T. Willingham, "Teachers Aren't Dumb," *New York Times*, September 8, 2015, https://www.nytimes.com/2015/09/08/opinion/teachers-arent-dumb.html.

48 **have added courses:** "A Closer Look at Early Reading: Undergraduate Elementary Programs," National Council on Teacher Quality, 2016, 2, http://www.nctq.org/dmsView/UE_2016_Reading_Findings. Sixty-four percent of undergraduate elementary teacher–training programs included coursework in phonics in 2016, compared to only 16 percent in 2006.

49 **rising from 15 percent in 2006 to 75 percent ten years later:** "A Closer Look," 2.

49 **have basically ignored it:** Dana Goldstein, "Why Kids Can't Write," *New York Times*, August 2, 2017, https://www.nytimes.com/2017/08/02/education/edlife/writing-education-grammar-students-children.html.

49 **practicalities like classroom management:** Willingham, "Unlocking the Science of How Kids Think"; "Landscapes in Teacher Prep: Undergraduate Elementary Ed," National Council on Teacher Quality, December 2016, 8, https://www.nctq.org/dmsView/UE_2016_Landscape_653385_656245.

49 **complain bitterly about a lack of rigor:** Peter Sipe, "At Ed Schools, a Low Degree of Difficulty," *Boston Herald*, June 20, 2014, http://www.bostonherald.com/news_opinion/opinion/op_ed/2014/06/at_ed_schools_a_low_degree_of_difficulty.

49 **a wealth of evidence:** Jean Stockard, et al., "The Effectiveness of Direct Instruction Curricula: A Meta-Analysis of a Half Century of Research," *Review of Educational Research* 88, no. 4 (January 2018), http://journals.sagepub.com/doi/pdf/10.3102/0034654317751919; Kirschner, Sweller, and Clark, "Why Minimal Guidance During Instruction Does Not Work."

50 **"the more prestige it carries with it":** David F. Labaree, *The Trouble with Ed Schools* (New Haven, CT: Yale University Press, 2006), 33.

50 **Willingham has come to see the problem:** Daniel T. Willingham, "Three Problems in the Marriage of Neuroscience and Education," *Cortex* 45 (2009): 544–545, retrieved on July 30, 2018, from http://amyalexander.wiki.westga.edu/file/view/3+problems-p.pdf.

50 **Another cognitive scientist:** Mark S. Seidenberg, "The Science of Reading and Its Educational Implications," *Language Learning and Development* 9, no. 4 (2013), 331–360, http://dx.doi.org/10.1080/15475441.2013.812017.

50 **argues that part of the problem:** Keith E. Stanovich, "Putting Children First by Putting Science First: The Politics of Early Reading Instruction," in *Progress in Understanding Reading: Scientific Foundations and New Frontiers* (New York: Guilford Press, 2000), 361–391.

51 **"Teaching Content Is Teaching Reading":** "Teaching Content Is Teaching Reading," YouTube video, 9:58, posted by "Daniel Willingham," January 9, 2009, accessed July 30, 2018, https://www.youtube.com/watch?v=RiP-ijdxqEc.

52 **"just Google them":** Anya Kamenetz, "Q&A: Exit Interview with a Nationally Known School Leader," *NPR*, February 15, 2015, http://www.npr.org/sections/ed/2015/02/15/385774711/q-a-exit-interview-with-a-nationally-known-school-leader. In the interview, Joshua Starr, the "nationally known school leader" in

question, remarked, "I ask teachers all the time, if you can Google it, why teach it? Because we have so much information today."

53 **"even alternative ones"**: Daniel T. Willingham, "You Still Need Your Brain," *New York Times*, May 19, 2017, https://www.nytimes.com/2017/05/19/opinion /sunday/you-still-need-your-brain.html?_r=0.

53 **"Much depended on . . . the two overnight batsmen"**: Ashis Ray, "Australia Brought Down to Earth," *Guardian Online*, January 19, 2008, https://www.the guardian.com/sport/2008/jan/20/cricket.sport.

54 **"the Inuit diet and way of life"**: Library and Archives Canada/www.collection scanada.gc.ca/The Kids' Site of Canadian Settlement, Inuit.

54 **By one estimate:** R. C. Atkinson and R. M. Shiffrin, "Human Memory: A Proposed System and Its Control Processes," in vol. 2 of *The Psychology of Learning and Motivation: Advances in Theory and Research*, ed. K. W. Spence and J. T. Spence (New York: Academic Press, 1968), 89–195.

55 **exactly what experiments have shown:** Daniel T. Willingham, "School Time, Knowledge, and Reading Comprehension," *Science and Education* (blog), March 7, 2012, http://www.danielwillingham.com/daniel-willingham-science -and-education-blog/school-time-knowledge-and-reading-comprehension.

55 **"knowledge tests in disguise"**: Willingham, *The Reading Mind*, 127.

56 **instructions are merely generic:** Daniel T. Willingham and Gail Lovette, "Can Reading Comprehension Be Taught?" *Teachers College Record*, September 26, 2014, http://www.danielwillingham.com/uploads/5/0/0/7/5007325/willingham &lovette_2014_can_reading_comprehension_be_taught_.pdf.

56 **called strategy instruction into question:** Sharon Walpole, et al., "The Promise of a Literacy Reform Effort in the Upper Elementary Grades," *The Elementary School Journal* 118, no. 2 (December 2017), http://www.journals.uchicago .edu/doi/abs/10.1086/694219; Marloes Muijselaar, et al., "The Effect of a Strategy Training on Reading Comprehension in Fourth-grade Students," *The Journal of Educational Research*, published online December 6, 2017, https://doi.org/10.108 0/00220671.2017.1396439.

56 **asking open-ended questions about content:** Margaret McKeown, Isabel L. Beck, and Ronette G. K. Blake, "Rethinking Reading Comprehension Instruction: A Comparison of Instruction for Strategies and Content Approaches," *Reading Research Quarterly* 44, no. 3 (July/August/September 2009): 242–243.

56 **said one of the authors:** Margaret McKeown, "Comprehension Instruction: Focus on Content or Strategies?," interview by Dr. Betsy Baker, podcast on *Voice of Literacy* (website), September 7, 2009, http://www.voiceofliteracy.org/posts /34422.

56 **yield no more benefit than ten:** Willingham, "The Usefulness of *Brief* Instruction in Reading Comprehension Strategies."

57 **according to one reading expert:** Timothy Shanahan, "Where Questioning Fits in Comprehension Instruction: Skills and Strategies Part II," *Shanahan on Literacy* (blog), May 28, 2018, http://www.shanahanonliteracy.com/blog/where -questioning-fits-in-comprehension-instruction-skills-and-strategies-part-ii#st hash.ipkTH3om.hW8xa1aD.dpbs.

57 **schools will adopt a curriculum:** Willingham, *The Reading Mind*, 195.

57 **aren't yet any reliable studies:** Numerous other variables make the effect of curriculum hard to isolate in a long-term study—for example, the fact that students tend to move from one school to another. However, two large-scale, multiyear studies of the knowledge-building aspects of the Core Knowledge curriculum are under way as of this writing. Sonia Cabell, "Efficacy of the Core Knowledge Language Arts Read Aloud Program in Kindergarten through Second Grade Classrooms," Institute of Education Sciences, U.S. Department of Education, 2016, https://ies.ed.gov/funding/grantsearch/details.asp?ID=1791; Audrey Breen, "U.VA. Researchers Receive $4.9M Grant to Study 'Core Knowledge' in Charter Schools," *UVA Today*, August 7, 2009, https://news.virginia.edu/content/uva-researchers -receive-49m-grant-study-core-knowledge-charter-schools.

September 2016

63 **far better when speaking than in writing:** The Core Knowledge curriculum includes a separate "strand" for building children's skills, including decoding and writing skills, but Center City doesn't use that strand systematically.

Chapter 4: The Reading Wars

64 **Flesch later recounted:** Rudolf Flesch, *Why Johnny Can't Read—And What You Can Do About It* (New York: Harper & Row, 1955), 18.

65 **"he was unfortunately exposed to an ordinary American school":** Flesch, *Why Johnny Can't Read*, 2.

65 **held sway since about 1935:** James S. Kim, "Research and the Reading Wars," in *When Research Matters: How Scholarship Influences Education Policy*, ed. Frederic M. Hess (Cambridge, MA: Harvard University Press, 2008), 93.

66 **"I don't wish that experience on anyone":** Flesch, *Why Johnny Can't Read*, 6–7.

66 **Flesch reported:** Rudolf Flesch, *Why Johnny* Still *Can't Read: A New Look at the Scandal of Our Schools* (New York: HarperCollins, 1981), 48.

67 **critics argue:** Louisa Cook Moats, *Whole Language Lives On: The Illusion of "Balanced" Reading Instruction* (Washington, D.C.: Thomas B. Fordham Foundation, 2000), http://files.eric.ed.gov/fulltext/ED449465.pdf.

67 **relying primarily on their own observations:** Seidenberg, *Language at the Speed of Sight*, 267–268.

67 **probably somewhere between half and a third:** Hanford, "Hard Words"; Phyllis Bertin, director of reading at the Windward Teacher Training Institute, email to author, March 14, 2018.

68 **children who speak a nonstandard dialect:** William Brennan, "Julie Washington's Quest to Get Schools to Respect African-American English," *The Atlantic*, April 2018, https://www.theatlantic.com/magazine/archive/2018/04/the-code -switcher/554099.

68 **best taught systematically:** David Liben and David D. Paige, "Why a Structured Phonics Program Is Effective," Student Achievement Partners, 5, retrieved July 30, 2018, https://www.google.com/url?sa=t&rct=j&q=&esrc=s&source=web&cd=1&v ed=0ahUKEwi0pZnckN7bAhXIxlkKHWbqAogQFggpMAA&url=https%3A%2

F%2Fachievethecore.org%2Faligned%2Fwp-content%2Fuploads%2F2017%2F03
%2FWhy-a-Structured-Phonics-Program-is-Effective.pdf&usg=AOvVaw1Gm
_o8zBWElj6e_vseMvJP. The sequence in structured phonics programs generally
begins with consonant sounds and then moves to short vowel sounds, long vowel
sounds, and consonant blends.

69 **An influential book:** Jeanne S. Chall, *Learning to Read: The Great Debate* (New
York: McGraw-Hill, 1967); Diane Ravitch, "Jeanne Chall's Historic Contribu-
tion," *American Educator*, Spring 2001, http://www.aft.org/periodical/american
-educator/spring-2001/tribute-jeanne-chall#ravitch.

69 **"They should not be taught at all":** Frank Smith, *Insult to Intelligence: The Bu-
reaucratic Invasion of Our Classrooms* (Portsmouth, NH: Heinemann, 1986), 211,
quoted in Greg Shafer, "Whole Language: Origins and Practice," *Language Arts
Journal of Michigan* 14, no. 1, (1998): 19, https://doi.org/10.9707/2168-149X.1429.

70 **one researcher observed:** Keith E. Stanovich, "Romance and Reality," *The Reading Teacher* 47, no. 4 (December, 1993–January 1994): 285–286.

70 **simply unaware of the data:** Anthony Pedriana, *Leaving Johnny Behind: Overcoming Barriers to Literacy and Reclaiming At-Risk Readers* (Lanham, Md: Row-
man & Littlefield Education, 2010), 36. Pedriana, a veteran educator, was
surprised to encounter the overwhelming evidence supporting systematic phonics instruction late in his career; he had never heard of most of it before, despite
the fact that he'd been trained as a reading specialist.

70 **a lack of fluency in reading:** Roxanne F. Hudson, Holly B. Lane, and Paige
C. Pullen, "Reading Fluency Assessment and Instruction: What, Why, and
How?," *The Reading Teacher* 58, no. 8 (May 2005): 702–714, https://doi.org
/10.1598/RT.58.8.1.

70 **were disfluent readers:** Liben and Paige, "Why a Structured Phonics Program Is
Effective," 2.

71 **wrote one reading expert in 1989:** P. David Pearson, "Reading the Whole-
Language Movement," *Elementary School Journal* 90, no. 2 (November 1989):
248, quoted in Kim, "Research and the Reading Wars," 97.

71 **many started freeing teachers:** Moats, *Whole Language Lives On*, 3.

71 **California changed course:** "California Leads Revival of Teaching by Phonics,"
New York Times, May 22, 1996, http://www.nytimes.com/1996/05/22/us/california
-leads-revival-of-teaching-by-phonics.html; Joan Beck, "Kids Are Victims in the
Phony War on Phonics," *Chicago Tribune*, May 23, 1996, http://articles.chicago tri-
bune.com/1996-05-23/news/9605230025_1_phonics-reading-scores-johnny
-can-t-read; Nicholas Lemann, "The Reading Wars," *The Atlantic*, November 1997,
https://www.theatlantic.com/magazine/archive/1997/11/the-reading-wars/376990.

72 **One phonics advocate charged:** "The Blumenfeld Education Letter," February
1992, 6, quoted in Kenneth Goodman, *Phonics Phacts* (Portsmouth, NH: Heinemann, 1993), 102.

72 **accused the phonics camp:** Diane Ravitch, *Left Back: A Century of Battles Over
School Reform* (New York: Touchstone, 2000), 447.

72 **thirty-three states had enacted legislation:** Kim, "Research and the Reading
Wars."

72 **"Reading First is the most effective federal program in history":** Shepard Barbash, "The Reading First Controversy," *Education Next* 8, no. 3 (Summer 2008), http://educationnext.org/the-reading-first-controversy.

73 **Reading First increased the amount of time teachers spent on reading:** William H. Teale, Kathleen A. Paciga, and Jessica L. Hoffman, "Beginning Reading Instruction in Urban Schools: The Curriculum Gap Ensures a Continuing Achievement Gap," *The Reading Teacher* 61, no. 4 (December 2007–January 2008): 346–347.

73 **a third-grader named Zulma Berrios:** Linda Perlstein, "School Pushes Reading, Writing, Reform," *Washington Post*, May 31, 2004, http://www.washingtonpost.com/wp-dyn/articles/A3179-2004May30.html.

73 **"comprehension [would] pretty much take care of itself":** Teale, Paciga, and Hoffman, "Beginning Reading Instruction in Urban Schools."

73 **aren't backed by evidence:** Dr. Deborah Glaser, educational consultant and professional development provider, and Kelly A. Butler, managing director for policy and partnerships at the Barksdale Reading Institute, conversations with the author, June 1 and 8, 2016; Hanford, "Hard Words." A review of hundreds of syllabi from more than eight hundred teacher-preparation programs showed that the general approach is to encourage prospective teachers to develop their own approaches to teaching reading rather than presenting evidence that any particlar approach is best. Kate Walsh, "21st-Century Teacher Education," *Education Next* 13, no. 3 (Summer 2013), https://www.educationnext.org/21st-century-teacher-education.

73 **numerous experiments have shown:** Daniel T. Willingham, "Does Tailoring Instruction to 'Learning Styles' Help Students Learn?," *American Educator*, Summer 2018, https://www.aft.org/ae/summer2018/willingham.

74 **once every three months:** Frederick Hess, *Letters to a Young Education Reformer* (Cambridge, MA: Harvard Education Press, 2017), 4.

74 **More than half of teachers surveyed in 2017:** Liana Loewus, "Majority of Teachers Say Reforms Have Been 'Too Much,'" *Education Week*, December 19, 2017, https://www.edweek.org/ew/articles/2017/12/19/majority-of-teachers-say-reforms-have-been.html.

74 **"the teachers' nightmare":** Steve Farkas and the FDR Group, "Building Teacher Enthusiasm for Core Knowledge," in Finn and Petrilli, *Knowledge at the Core*, 73.

74 **they dismiss the mandate to teach it:** Anne Castles, Kathleen Rastle, and Kate Nation, "Ending the Reading Wars: Reading Acquisition from Novice to Expert," *Psychological Science in the Public Interest* 19, no. 1 (June 2018): 38, https://doi.org/10.1177/1529100618772271.

75 **"like asking a Christian fundamentalist to embrace the spirit of Allah":** Pedriana, *Leaving Johnny Behind*, 18.

75 **members of the helping professions:** Carol Tavris and Elliot Aronson, *Mistakes Were Made (but Not by Me)* (New York: Harcourt, 2007), 8, 101–102.

75 **Doctors in mid-nineteenth-century Vienna:** Rebecca Davis, "The Doctor Who Championed Hand-Washing and Briefly Saved Lives," *NPR*, January 12, 2015, http://www.npr.org/sections/health-shots/2015/01/12/375663920/the-doctor-who-championed-hand-washing-and-saved-women-s-lives; Tavris and Aronson, *Mistakes Were Made*, 101–102.

76 **Better to focus on their existing goals:** Tavris and Aronson, *Mistakes Were Made*, 231–232.

October 2016

81 **readers actually learn better:** Danielle S. McNamara and Walter Kintsch, "Learning from Texts: Effects of Prior Knowledge and Text Coherence," *Discourse Processes* 22, no. 3 (1996): 247–288, https://doi.org/10.1080/01638539609 544975.

Chapter 5: Unbalanced Literacy

82 **Some defenders of whole language:** Alfie Kohn, *The Schools Our Children Deserve: Moving Beyond Traditional Classrooms and "Tougher Standards"* (New York: Houghton Mifflin, 1999), 166.

83 **had adopted her version of balanced literacy:** Robert Kolker, "A Is for Apple, B Is for Brawl: Why New York's Reading Wars Are So Contentious," *New York*, May 1, 2006, http://nymag.com/news/features/16775/index2.html.

84 **were reading below grade level:** James Traub, "New York's New Approach," *New York Times*, August 3, 2003, http://www.nytimes.com/2003/08/03/education /new-york-s-new-approach.html.

84 **doing far worse than white and Asian ones:** Anemona Hartocollis, "Racial Gap in Test Scores Found Across New York," *New York Times*, March 28, 2002, http:// www.nytimes.com/2002/03/28/nyregion/racial-gap-in-test-scores-found -across-new-york.html.

84 **Bloomberg had called for just that:** Karla Scoon Reid, "Mayor Outlines Major Overhaul of N.Y.C. System," *Education Week*, January 22, 2003, http://www .edweek.org/ew/articles/2003/01/22/19nyc.h22.html.

85 **the only regret he had:** Geoff Decker, "Joel Klein Says Curriculum Is His Legacy's Lone Dark Spot," *Chalkbeat*, December 13, 2013, http://www.chalkbeat.org /posts/ny/2013/12/13/joel-klein-says-curriculum-is-his-legacys-lone-dark-spot.

85 **has been challenged:** Timothy Shanahan, "The Instructional Level Concept Revisited: Teaching with Complex Text," *Shanahan on Literacy* (blog), February 7, 2017, http://shanahanonliteracy.com/blog/the-instructional-level-concept-revisited -teaching-with-complex-text#sthash.achTbyYi.dpbs; Shanahan, "The Informal Reading Inventory and the Instructional Level: The Study That Never Took Place," 577–580.

85 **listening for the number of mistakes:** If a student reads 95 percent or more of the words correctly, a book is deemed easy enough for him to read on his own—or, if he answers all the comprehension questions correctly, *too* easy. If he reads less than 90 percent of the words correctly, the book is too difficult. But if he can read between 90 and 95 percent of the words and answer most of the comprehension questions correctly, the book is at his "instructional level," meaning that he should read books at that level with the teacher's support during guided reading.

85 **ten different factors:** "Ten Text Characteristics for Guided Reading," Fountas & Pinnell Leveled Books Website, accessed July 31, 2018, http://www.fountasand pinnellleveledbooks.com/aboutleveledtexts.aspx#TC. The factors are genre/ form, text structure, content, themes and ideas, language and literary features, sentence complexity, vocabulary, difficulty of words used (e.g., the amount of repetition of high-frequency words), illustrations, and book and print features (length, size, layout, table of contents, etc.).

86 **don't reliably predict comprehensibility:** James W. Cunningham, Elfrieda H. Hiebert, and Heidi Anne Mesmer, "Investigating the Validity of Two Widely Used Quantitative Text Tools," *Reading and Writing: An Interdisciplinary Journal* 31, no. 4 (April 2018): 813–833, https://eric.ed.gov/?id=EJ1171526; Daniel Willingham, "Reading Is Not Formulaic: Why Equations Can't Be Sole Determinants of Student Texts," *Real Clear Education*, March 26, 2014, https://www.realcleareduca tion. com/articles/2014/03/26/reading_is_not_formulaic_why_equations_cant _be_920.html.

87 **the approach was deeply entrenched:** P. David Pearson and Janice A. Dole, "Explicit Comprehension Instruction: A Review of Research and a New Conceptualization of Instruction," Center for the Study of Reading, University of Illinois at Urbana-Champaign, May 1988, https://www.ideals.illinois.edu/bit stream/ handle/2142/17914/ctrstreadtechrepv01988i00427_opt.pdf?sequence=1; Timothy Shanahan, "Comprehension Skills or Strategies: Is There a Difference and Does It Matter?," *Shanahan on Literacy* (blog), May 19, 2018, http://www .shanahanonliteracy.com/blog/comprehension-skills-or-strategies-is-there-a -difference-and-does-it-matter#sthash.BWBhTyQ4.fvdCh7ok.dpbs.

87 **academics debated:** P. David Pearson, et al., "Developing Expertise in Reading Comprehension: What Should Be Taught? How Should It Be Taught?," Center for the Study of Reading, University of Illinois at Urbana-Champaign, September 1990, https://www.ideals.illinois.edu/bitstream/handle/2142/17648/ctrstread techrepv01990i00512_opt.pdf?sequence=1.

87 **"introspective nightmares":** Pearson and Dole, "Explicit Comprehension Instruction," 12.

87 **"We can only infer, predict, and think critically":** Frank Smith, *Joining the Literacy Club: Further Essays into Education* (Portsmouth, NH: Heinemann, 1987), 49.

88 **"Nagging questions":** Debbie Miller, *Reading with Meaning: Teaching Comprehension in the Primary Grades* (Portsmouth, NH: Stenhouse, 2002), ii.

88 **"The record remained stuck":** Ellin Oliver Keene and Susan Zimmermann, *Mosaic of Thought: Teaching Comprehension in a Reader's Workshop* (Portsmouth, NH: Heinemann, 1997).

89 **an article she'd come across:** Pearson, et al., "Developing Expertise in Reading Comprehension."

89 **"construct their own meaning":** Pearson, et al., "Developing Expertise in Reading Comprehension," 4.

90 **"it's as if this fog bank rolls in":** Keene and Zimmermann, *Mosaic of Thought*, 81–87.

91 **"very different things":** Shanahan, "Comprehension Skills or Strategies."

91 **one of the most frequently assigned books:** The Open Syllabus Project (website), accessed July 31, 2018, https://opensyllabusproject.org.

91 **partners with "scores of schools":** "Our History," Reading & Writing Project, Teachers College, Columbia University (website), accessed July 31, 2018, https://readingandwritingproject.org/about/history.

91 **a transformative trip to San Diego:** Joel Klein, *Lessons of Hope* (New York: HarperCollins, 2014), 42–43.

92 **"in every school I go to":** Kelly Butler, conversation with author, June 8, 2016.

93 **one teacher complained:** Barbara Feinberg, "The Lucy Calkins Project: Parsing a Self-Proclaimed Literacy Guru," *Education Next* 7, no. 3 (Summer 2007), http://educationnext.org/the-lucy-calkins-project.

94 **Keene herself expressed dismay:** Ellin Oliver Keene and Susan Zimmermann, "Years Later, Comprehension Strategies Still at Work," *The Reading Teacher* 66, no. 8 (May 2013): 605. Zimmermann was also Keene's coauthor for *Mosaic of Thought*.

94 **He and others were questioning:** "Is Lucy Calkins Legally Insane?," *South Bronx School: Reality Meets the NYC DOE* (blog), February 28, 2013, http://south-bronxschool.blogspot.com/2013/02/is-lucy-calkins-legally-insane.html; Alexander Nazaryan, "The Fallacy of 'Balanced Literacy,'" *New York Times*, July 6, 2014, https://www.nytimes.com/2014/07/07/opinion/the-fallacy-of-balanced-literacy.html; Robert Pondiscio, "How Self-Expression Damaged My Students," *The Atlantic*, September 25, 2012, https://www.theatlantic.com/national/archive/2012/09/how-self-expression-damaged-my-students/262656; Javier C. Hernández, "New York Schools Chief Advocates More 'Balanced Literacy,'" *New York Times*, June 26, 2014, https://www.nytimes.com/2014/06/27/nyregion/new-york-schools-chancellor-carmen-farina-advocates-more-balanced-literacy.html.

95 **"never got back to discussing the Civil War":** Klein, *Lessons of Hope*, 263–264.

95 **something she'd seen in the news:** Klein doesn't remember what the news item was, but it may have been about an internal reorganization that gave New York City schools the option of contracting with a "Knowledge Network" group, which would help them implement a "content-rich" curriculum. David M. Herszenhorn, "Klein Specifies Restructuring of City Schools," *New York Times*, April 17, 2007, http://www.nytimes.com/2007/04/17/nyregion/17schools.html.

95 **they would bring history and science to language arts:** In 2017, the Core Knowledge Foundation also released a history and geography curriculum covering third to fifth grade, with plans to expand to sixth. Both the Core Knowledge Language Arts curriculum and the history and geography one are currently available for free online at https://www.coreknowledge.org/curriculum/download-curriculum/. Stephen Sawchuk, "'Open' Curricula Offerings Expand to Social Studies," *Education Week*, October 10, 2017, http://blogs.edweek.org/edweek/curriculum/2017/10/open_curricula_offerings_expand_to_social_studies.html.

96 **scored significantly higher:** Anna M. Phillips, "Nonfiction Curriculum Enhanced Reading Skills, Study Finds," *New York Times*, March 11, 2012, https://www.nytimes.com/2012/03/12/nyregion/nonfiction-curriculum-enhanced-reading-skills-in-new-york-city-schools.html.

96 **"we learn thinking to get on in life"**: Liz Willen, "Analysis: New NYC Schools Chancellor Wants Dramatic—Even Joyful—Departure from Bloomberg Era," *The Hechinger Report*, December 31, 2013, http://hechingerreport.org/new-nyc-schools -chancellor-wants-dramatic-even-joyful-departure-from-bloomberg-era.

97 **"They're going to feel frustrated, alienated"**: Hernández, "New York Schools Chief."

97 **send their "best and brightest"**: Patrick Wall, "In Struggling Schools, Fariña Looks to Shape How Students Read and Write," *Chalkbeat*, January 9, 2015, http://www.chalkbeat.org/posts/ny/2015/01/09/in-struggling-schools-farina -looks-to-shape-how-students-read-and-write.

97 **continued to grow**: David Cantor, "New Study of 70,000 NYC Kids Shows Achievement Gaps Widening over Time—Except for Asian Students," *The 74*, December 5, 2017, https://www.the74million.org/article/new-study-of-70000-nyc -kids-shows-achievement-gaps-widening-over-time-except-for-asian-students.

97 **credited it for raising test scores**: The reading proficiency rate at each school was 58 percent, twenty points above the rate for the city overall.

97 **the kids replied**: The teacher then turned to the next chapter, "A Foal Is Born," and repeated the exercise. Unfortunately, this time she consistently mispronounced *foal* as *foil*, and the children followed her lead.

98 **"one of the most interesting crustaceans"**: Leanne Guenther, "Mantis Shrimp," *KidZone Animals* (website), accessed July 31, 2018, http://www.kidzone.ws/animals /mantis-shrimp.htm.

98 **do even better**: "Our Data," http://readingandwritingproject.org/about/our-data.

Chapter 6: Billions for Education Reform, but Barely a Cent for Knowledge

104 **with assets of more than $40 billion**: "Who We Are: Foundation Fact Sheet," Bill & Melinda Gates Foundation (website), accessed July 31, 2018, http://www.gates foundation.org/Who-We-Are/General-Information/Foundation-Factsheet.

105 **one of many foundations**: Others include the Walton Family Foundation, the Eli and Edythe Broad Foundation, and the Michael & Susan Dell Foundation, to name just a few.

105 **"it's easier to name which groups Gates doesn't support"**: Sam Dillon, "Behind Grass-Roots School Advocacy, Bill Gates," *New York Times*, May 21, 2011, http:// www.nytimes.com/2011/05/22/education/22gates.html.

105 **a kind of R&D lab**: Lyndsey Layton, "How Bill Gates Pulled off the Swift Common Core Revolution," *Washington Post*, June 7, 2014, https://www.washingtonpost.com /politics/how-bill-gates-pulled-off-the-swift-common-core-revolution/2014/06/07 /a830e32e-ec34-11e3-9f5c-9075d5508f0a_story.html.

106 **Lemov took a part-time job**: This account of Doug Lemov's interactions with Alphonso is taken from Elizabeth Green, *Building a Better Teacher: How Teaching Works (and How to Teach It to Everyone)* (New York: W. W. Norton, 2014), 150–154.

107 **the ubiquitous direction to "SLANT"**: SLANT, as Lemov makes clear in his book, was first used at the KIPP network of charter schools.

108 **a 2005 speech to governors:** "Bill Gates—National Education Summit on High Schools," Bill & Melinda Gates Foundation (website), February 26, 2005, accessed July 31, 2018, http://www.gatesfoundation.org/media-center/speeches/2005/02/bill -gates-2005-national-education-summit.

108 **spending more than $650 million:** Mary Beth Lambert, Gates Foundation, email to author, April 18, 2017.

108 **only a slight improvement:** Patricia Willens, "New Research Suggests Small High Schools May Help After All," *NPR*, October 17, 2014, http://www.npr.org /sections/ed/2014/10/17/356661018/new-research-suggests-small-high-schools -may-help-after-all.

109 **"school reform is a futile exercise":** Robert Gordon, Thomas J. Kane, and Douglas O. Staiger, *Identifying Effective Teachers Using Performance on the Job* (Washington, D.C.: The Brookings Institution, 2006), 5. https://www.dartmouth .edu/~dstaiger/Papers/200604hamilton_1.pdf. It's notable that the "everything else" the researchers listed didn't mention curriculum.

109 **at a time when it received $20 million:** Layton, "How Bill Gates Pulled off the Swift Common Core Revolution."

109 **had almost tripled:** *State of the States 2015: Evaluating Teaching, Leading and Learning* (Washington, D.C.: National Council on Teacher Quality, 2015) i, http://www.nctq.org/dmsView/StateofStates2015.

109 **States have also been required:** Zoë Gioja, "Texplainer: What if Texas Schools Don't Meet Federal Benchmarks?," *Texas Tribune*, August 21, 2012, https://www .texastribune.org/2012/08/21/texplainer-what-if-schools-dont-meet-bench marks.

109 **were rated effective or highly effective:** *State of the States 2015*, iii; Frederick Hess, *Letters to a Young Education Reformer*, 25–26.

110 **"What counts for teachers":** Brittany Perna, Watkins Elementary School, conversation with author, May 30, 2016.

111 **"The hope that collecting more test scores":** Dana Goldstein, *The Teacher Wars: A History of America's Most Embattled Profession* (New York: Doubleday, 2014), 231–232.

111 **it failed to boost teacher quality or student learning:** Matt Barnum, "The Gates Foundation Bet Big on Teacher Evaluation. The Report It Commissioned Explains How Those Efforts Fell Short," *Chalkbeat*, June 21, 2018, https://www .chalkbeat.org/posts/us/2018/06/21/the-gates-foundation-bet-big-on-teacher -evaluation-the-report-it-commissioned-explains-how-those-efforts-fell-short; Jay P. Greene, "The Gates Effective Teaching Initiative Fails to Improve Student Outcomes," *Education Next*, June 22, 2018, http://educationnext.org/gates-effective-teaching-initiative-fails-improve-student-outcomes.

112 **as much as $18 billion a year:** Karen Hawley Miles, David Rosenberg, and Genevieve Quist Green, *Igniting the Learning Engine: How School Systems Accelerate Teacher Effectiveness and Student Growth Through Connected Professional Learning* (Watertown, MA: Education Resource Strategies, 2017), 13, https:// www.erstrategies.org/cms/files/3560-igniting-the-learning-engine.pdf.

112 **see it as a waste of time:** Christina Samuels, "Teachers Like Common Planning Time, Survey Shows," *Education Week*, April 25, 2017, https://www.edweek.org

/ew/section/multimedia/teachers-like-common-planning-time-survey-shows
.html; Madeline Will, "Educators Are More Stressed at Work Than Average People, Survey Finds," *Education Week*, October 30, 2017, http://blogs.edweek.org
/teachers/teaching_now/2017/10/educator_stress_aft_bat.html.

112 **the Gates Foundation reported:** *Teachers Know Best: Teachers' Views on Professional Development* (Bill and Melinda Gates Foundation, 2015), 3, http://k12e
ducation.gatesfoundation.org/resource/teachers-know-best-teachers-views-on
-professional-development .

112 **"mostly a mirage":** *The Mirage: Confronting Hard Truths About Our Quest for Teacher Development* (TNTP, 2015), 4, 22, and 34, https://tntp.org/assets/docu
ments/TNTP-Mirage_2015.pdf.

113 **for PD to be effective:** Ross Wiener and Susan Pimentel, *Practice What You Teach: Connecting Curriculum & Professional Learning in Schools* (Washington, D.C.: Aspen Institute, 2017), http://www.aspendrl.org/portal/browse/DocumentDetail?do
cumentId=2969&download&admin=2969%7C3571821; Miles, Rosenberg, and Green, *Igniting the Learning Engine*.

113 **figuring out both what to teach *and* how to teach it:** Nonie K. Lesaux, Emily Phillips Galloway, and Sky H. Marietta, *Teaching Advanced Literacy Skills: A Guide for Leaders in Linguistically Diverse Schools* (New York: Guilford, 2016), 40.

113 **"all the shopping and prepping the night before":** Robert Pondiscio, "Failing by Design: How We Make Teaching Too Hard for Mere Mortals," *Flypaper* (blog), Thomas B. Fordham Institute, May 10, 2016, https://edexcellence.net/articles
/failing-by-design-how-we-make-teaching-too-hard-for-mere-mortals.

114 **discourage teacher-candidates from relying on textbooks:** Dewitz and Jones, "Using Basal Readers"; Hannah Putnam, Julie Greenberg, and Kate Walsh, *Training Our Future Teachers: Easy A's and What's Behind Them* (Washington, D.C.: National Council on Teacher Quality, 2014), 34–35. Generally, teacher-training programs encourage their students to develop their own personal philosophies of teaching, reflecting the assumption that a teacher's own judgment is superior to any knowledge transmitted by a professor or a curriculum.

114 **losing 20 percent of their faculty every year:** "Keeping the Teachers: The Problem of High Turnover in Urban Schools," NYU/Steinhardt School of Education (website), December 19, 2017, accessed July 31, 2018, http://teachereducation
.steinhardt.nyu.edu/high-teacher-turnover; Brenda Iasevoli, "Today's Teaching Force Is Larger, Less Experienced, More Diverse Than Ever," *Education Week*, April 13, 2017, http://blogs.edweek.org/edweek/teacherbeat/2017/04/teaching
_force_of_today_is_large.html.

114 **little or no research basis:** Jay P. Greene, "Buckets into Another Sea," in *The New Education Philanthropy: Politics, Policy, and Reform*, ed. Frederick M. Hess and Jeffrey R. Henig (Cambridge, MA: Harvard Education Press, 2015), 27–28.

115 **Nine countries that consistently outrank the United States:** *Why We're Behind: What Top Nations Teach Their Students But We Don't* (Washington, D.C.: Common Core, 2009), iii–v, https://www.giarts.org/sites/default/files/Why-Were-Behind.
pdf. One of the geographic entities studied was Hong Kong, which is a territory rather than a country. There is also, of course, the unintentional experiment that occurred when the French government decreed that the nation's elementary

schools should abandon their hitherto content-focused curriculum and switch to a focus on skills, which I described in Chapter 2.

115 **the impact of a high-quality curriculum can be greater:** Matthew M. Chingos and Grover J. "Russ" Whitehurst, *Choosing Blindly: Instructional Materials, Teacher Effectiveness, and the Common Core* (Washington, D.C.: Brookings, 2012), 5; C. Kirabo Jackson and Alexey Makarin, "Can Online Off-the-Shelf Lessons Improve Student Outcomes?: Evidence from a Field Experiment," *American Economic Journal: Economic Policy* 10, no. 3 (August 2018): 226–254, https://doi.org/10.1257/pol.20170211.

115 **she couldn't find any takers:** Katherine Bradley, founder and executive chair of CityBridge Education, conversation with author, March 30, 2016.

116 **"The last thing we're going to do":** Robert Pondiscio, "The Fierce Urgency of Eventually," *Flypaper* (blog), Thomas B. Fordham Institute, December 23, 2010, accessed August 1, 2018, https://edexcellence.net/commentary/education-gadfly-daily/flypaper/2010/the-fierce-urgency-of-eventually.html.

116 **suffered from groupthink:** Jeffrey W. Snyder, "How Old Foundations Differ from New Foundations," in Hess and Henig, *The New Education Philanthropy*, 32–34; Hess, *Letters to a Young Education Reformer*, 103–105.

116 **an assertion that has been challenged:** Seidenberg, *Language at the Speed of Sight*, 230–235.

116 **"poverty is a bigger problem than curriculum":** Diane Ravitch, email to author, March 14, 2017.

116 **she now ridicules Core Knowledge:** Diane Ravitch, "Are You As Smart As a First-Grader?," *Diane Ravitch's Blog*, August 23, 2013, https://dianeravitch.net/2013/08/23/can-you-explain-the-code-of-hammurabi-and-a-ziggurat/comment-page-1.

117 **they began retooling their elementary curricula:** Natalie Wexler, "High Test Scores at Many Charter Schools May Actually Be 'False Positives,'" *Greater Greater Washington* (blog), January 20, 2015, https://ggwash.org/view/37045/high-test-scores-at-many-charter-schools-may-actually-be-false-positives; Michael J. Petrilli, "Knowledge Is Power: How KIPP and Other High-Performing Charter Networks Are Making an Impact Through Well-Rounded Curricula," *Principal* 97, no. 1 (September/October 2017): 14–16.

117 **"it doesn't matter what questions you're asking":** Elizabeth Green, "Building a Better Teacher," *New York Times Magazine*, March 2, 2010, http://www.nytimes.com/2010/03/07/magazine/07Teachers-t.html.

118 **a model of knowledge-building:** Karin Chenoweth, "Kids Love Knowing Stuff," *Huffington Post*, September 10, 2015 (updated September 9, 2016), https://www.huffingtonpost.com/Karin-Chenoweth/kids-love-knowing-stuff_b_8117398.html.

120 **students "choose their own curriculum":** Katie Pisa, "Are These the Schools of the Future?," CNN, September 28, 2017, http://www.cnn.com/2017/09/27/health/future-schools/index.html.

120 **a surge of interest:** Jackie Zubrzycki, "As Project-Based Learning Gains in Popularity, Experts Offer Caution," *Education Week*, July 22, 2016, http://blogs.edweek.org/edweek/curriculum/2016/07/as_project-based_learning_gain.html.

120 **do best when they receive direct instruction:** Russell Gersten and Thomas Keating, "Long-Term Benefits from Direct Instruction," *Educational Leadership*, March 1987, 28–31, http://www.ascd.org/ASCD/pdf/journals/ed_lead/el_198703 _gersten.pdf; Kirschner, Sweller, and Clark, "Why Minimal Guidance During Instruction Does Not Work."

121 **have made it the prime focus:** Benjamin Herold, "Zuckerberg Talks Personalized Learning, Philanthropy, and Lessons from Newark," *Education Week*, March 7, 2016, http://www.edweek.org/ew/articles/2016/03/07/zuckerberg-talks-personalized -learning-philanthropy-and-lessons.html; Matt Barnum, "Why 'Personalized Learning' Advocates Like Mark Zuckerberg Keep Citing a 1984 Study—and Why It Might Not Say Much about Schools Today," *Chalkbeat*, January 29, 2018, https:// www.chalkbeat.org/posts/us/2018/01/29/why-personalized-learning-advocates -like-mark-zuckerberg-keep-citing-a-1984-study-and-why-it-might-not-say-much -about-schools-today.

121 **also its content:** Bill Gates, "I Love This Cutting-Edge School Design," *Gates Notes* (blog), August 22, 2016, https://www.gatesnotes.com/Education/Why-I -Love-This-Cutting-Edge-School-Design.

121 **"an expert in princesses and dogs":** Lisa Hansel, "Why I'm Afraid of Personalized Learning," *The 74*, September 29, 2015, https://www.the74million.org /article/why-im-afraid-of-personalized-learning-opinion.

121 **if it's attached to a skills-focused curriculum:** Benjamin Herold, "RAND Researchers Make It Clear: Personalized Learning Is Difficult to Do," *Education Week*, October 4, 2017, https://www.edweek.org/ew/articles/2017/10/04 /rand-researchers-make-it-clear-personalized-learning.html; Frederick Hess, "A Confession and a Question on Personalized Learning," *Education Next*, February 13, 2018, http://educationnext.org/confession-question-personalized -learning.

121 **we'll lose the essence:** Benjamin Riley, "Bursting the 'Personalization' Bubble: An Alternative Vision for Our Public Schools," *EdSurge*, May 18, 2016, https:// www.edsurge.com/news/2016-05-18-bursting-the-personalization-bubble-an -alternative-vision-for-our-public-schools.

121 **what really promotes perseverance and a growth mind-set:** Tough, *Helping Children Succeed*, 91–104.

122 **Bill Gates announced:** Bill Gates, "Our Education Efforts Are Evolving," *Gates Notes* (blog), October 19, 2017, https://www.gatesnotes.com/Education/Council -of-Great-City-Schools.

123 **when the foundation identified the subjects:** Matt Barnum, "With New Focus on Curriculum, Gates Foundation Wades into Tricky Territory," *Chalkbeat*, February 6, 2018, https://www.chalkbeat.org/posts/us/2018/02/06/with-new-focus -on-curriculum-gates-foundation-wades-into-tricky-territory.

Chapter 7: Émile Meets the Common Core

130 **as the English poet William Wordsworth put it:** William J. Reese, "The Origins of Progressive Education," *History of Education Quarterly* 41, no. 1 (Spring 2001): 6, 23–24.

131 **"the burden of proof should be on the teacher":** Kohn, *The Schools Our Children Deserve*, 136. The one area where Kohn believes direct instruction *can* work is "reading and thinking skills."

131 **these "common schools":** Ravitch, *Left Back*, 19–25.

132 **Mann deliberately recruited women:** Goldstein, *Teacher Wars*, 26–27.

132 **don't acquire much in the way of subject-matter knowledge:** *Landscapes in Teacher Prep*, 6-7.

132 **a host of aims:** Ravitch, *Left Back*, 53–55; *Educational Psychology: A Century of Contributions*, ed. Barry J. Zimmerman and Dale H. Schunk (New York: Taylor and Francis, 2003), 105.

133 **"If you provide a sufficient variety of activities":** Max Eastman, quoted in Ravitch, *Left Back*, 171.

133 **Some of his followers:** Ravitch, *Left Back*, 69–74, 178–183.

134 **old-fashioned drills:** Ravitch, *Left Back*, 247–252.

134 **"less-connected content of history, civics, and geography":** James A. Duplass, "Elementary Social Studies: Trite, Disjointed, and in Need of Reform?," *The Social Studies* 98, no. 4 (July–August 2007): 137.

135 **"a dozen leading scholars":** Diane Ravitch, "Tot Sociology," *The American Scholar* 56, no. 3 (Summer 1987): 352.

136 **Between 1870 and 1940:** Diane Ravitch, *The Troubled Crusade: American Education, 1945–1980* (New York: Basic Books, 1983), 5.

136 **some high schools began to submerge:** Ravitch, *Troubled Crusade*, 55.

136 **the bulk of students:** Ravitch, *Left Back*, 197.

137 **were dismissed as being unfamiliar:** Ravitch, *Troubled Crusade*, 55.

137 **Neill argued:** A. S. Neill, *Summerhill: A Radical Approach to Child Rearing* (New York: Hart, 1960), 9.

137 **it was selling two hundred thousand copies a year:** Ravitch, *Left Back*, 387–389.

137 **other popular books:** These books included John Holt's *How Children Fail*, Herbert Kohl's *36 Children*, James Herndon's *The Way It Spozed to Be*, and Jonathan Kozol's *Death at an Early Age*, which won the National Book Award.

138 **"The severest critics of the school":** Thomas Powers, *Diana: The Making of a Terrorist* (Boston: Houghton Mifflin, 1971), 64–67, quoted in Ravitch, *Left Back*, 394.

138 **the open-classroom model:** Larry Cuban, "The Open Classroom," *Education Next* 4, no. 2 (Spring 2004), https://www.educationnext.org/theopenclassroom; Cuban, "Whatever Happened to Open Classrooms?," *Larry Cuban on School Reform and Classroom Practice* (blog), September 11, 2017, https://larrycuban .wordpress.com/2017/09/11/whatever-happened-to-open-classrooms/amp.

138 **"children's own experiences":** Beatrice and Ronald Gross, "A Little Bit of Chaos," *Saturday Review*, May 16, 1970, 84, quoted in Ravitch, *Troubled Crusade*, 245.

138 **one parent chided a teacher:** Ravitch, *Troubled Crusade*, 250.

139 **textbooks had been getting simpler:** Adams, "Advancing Our Students' Language and Literacy," 5.

140 **It's hugely important:** Daniel T. Willingham, "Inflexible Knowledge: The First Step to Expertise," *American Educator*, Winter 2002, https://www.aft.org/peri odical/american-educator/winter-2002/ask-cognitive-scientist.

140 **it has been surfacing in various forms:** The prominent progressive William Heard Kilpatrick invented the claim in the 1920s, according to E. D. Hirsch Jr., *The Schools We Need: And Why We Don't Have Them* (New York: Anchor Books, 1996), 125.

140 **In fact, Bloom meant:** Doug Lemov, "Bloom's Taxonomy—That Pyramid Is a Problem," *Doug Lemov's Field Notes* (blog), Teach Like a Champion (website), April 3, 2017, http://teachlikeachampion.com/blog/blooms-taxonomy-pyramid-problem.

140 **skipping over basic, concrete aspects:** Jere Brophy, "Teacher Influences on Student Achievement," *American Psychologist* 41, no. 10 (October 1986): 1071–72.

141 **most teachers say:** "Learning Less," 8. Elementary teachers were the most likely to say that formal tracking exists—not surprisingly, since leveled reading is a form of tracking used in virtually every elementary classroom in the country.

142 **enrollment in AP and other college-level classes:** Emily Tate, "AP Participation Is Up," *Inside Higher Ed*, February 22, 2017, https://www.insidehighered.com/news/2017/02/22/ap-program-results-show-more-students-taking-classes-and-succeeding.

142 **AP classes at high-poverty schools:** Alina Tugend, "Who Benefits from the Expansion of A.P. Classes?," *New York Times Magazine*, September 7, 2017, https://www.nytimes.com/2017/09/07/magazine/who-benefits-from-the-expansion-of-ap-classes.html; Natalie Wexler, "DCPS Schools Put Unmotivated Students in AP Classes. That Doesn't Work," *Greater Greater Washington* (blog), November 17, 2015, https://ggwash.org/view/39976/dcps-schools-put-unmotivated-students-in-ap-classes-that-doesnt-work.

142 **end up failing the exams:** Liz Bowie, "Maryland Schools Have Been Leader in Advanced Placement, but Results Are Mixed," *Baltimore Sun*, August 17, 2013, http://www.baltimoresun.com/news/maryland/bs-md-advanced-placement-classes-20130817-story.html.

142 **one article asked:** Timothy Pratt, "The Open Access Dilemma," *Education Next* 17, no. 4 (Fall 2017), http://educationnext.org/open-access-dilemma-community-college-better-server-underprepared-students.

143 **the Michaela Community School:** I am indebted to Doug Lemov for telling me about Michaela and urging me to visit.

144 **used across the curriculum at Michaela:** Katie Ashford, "How Reluctant Readers Learn to Love Reading," in *Battle Hymn of the Tiger Teachers*, ed. Katharine Birbalsingh (Melton, UK: John Catt Educational Ltd., 2016), 40–45.

145 **the inspectors reported:** Ofsted School Report, Michaela Community School, May 23–24, 2017, http://mcsbrent.co.uk/wp-content/uploads/2017/06/Michaela-Community-School-OFSTED-report-final.pdf.

January 2017

149 **One class had a heated debate:** "Knowledge Matters: Abril's Class, 2nd Grade, Westergard Elementary School in Reno, NV," TNTP (website), accessed August 2, 2018, https://tntp.org/room-to-run/knowledge-matters.

Chapter 8: Politics and the Quest for Content

151 **"These kids had been cheated":** Drew Lindsay, "Against the Establishment," *Washington Post*, November 11, 2001, https://www.washingtonpost.com/archive /lifestyle/magazine/2001/11/11/against-the-establishment/1ca7f81e-80af-483e -84f7-c425c165d1a0/?utm_term=.ff2bd75e7363.

152 **"practically a socialist":** Peg Tyre, "I've Been a Pariah for So Long," *Politico*, September/October 2014, https://www.politico.com/magazine/politico50/2014 /ive-been-a-pariah-for-so-long.html#.W2NhUrgnaMo.

152 **his eyes were opened:** Lindsay, "Against the Establishment."

152 **"Only by accumulating shared symbols":** E. D. Hirsch Jr., *Cultural Literacy: What Every American Needs to Know* (New York: Vintage, 1988), xvii.

153 **pirated editions of the List alone:** Hirsch, *Why Knowledge Matters*, 126.

153 **memorize disconnected facts:** R. E. Stratton, "Cultural Literacy, Standardized Testing, and Charlottesville Arrogance," *Radical Teacher* 35 (Summer 1988): 45–46.

154 **many publications excoriated Hirsch:** Robert Pattison, "On the Finn Syndrome and the Shakespearean Paradox," *The Nation*, May 30, 1987; Wayne J. Urban, "Book Reviews: *The Closing of the American Mind; Cultural Literacy;* and *What Do Our 17-Year-Olds Know?*," *The Journal of American History* 75, no. 3 (December, 1988): 869–874.

154 **opined two left-wing academics:** Stanley Aronowitz and Henry A. Giroux, "Schooling, Culture, and Literacy in the Age of Broken Dreams: A Review of Bloom and Hirsch," *Harvard Educational Review* 58, no. 2 (July 1988): 191.

155 **the top choice, at 19 percent:** Michael J. Petrilli, "Why Don't Districts Do the Easy Things to Improve Student Learning?," *Flypaper* (blog), Thomas B. Fordham Institute, June 20, 2018, https://edexcellence.net/articles/why-dont-districts -do-the-easy-things-to-improve-student-learning.

155 **more likely to switch schools frequently:** Sarah D. Sparks, "Student Mobility: How It Affects Learning," *Education Week*, August 11, 2016, https://www .edweek.org/ew/issues/student-mobility/index.html.

155 **A student may find herself:** Charles M. Payne, *So Much Reform, So Little Change: The Persistence of Failure in Urban Schools* (Cambridge, MA: Harvard Education Press, 2008), 87–88.

156 **swiftly yanked from classrooms:** Ronald W. Evans, *The Social Studies Wars: What Should We Teach the Children?* (New York: Teachers College Press, 2004), 77–79.

156 **"Man: A Course of Study":** David J. Hoff, "The Race to Space Rocketed NSF into Classroom," *Education Week*, May 19, 1999, http://www.edweek.org/ew /articles/1999/05/19/36nsf.h18.html; Geoff Alexander, *Academic Films for the Classroom: A History* (Jefferson, NC: McFarland, 2010), 88–90; Evans, *The Social Studies Wars*, 142–145.

156 **a "mythical national crisis":** Julie A. Miller, "Report Questioning 'Crisis' in Education Triggers an Uproar," *Education Week*, October 9, 1991, http://www .edweek.org/ew/articles/1991/10/09/06crisis.h11.html.

157 **Within a little over a year:** Richard D. Kahlenberg, *Tough Liberal: Albert Shanker and the Battles Over Schools, Unions, Race, and Democracy* (New York: Columbia University Press, 2007), 278.

157 **70 percent of Americans wanted:** Kahlenberg, *Tough Liberal*, 332.

157 **on a national test of history and literature:** Diane Ravitch and Chester E. Finn Jr., *What Do Our 17-Year-Olds Know?* (New York: Harper & Row, 1987), 132.

158 **"was a nonpartisan issue":** Diane Ravitch, *The Death and Life of the Great American School System: How Testing and Choice Are Undermining Education* (New York: Basic Books, 2010), 7.

158 **"walking into a buzz saw":** Gary B. Nash, interview by Bob Frost, HistoryAccess.com (website), 2001, accessed August 2, 2018, http://www.historyaccess.com/garyb.nashinterv.html.

158 **were jolted from their sleep:** Gary B. Nash, Charlotte Crabtree, and Ross E. Dunn, *History on Trial: Culture Wars and the Teaching of the Past* (New York: Vintage, 1997), 3.

160 **speculating that the real reason:** Nash, Crabtree, and Dunn, *History on Trial*, 221; Mary Jacoby, "Madame Cheney's Cultural Revolution," *Salon*, August 26, 2004, https://www.salon.com/2004/08/26/lynne_cheney.

160 **led her to mock the standards:** "Standards Push Wider View of World History," *USA Today*, November 11, 1994, quoted in Nash, Crabtree, and Dunn, *History on Trial*, 210.

160 **Nash also believed:** Gary B. Nash, interview by Jane Pauley, 1995, quoted in Robert Sullivan, "The Hamilton Cult," *Harper's Magazine*, October 2016, https://harpers.org/archive/2016/10/the-hamilton-cult/4.

161 **"If we do not teach our children these things":** Lynne V. Cheney, *Telling the Truth* (New York: Touchstone, 1995), 30.

161 **tore up a history book:** Nash, Crabtree, and Dunn, *History on Trial*, 5–6.

162 **"Students use experiences":** Quoted in E. D. Hirsch Jr., *The Making of Americans: Democracy and Our Schools* (New Haven, CT: Yale University Press, 2009), 66.

163 **"a variety of traditional and contemporary literature":** Chester E. Finn Jr., Michael J. Petrilli, and Gregg Vanourek, *The State of State Standards* (Washington, D.C.: Thomas B. Fordham Foundation, 1998), 7.

163 **are particularly dismal:** Barbara Davidson, "Historical Change," Thomas B. Fordham Institute (website), October 15, 2008, https://edexcellence.net/commentary/education-gadfly-weekly/2008/october-16/historical-change.html.

163 **has only *expanded* in recent years:** Peter Balonen-Rosen, "Massachusetts Education Again Ranks No. 1 Nationally," *Learning Lab*, WBUR (website), January 7, 2016, http://learninglab.legacy.wbur.org/2016/01/07/massachusetts-education-again-ranks-no-1-nationally; Alia Wong, "What Are Massachusetts Public Schools Doing Right?," *The Atlantic*, May 23, 2016, http://www.theatlantic.com/education/archive/2016/05/what-are-massachusetts-public-schools-doing-right/483935.

163 **the same high school–level disparities:** Michael Jonas, "Report Rips Boston Record with 'Off-Track' High School Students," *CommonWealth*, May 23, 2018, https://commonwealthmagazine.org/education/report-rips-boston-record-with-off-track-high-school-students.

163 **one group of researchers concluded:** Nonie K. Lesaux, et al., *Turning the Page: Refocusing Massachusetts for Reading Success* (Boston: Strategies for Children, Inc., 2010), 15–16, http://www.strategiesforchildren.org/docs_research/10_TurningThePageReport.pdf.

163 **test scores there are no better:** Daniel Hamlin and Paul E. Peterson, "Have States Maintained High Expectations for Student Performance?," *Education Next* 18, no. 4 (Fall 2018), http://educationnext.org/have-states-maintained-high -expectations-student-performance-analysis-2017-proficiency-standards.

164 **a detailed national curriculum:** *No Time to Lose: How to Build a World-Class Education System State by State* (Denver, CO: National Conference of State Legislatures, 2016), 11, http://www.ncsl.org/documents/educ/Edu_International _Final_V2.pdf.

164 **Florida passed a law:** Greg Allen, "New Florida Law Lets Residents Challenge School Textbooks," *NPR*, July 31, 2017, http://www.npr.org/2017/07/31/540041860 /new-florida-law-lets-residents-challenge-school-textbooks.

164 **a compromise was reached:** Jay Mathews, "In a divided nation, left and right educators found common ground," *Washington Post*, November 10, 2017, https:// www.washingtonpost.com/local/education/in-a-divided-nation-left-and-right -educators-found-common-ground/2017/11/10/a30088e2-c3f8-11e7-84bc-5e285 c7f4512_story.html.

165 **the materials for kindergarten through fourth grade:** Charlotte Crabtree and Gary B. Nash, *National Standards for History for Grades K-4: Expanding Children's World in Time and Space* (Los Angeles: National Center for History in the Schools, 1994).

166 **a few key historical documents:** The four documents mentioned by name in the Common Core are the Declaration of Independence, the Preamble to the Constitution, the Bill of Rights, and Lincoln's second inaugural address.

Chapter 9: The Common Core

171 **He was dismayed to find:** Dana Goldstein, "The Schoolmaster," *The Atlantic*, October 2012, https://www.theatlantic.com/magazine/archive/2012/10/the-school master/309091.

173 **its primary focus has been reading and math:** Daniel Koretz, *The Testing Charade: Pretending to Make Schools Better* (Chicago: University of Chicago Press, 2017), 176.

174 **"Americans must recognize":** Diane Ravitch, "Every State Left Behind," *New York Times*, November 7, 2005, http://www.nytimes.com/2005/11/07/opinion /every-state-left-behind.html.

174 **three groups:** One group was the National Governors Association, led by then governor of Arizona Janet Napolitano. Another was the Council of Chief State School Officers, which was basically a group of state school superintendents. The third was a bipartisan coalition of state officials and business leaders called Achieve, which had been formed specifically to push for more rigorous state standards.

174 **"fewer, clearer, and higher":** Joy Resmovits, "David Coleman, the Most Influential Education Figure You've Never Heard Of," *Forward*, August 25, 2013, http://for ward.com/culture/182587/david-coleman-the-most-influential-education-figur.

175 **"dysfunctional state standards already in place":** Quoted in Sean Cavanagh and Catherine Gewertz, "Draft Content Standards Elicit Mixed Reviews," *Education*

Week, July 23, 2009, http://www.edweek.org/ew/articles/2009/07/23/37standards. h28.html. The blog post itself is no longer on the Core Knowledge Foundation website.

175 **consisted of skills:** Kathleen Kennedy Manzo, "Achieve Finds Common Core of Standards in States," *Education Week,* July 31, 2008, http://www.edweek.org/ew /articles/2008/08/13/45achieve.h27.html.

176 **"like giving children various pieces of a puzzle":** *Common Core State Standards for English Language Arts & Literacy in History/Social Studies, Science, and Technical Subjects* (Common Core State Standards Initiative, 2010), 33.

177 **"By reading texts in history/social studies":** *Common Core State Standards,* 10.

177 **"The document has been criticized":** Valerie Strauss, "E. D. Hirsch Jr.: Common Core Standards Could Revolutionize Reading Instruction," *Washington Post,* April 6, 2010, http://voices.washingtonpost.com/answer-sheet/guest-bloggers /ed-hirsch-jr-common-core-stand.html.

177 **Within six months of their release:** "Common Core History and Timeline," HotChalk Education Network (website), April 3, 2014, http://www.hotchalkedu cationnetwork.com/common-core-history-timeline.

178 **teachers hadn't played enough of a role:** Jeffrey S. Solochek, "Teachers Were Not Involved in Developing the Common Core State Standards, Say Common Core Opponents," *Politifact Florida,* October 21, 2013, http://www.politifact.com/flor ida/statements/2013/oct/21/public-comments-common-core-hearing/teachers -were-not-involved-developing-common-core-. The official website of the Common Core says that teachers "played a critical role" in developing the standards and lists examples of their involvement. "Development Process," Common Core State Standards Initiative (website), accessed August 2, 2018, http://www.cores tandards.org/about-the-standards/development-process.

178 **a terrible mistake:** Ravitch, *Death and Life,* 1–4.

179 **and their difficulty:** Or in some cases, their absurdity. Eyder Peralta, "The Pineapple and the Hare: Can You Answer Two Bizarre State Exam Questions?," *NPR,* April 20, 2012, http://www.npr.org/sections/thetwo-way/2012/04/20/151044647 /the-pineapple-and-the-hare-can-you-answer-two-bizarre-state-exam-questions; Natalie Wexler, "DC Students May Find Themselves Stumped by Common Core Tests Next Year," *Greater Greater Washington* (blog), May 5, 2014, https://ggwash. org/view/34625/dc-students-may-find-themselves-stumped-by-common-core -tests-next-year.

179 **test anxiety and feelings of failure:** Rhema Thompson, "Too Much Test Stress? Parents, Experts Discuss High-Stakes Standardized Test Anxiety," WJCT (website), April 23, 2014, http://news.wjct.org/post/too-much-test-stress-parents- experts-discuss-high-stakes-standardized-test-anxiety; Marion Brady, "One Mother's Story: How Overemphasis on Standardized Tests Caused Her 9-Year-Old to Try to Hang Himself," AlterNet (website), August 1, 2016, https://www.alternet .org/education/perils-standardized-tests.

179 **Educators complained:** Valerie Strauss, "N.Y. School Principals Write Letter of Concern about Common Core Tests," *Washington Post,* November 21, 2013, https://www.washingtonpost.com/news/answer-sheet/wp/2013/11/21/n -y-school-principals-write-letter-of-concern-about-common-core-tests; Katrina

vanden Heuvel, "Stakes on Standardized Testing Are Too High," *Washington Post*, April 30, 2013, https://www.washingtonpost.com/opinions/katrina-vanden -heuvel-stakes-on-standardized-testing-are-too-high/2013/04/29/16e9e9d8-b0d5 -11e2-bbf2-a6f9e9d79e19_story.html.

179 **20 percent of students:** Andrew Ujifusa, "N.Y. Opt-Out Rate Hits 20 Percent on Common-Core Tests," *Education Week*, August 12, 2015, http://blogs.edweek .org/edweek/state_edwatch/2015/08/ny_opt-out_rate_hits_20_percent_on _common-core_tests.html.

179 **were in the process of revising them:** Sarah D. Sparks, "Common Core Revisions: What Are States Really Changing?," *Education Week*, January 18, 2017, http://blogs.edweek.org/edweek/curriculum/2017/01/common_core_revisions _what_are.html.

179 **just twenty states and the District of Columbia:** Catherine Gewertz, "Which States Are Using PARCC or Smarter Balanced?," *Education Week*, February 15, 2017 (updated June 15, 2018), http://www.edweek.org/ew/section/multimedia /states-using-parcc-or-smarter-balanced.html.

179 **"should *know* and be able to do":** *Common Core*, 40 (emphasis added).

179 **"the three shifts":** "Key Shifts in English Language Arts," Common Core State Standards Initiative (website), accessed August 2, 2018, http://www.corestan dards.org/other-resources/key-shifts-in-english-language-arts.

181 **"The author says Maria loved":** "Making Inferences, Too Many Tamales," TeacherVision (website), accessed August 2, 2018, https://www.teachervision .com/making-inferences-too-many-tamales.

183 **more than two-thirds of elementary teachers:** Opfer, Kaufman, and Thompson, *Implementation of K–12 State Standards*, 35.

183 **the most commonly used type:** Julia H. Kaufman, et al., *Use of Open Educational Resources in an Era of Common Standards: A Case Study on the Use of EngageNY* (Santa Monica, CA: RAND Corporation, 2017), 26. In answers to a question about "the frequency with which you draw upon the following instructional materials," leveled readers scored 98 percent in percentage use among elementary ELA teachers and 84 percent among secondary ELA teachers. Another report showed that after the Common Core, it was actually *more* common for teachers to choose texts at students' individual levels rather than on grade level, even though the standards encourage the opposite. David Griffith and Ann M. Duffett, *Reading and Writing Instruction in America's Schools* (Washington, D.C.: Thomas B. Fordham Institute, 2018), 21.

183 **silencing student voices:** Daniel E. Ferguson, "Martin Luther King Jr. and the Common Core," *rethinking schools* 28, no. 2 (Winter 2013–14), http://www .rethinkingschools.org/articles/martin-luther-king-jr-and-the-common-core.

184 **"makes school wildly boring":** Jeremiah Chaffee, "Teacher: One (Maddening) Day Working with the Common Core," *Washington Post*, March 23, 2012, https://www.washingtonpost.com/blogs/answer-sheet/post/teacher-one -maddening-day-working-with-the-common-core/2012/03/15/gIQA8J4WUS _blog.html.

184 **"Imagine learning about the Gettysburg Address":** Valerie Strauss, "Common Core's Odd Approach to Teaching the Gettysburg Address," *Washington Post*,

November 19, 2013, https://www.washingtonpost.com/news/answer-sheet/wp /2013/11/19/common-cores-odd-approach-to-teaching-gettysburg-address.

185 **"squarely into the hands of teachers":** Lucy Calkins, Mary Ehrenworth, and Christopher Lehman, *Pathways to the Common Core: Accelerating Achievement* (Portsmouth, NH: Heinemann, 2012), 17, 34.

186 **a CliffsNotes version of *Romeo and Juliet*:** E. D. Hirsch Jr., "'Cultural Literacy' Does Not Mean 'Canon,'" *Salmagundi* 72 (Fall 1986): 120.

Chapter 10: No More Jackpot Standards

194 **One researcher has estimated:** Robert J. Marzano and Mark W. Haystead, *Making Standards Useful in the Classroom* (Alexandria, VA: ASCD, 2008), 7.

196 **were otherwise largely unchanged:** Benjamin Herold, "Boasts about Textbooks Aligned to Common Core a 'Sham,' Say Researchers," *Education Week*, February 21, 2014, http://blogs.edweek.org/edweek/DigitalEducation/2014/02/claims_of _common_core-aligned_.html.

198 **to be "like shackles":** Emily Hanford, "Teachers Embrace the Common Core," *American RadioWorks*, August 31, 2014, http://www.americanradioworks.org /segments/teachers-embrace-the-common-core.

198 **an essay by the physicist Richard Feynman:** While the Feynman example is now classified as a sixth-grade lesson, at the time of the Core Task Project meeting in 2011, it was labeled a fourth- or fifth-grade lesson.

200 **"Ben Franklin started the nation":** Hanford, "Teachers Embrace the Common Core."

202 **"You gotta be freaking kidding me":** Emily Hanford, "Common Core Reading: 'The New Colossus,'" *NPR*, November 11, 2014, http://www.npr.org/sections /ed/2014/11/11/356357971/common-core-reading-the-new-colossus.

204 **a spot-on David Coleman impression:** Aaron Grossman, "Homegrown Common Core Implementation: A Good Bet for Reno," *Common Core Watch* (blog), Thomas B. Fordham Institute (website), March 10, 2014, https://edexcellence .net/commentary/education-gadfly-daily/common-core-watch/homegrown -common-core-implementation-a-good-bet.

210 **"There's no discussion there":** "Knowledge Matters: Abril's Class."

210 **all kids benefit from attending diverse schools:** Anya Kamenetz, "Try This One Trick to Improve Student Outcomes," *NPR*, March 16, 2017, https://www.npr .org/sections/ed/2017/03/16/515788673/try-this-one-trick-to-improve-student -outcomes.

210 **a disturbing trend:** Aris Folley and Brian Latimer, "Public Schools Becoming More Racially Segregated: Report," *NBC News*, May 18, 2016, http://www .nbcnews.com/news/latino/public-schools-becoming-more-racially-segregated -report-n576121.

212 **forgotten books and materials:** In 2001, before the development of the Core Knowledge Language Arts curriculum, the Core Knowledge Foundation teamed up with a major textbook publisher, Pearson, to create a series of textbooks based on the "sequence" of topics that the foundation had developed. Eventually those books went out of print and needed revising. In 2017, the foundation, having re-

trieved the copyright from the publisher, released a free, online, and updated version of the history and geography textbooks. Stephen Sawchuk, "'Open' Curricula Offerings Expand to Social Studies," *Education Week*, October 10, 2017, http://blogs.edweek.org/edweek/curriculum/2017/10/open_curricula_offerings _expand_to_social_studies.html.

April 2017

216 **a way to enliven science:** Joy Hakim, "You Don't Have to Be a Boring Teacher," *Education Week*, February 6, 2018, https://www.edweek.org/ew/articles/2018 /02/07/you-dont-have-to-be-a-boring.html.

Chapter 11: Don't Forget to Write

218 **were struggling to write coherently:** National Center for Education Statistics, "The Nation's Report Card: Writing 2011," 10, 11, 14, 28, 29, 31. Tests in 2011 showed that only 27 percent of eighth- and twelfth-graders scored at or above the proficient level in writing. Among low-income eighth-graders, only 12 percent scored proficient or above.

221 **Excellent readers can still struggle:** Steve Graham and Dolores Perin, *Writing Next: Effective Strategies to Improve Writing of Adolescents in Middle and High Schools—A Report to Carnegie Corporation of New York* (Washington, D.C.: Alliance for Excellent Education, 2007), 7–8.

222 **decreasing their cognitive power:** Ulrich Boser, *Learn Better: Mastering the Skills for Success in Life, Business, and School, or, How to Become an Expert in Just About Anything* (New York: Rodale, 2017), 43.

222 **the *protégé effect*:** Boser, *Learn Better*, 127.

223 **tantamount to teaching students how to think critically:** Judith A. Langer and Arthur N. Applebee, *How Writing Shapes Thinking: A Study of Teaching and Learning* (Urbana, IL: National Council of Teachers of English, 1987), 3.

223 **can easily obscure the learning objectives:** Zubrzycki, "As Project-Based Learning Gains in Popularity, Experts Offer Caution."

223 **Group work:** Tom Bennett, "Group Work for the Good," *American Educator* 39, no. 1 (Spring 2015): 32–37, https://www.aft.org/ae/spring2015/bennett.

223 **one internet meme:** Maureen Downey, "What Teens Resent: Classrooms Controlled by Students Rather Than Teachers," June 2, 2016, *Atlanta Journal-Constitution*, https://www.myajc.com/blog/get-schooled/what-teens-resent-classrooms-controlled-students-rather-than-teachers/29dRwFm2OirB5utfYlVieM.

224 **deliberate practice:** Anders Ericsson and Robert Pool, *Peak: Secrets from the New Science of Expertise* (New York: Houghton Mifflin Harcourt, 2016), 14; Nell Scharff Panero, "Progressive Mastery Through Deliberate Practice: A Promising Approach for Improving Writing," *Improving Schools* 19, no. 3 (2016): 228–245.

224 **what the research indicates will work:** Steve Graham, et al., "A Meta-Analysis of Writing Instruction for Students in the Elementary Grades," *Journal of Educational Psychology* 10, no. 4 (November 2012): 879–896.

225 **a small negative effect:** Graham and Perin, *Writing Next*, 21.

226 **"She needs to be supported":** Lucy McCormick Calkins, *The Art of Teaching Writing* (Portsmouth, NH: Heinemann, 1986), 306.

226 **have found it to be a disaster:** Robert Pondiscio, "How Self-Expression Damaged My Students," *The Atlantic*, September 25, 2012, https://www.theatlantic.com /national/archive/2012/09/how-self-expression-damaged-my-students/262656.

227 **"lost dolphins":** Lucy McCormick Calkins, *Lessons from a Child: On the Teaching and Learning of Writing* (Portsmouth, NH: Heinemann, 1983), 24–25. Whether the basal reader actually included any information about "lost dolphins" is unclear.

227 **"It becomes an independent study":** Sarah Webb, conversation with author, August 4, 2017.

229 **"Our kids *are* fluent":** Lisa Delpit, *Other People's Children: Cultural Conflict in the Classroom* (New York: The New Press, 1995), 16.

230 **"knowing a set of rules":** Delpit, *Other People's Children*, 31.

230 **"The only problem with those two forms of writing":** "David Coleman, 'Bringing the Common Core to Life,'" YouTube video, 0:37, posted by "Tim Furman," March 2, 2012, accessed August 3, 2018, https://www.youtube.com/watch?v=Pu6lin88YXU.

230 **"Johnson, I need a market analysis by Friday":** Tamar Lewin, "Backer of Common Core School Curriculum Is Chosen to Lead College Board," *New York Times*, May 16, 2012, http://www.nytimes.com/2012/05/16/education/david-coleman -to-lead-college-board.html.

231 **Examples of student work in an appendix:** *Common Core State Standards*, Appendix C, http://www.corestandards.org/assets/Appendix_C.pdf.

231 **defines goals in terms of the number of pages:** At a teacher training I attended, Calkins told teachers to expect "at least a notebook page full of writing" per fifty-minute teaching session in third grade, closer to a page and a half in fourth, and "easily two pages in one class period" in fifth. Students should be producing the same number of pages as homework, she added.

232 **the more demanding genres of informational and argumentative writing:** For a discussion of the cognitive demands posed by argumentative writing, see Judith C. Hochman and Natalie Wexler, *The Writing Revolution: A Guide to Advancing Thinking Through Writing in All Subjects and Grades* (San Francisco: Jossey-Bass, 2017), 181–183.

232 **cries for help:** Madeline Will, "As Teachers Tackle New Student-Writing Expectations, Support Is Lacking," *Education Week*, June 20, 2016, http://www .edweek.org/tm/articles/2016/06/20/as-teachers-tackle-new-student-writing -expectations-support.html.

233 **"that student had writing *down*":** Peg Tyre, "The Writing Revolution," *The Atlantic*, October 2012, https://www.theatlantic.com/magazine/archive/2012/10 /the-writing-revolution/309090.

233 **"We *have* to do this":** "Principal Deirdre DeAngelis," Vimeo video, 1:46, posted by "The Writing Revolution," June 7, 2017, accessed August 3, 2018, https:// vimeo.com/220587043.

234 **passed with a score of four or five:** Panero, "Progressive Mastery Through Deliberate Practice," 233.

234 **attracting educators from across the country:** Tyre, "The Writing Revolution."

234 **phenomenal success:** Jay Mathews, "Deep thinking and writing bloom at an un-

likely high school in the District," *Washington Post*, April 23, 2017, https://www
.washingtonpost.com/local/education/deep-thinking-and-writing-bloom-at
-an-unlikely-high-school-in-the-district/2017/04/23/e89b271c-2610-11e7-b503
-9d616bd5a305_story.html; Liz Braganza, Eastern Senior High School, conversation with author, June 22, 2017.

235 **the transformation they've seen:** Lauren Castillo and Adam Zimmerman,
"How a Writing Program Helped Daniel and Other Struggling Middle-Grade
DCPS Students," *Greater Greater Washington* (blog), July 21, 2014, https://
ggwash.org/view/35416/how-a-writing-program-helped-daniel-and-other
-struggling-middle-grade-dcps-students.

May 2017

238 **votes to revoke the school's charter:** Perry Stein, "City Charter Board Votes to
Shut Down DC's Only All-Girls Public School," *Washington Post*, January 12, 2018,
https://www.washingtonpost.com/local/education/city-charter-board-votes-to
-shut-down-dcs-only-all-girls-public-school/2018/01/12/a3a6176e-f7b8-11e7
-beb6-c8d48830c54d_story.html. On the 2017 PARCC tests, only 9 percent of Excel students met or exceeded expectations in math, compared with 27 percent city-
wide. Reading scores were only slightly better: 19 percent of Excel students scored
proficient or above, compared with 31 percent for the city as a whole. Ultimately,
the school was taken over by the D.C. Public School system.

241 **many other talented teachers:** Madeline Will, "Teachers Are Quitting Because
They're Dissatisfied. That's a Crisis, Scholars Say," *Education Week*, September
20, 2017, http://blogs.edweek.org/teachers/teaching_now/2017/09/teacher_turn
over_data.html; Frederick Hess, "Has Evaluation Reform Chased Away Compe-
tent Would-Be Teachers?," *Education Next*, February 16, 2018, http://education
next.org/evaluation-reform-chased-away-competent-teachers.

Chapter 12: Scaling Up

244 **"I had tears in my eyes":** Peter Meyer, "Assessing New York's Commissioner of
Education," *Education Next* 11, no. 3 (Summer 2011), http://educationnext.org
/assessing-new-yorks-commissioner-of-education.

244 **among the most commonly used materials:** Kaufman, et al., *Use of Open Education Resources*, xi.

247 **One survey that year:** Kaufman, et al., *Use of Open Education Resources*, 2–3.

247 **most states were sharing instructional materials:** Lindsey Tepe and Teresa
Mooney, *Navigating the New Curriculum Landscape: How States Are Using and
Sharing Open Educational Resources* (Washington, D.C.: New America, 2018),
https://www.newamerica.org/education-policy/reports/navigating-new
-curriculum-landscape/introduction.

248 **a large plurality of districts:** Marc Tucker, "The 'Creative Destruction' of the
American School Publishing Industry," *Education Week*, May 17, 2018, http://
blogs.edweek.org/edweek/top_performers/2018/05/the_creative_destruction

_of_the_american_school_publishing_industry.html; Michael J. Petrilli, "Why Don't Districts Do the Easy Things to Improve Student Learning?," *Flypaper* (blog), Thomas B. Fordham Institute, June 20, 2018, https://edexcellence.net /articles/why-dont-districts-do-the-easy-things-to-improve-student-learning.

248 **are regularly resorting to Google:** Liana Heitin Loewus, "The Search for Common-Core Curricula: Where Are Teachers Finding Materials?," *Education Week*, April 19, 2016, http://blogs.edweek.org/edweek/curriculum/2016/04/com mon_core_curricula_teacher_materials.html.

250 **can significantly increase reading comprehension:** David Liben, Student Achievement Partners, email to author, September 23, 2018; Sharon Walpole, et al., "The Promise of a Literacy Reform Effort in the Upper Elementary Grades," *The Elementary School Journal* 118, no. 2 (October 2017): 257–280, https://www .researchgate.net/publication/320723732_The_Promise_of_a_Literacy_Reform _Effort_in_the_Upper_Elementary_Grades.

250 **Louisiana's is freely available:** While Louisiana's curriculum is content-rich, it doesn't begin until third grade. The state does, however, recommend several knowledge-building curricula for lower grade levels.

250 **Michigan's social studies curriculum:** Michigan Open Book Project (website), accessed August 3, 2018, http://textbooks.wmisd.org/projectbacon.html.

250 **have started rating literacy curricula:** A leading site that rates curricula in this way is EdReports.org.

250 **Detroit recently adopted EL Education:** Amanda Rahn, "Eight Things to Know about Detroit's Big Math and Reading Curriculum Shift," *Chalkbeat*, April 25, 2018, https://www.chalkbeat.org/posts/detroit/2018/04/25/eight-things-to-know -about-detroits-big-math-and-reading-curriculum-shift.

251 **the district has done little or nothing:** Natalie Wexler, "The DCPS Scandal That (Almost) No One Is Talking About," *DC Eduphile* (blog), January 19, 2018, http://www.dceduphile.org/dc-public-schools/the-dcps-scandal-that-almost-no -one-is-talking-about.

251 **many erupted in anger at John King:** Carol Burris, "How New York's Education Commissioner Blew It Big Time—Principal," *Washington Post*, October 13, 2013, https://www.washingtonpost.com/news/answer-sheet/wp/2013/10/13/how-new -yorks-education-commissioner-blew-it-principal/?utm_term=.ffd75a765de7; Al Baker, "At Forums, New York State Education Commissioner Faces a Barrage of Complaints," *New York Times*, November 17, 2013, http://www.nytimes .com/2013/11/18/nyregion/at-forums-state-education-commissioner-faces-a -barrage-of-complaints.html.

252 **called for his resignation:** Geoff Decker, Patrick Wall, and Sarah Darville, "After Turbulent Tenure, State Ed Commissioner John King Stepping Down for Federal Ed Job," *Chalkbeat*, December 10, 2014, https://www.chalkbeat.org/posts /ny/2014/12/10/state-education-commissioner-john-king-stepping-down.

252 **65 percent of downloads:** Kaufman, et al., *Use of Open Education Resources*, 14.

252 **"complicated and difficult to use":** *New York Common Core Task Force Final Report*, December 2015, 8, https://www.governor.ny.gov/sites/governor.ny.gov /files/atoms/files/NewYorkCommonCoreTaskForceFinalReport2015.pdf.

252 **at least 70 percent were using them:** Rebecca Kockler, Assistant Superintendent of Academic Content, Louisiana Department of Education, "High Quality Curricula and Student Success," Johns Hopkins Insitute for Education Policy panel discussion, September 14, 2016, http://edpolicy.education.jhu.edu/wordpress/?p=318.

253 **just under half hold those views:** Kaufman, et al., *Use of Open Education Resources*, 7–8.

253 **"It was one of the most powerful visits I've ever taken":** Robert Pondiscio, "Louisiana Threads the Needle on Ed Reform," *Education Next* 17, no. 4 (Fall 2017), http://educationnext.org/louisiana-threads-the-needle-ed-reform-launching-coherent-curriculum-local-control.

253 **look more like Louisiana's:** For an overview of Lousiana's efforts to transform its education system, see Julia H. Kaufman, et al., *Raising the Bar: Louisiana's Strategies for Improving Student Outcomes* (Santa Monica, CA: RAND, 2018), https://www.rand.org/pubs/research_reports/RR2303.html.

253 **suspended the practice of tying teacher evaluations to test scores:** Will Sentell, "Louisiana Teachers to Face Tougher Job Reviews in New School Year under Controversial Evaluations," *The Advocate* (Baton Rouge), August 5, 2017, http://www.theadvocate.com/baton_rouge/news/politics/article_b80af760-76d5-11e7-b99a-9b931f3ecda5.html.

253 **only four states had done so:** Kaitlin Pennington, "Will States Keep Student Growth in Teacher Evaluation Systems After ESSA?," *Ahead of the Heard* (blog), Bellwether Education Partners (website), March 30, 2018, https://aheadofthe-heard.org/will-states-keep-student-growth-in-teacher-evaluation-systems-after-essa.

253 **"to broaden their definition of educational excellence":** Emma Brown, "Not Just Reading and Math: Education Secretary to Call for Return to a 'Well-Rounded Education,'" *Washington Post*, April 14, 2016, https://www.washingtonpost.com/local/education/not-just-reading-and-math-education-secretary-to-call-for-return-to-a-well-rounded-education/2016/04/13/b6cb3498-0190-11e6-9203-7b8670959b88_story.html.

254 **has even discouraged states:** Andrew Ujifusa, "How One State Changed Its ESSA Plan in Response to the Trump Team," *Education Week*, July 10, 2017, http://blogs.edweek.org/edweek/campaign-k-12/2017/07/essa_plan_changes_response_to_trump_team.html.

254 **received federal approval:** Alyson Klein, "Betsy DeVos OKs Louisiana Pitch to Use Innovative Tests Under ESSA," *Education Week*. July 27, 2018, https://blogs.edweek.org/edweek/campaign-k-12/2018/07/betsy_devos_louisiana_test_innovative.html.

254 **"reading tests have contributed to the false impression":** John C. White, "States Don't Measure What Kids Actually Know. That Needs to Change," *The Hill*, April 3, 2018, http://thehill.com/opinion/education/381285-states-dont-measure-what-kids-actually-know-that-needs-to-change.

256 **some teachers complain:** Mark Simon, "Is DCPS Really Redesigning Teaching?" *Washington Post*, August 11, 2017, https://www.washingtonpost.com/opinions/is-dcps-really-redesigning-teaching/2017/08/11/880c43fc-7c70-11e7-9d08-b79f191668ed_story.html.

259 **"I could never go back to what we did before":** Barbara Davidson, "Innovation Road Trip: At This Rust Belt Grade School, a Curriculum Centered on Texts Is Defying the Effects of Generational Poverty," *The 74*, March 18, 2018, https://www.the74million.org/article/innovation-road-trip-at-this-rust-belt-grade-school-a-curriculum-centered-around-texts-is-defying-the-effects-of-generational-poverty.

Epilogue

260 **an American school:** The Michaela Community School in London certainly seems like it could be a model, but it exists outside the American education system.

260 **"on my gluteus maximus?":** Chris Daniels and Courtney Seiler, "Knowledge-Rich Texts Lay the Foundation for Early-Literacy Progress," Lift Education: Leading Innovation for Tennessee (website), January 18, 2017, https://lifteducationtn.com/knowledge-rich-texts-lay-foundation-early-literacy-progress.

260 **saying they feel more supported:** *Early Literacy Implementation Work Annual Report* (Nashville: Lift Education, 2017), 2, https://lifteducationtn.com/wp-content/uploads/2017/11/LIFT-Education-Annual-Report-2017_FINAL.pdf.

262 **One scientist has gone so far as to suggest:** Alan G. Kamhi, "Knowledge Deficits: The True Crisis in Education," *The ASHA Leader* 12, no. 7 (May 2007): 28–29, http://leader.pubs.asha.org/article.aspx?articleid=2278173.

262 **could announce in advance a list of topics:** David M. Steiner, "The New Common Core Assessments: How They Could Stop Patronizing Our Students," *Huffington Post*, February 21, 2014 (updated April 23, 2014), https://www.huffingtonpost.com/david-m-steiner/the-new-common-core-asses_b_4809973.html.

INDEX

The
KNOWLEDGE
GAP

The Hidden Cause of America's
Broken Education System—and
How to Fix It

by Natalie Wexler

Reading Guide

AVERY

PART ONE:
The Way We Teach Now:
All You Need Is Skills

Covering Chapter 1: The Water They've Been Swimming In, and
Chapter 2: A Problem Hiding in Plain Sight

1. Why did you find yourself drawn to this book? What did you think the term "knowledge gap" would refer to? As a parent, educator, administrator, and/or community member, what was your starting perspective on the state of education in the United States, and did it differ from the view presented in the book so far?

2. If you're a teacher or a parent, do you see connections between your own experience of the education system and Ms. Arredondo's, Ms. Bauer's, and/or Ms. Williams's classrooms? Have you seen the curriculum narrowing to reading and math, as described in the book? Have you believed that that focus was necessary to boost test scores, or have you felt that too much time has been spent on test prep and testing?

3. How did the passage of the No Child Left Behind legislation bring to light inequities in the education system? In what ways might it have unintentionally perpetuated or even exacerbated those inequities?

4. "An understanding of civics fundamentally depends on an understanding of history. It's hard to grasp how the system operates if you have no idea where it came from and no context in which to place it." [p. 10] Were you surprised by the kinds of things some students in high-poverty high schools—and even college—don't know about history and geography? Have you seen evidence that Americans lack this kind of knowledge? Do you see connections between the current state of politics and Americans' generally weak grasp of civics?

5. "For the most part, parent activism has been focused on getting rid of or reducing testing rather than on what the curriculum should look like if testing disappeared." [p. 18] Did you find this observation to ring true? When it comes to reforming the education system, where do

you think parent activism has been focused, and do you feel it's been effective?

6. "[Education] represents our best hope for breaking the cycle of multigenerational poverty. Really, it is our *only* hope." [p. 22] Do you agree? Are there other avenues that you feel are more promising in addressing multigenerational poverty?

7. "At the same time, teaching disconnected comprehension skills boosts neither comprehension nor reading scores. It's just empty calories. In effect, kids are clamoring for broccoli and spinach while adults insist on a steady diet of donuts." [p. 29] What does the author mean by this metaphor? Do you feel that it's apt?

8. The author quotes another commentator as saying that people need to have enough facts in their heads to have a "knowledge party." [p. 31] What do think the phrase means, and do you agree that it's important for people to have a critical mass of factual information stored in their long-term memories?

9. "The bottom line is that the test-score gap is, at its heart, a knowledge gap." [p. 31] Does this core observation make sense to you and align with what you've seen in the classroom? How might a lack of knowledge hold students back on standardized tests? How do teachers try to compensate for gaps in their students' background knowledge, and how effective do you think those efforts can be? What are the risks of either overestimating or underestimating what students are capable of understanding?

10. "Children of wealthier and more educated parents may not be gaining much knowledge of the world at school, but they typically acquire more of it *outside* school than their disadvantaged peers." [p. 31] While Ms. Arredondo and Ms. Bauer adopt similar approaches to teaching reading comprehension, do you think the long-term effects will be different because of their students' different experiences outside of school? How does this relate to "the Matthew effect"? [p. 35] How might a knowledge-building curriculum like the one used at Center City help to reverse that effect?

11. "What the vast majority of educators, reformers, commentators,

and government officials still haven't realized is that elementary school is where the real problem has been hiding, in plain sight." [p. 36] What does the author mean by this? If this is true, why do you think "the real problem" has been overlooked by so many observers?

12. For decades, education experts have debated whether it's reasonable to expect schools to compensate for societal inequality. [pp. 37–39] Why do you think the recent wave of education reformers rejected the argument that the home and neighborhood environments were more important than anything schools could accomplish? Why have some now apparently changed their minds? What light does cognitive science shed on this debate? What does the example of France imply about the power of education to reduce inequality, and do you find it convincing?

13. While Ms. Arredondo's students are mostly from low-income native-born families, the students in Ms. Williams's and then Ms. Masi's class are mostly from low-income immigrant families. Do you think that demographic difference makes it difficult to compare the two classrooms? Do you think it's important for children still learning English—like some in Ms. Williams's classroom—to learn words like *bacteria, soil,* and *crops*? Do you think it's important for any first-graders to learn words of that kind?

14. If you're a parent, which of the classrooms described in the book so far would you prefer for your own children? If you're a teacher, which would you prefer to teach in? As a member of the public, which would you prefer your tax dollars to support? Why?

Covering Chapter 3: Everything Was Surprising and Novel

15. What are the key differences between what cognitive scientists have discovered about the process of reading and the way most educators have been trained to view it? In what ways have the two groups come to "exactly the opposite conclusions" about what is involved? [p. 47] How do these different perspectives lead to different conclusions about the best way to teach reading?

16. The divergence between cognitive scientists and educators on reading instruction is just one aspect of a broader disagreement between the two groups. What theories have been offered to explain this divergence? [p. 50] Do you find them convincing?

17. According to Daniel Willingham, problems in comprehension generally arise because "authors inevitably leave out information." [p. 52] In your own writing, how aware are you of the assumptions you're making about a reader's background knowledge? Do your assumptions vary depending on the intended audience? When you read, how aware are you of the background knowledge you're using to make sense of the text? Does your comprehension vary depending on your familiarity with the topic?

18. What are the advantages and disadvantages of Willingham's stance as a neutral scientist when it comes to communicating with teachers? Do you think his strategy of taking his message directly to teachers and bypassing schools of education makes sense? Why or why not?

Covering Chapter 4: The Reading Wars, and
Chapter 5: Unbalanced Literacy

19. Why have proponents of whole language and its successor, balanced literacy, argued that drilling children in phonics isn't necessary—and isn't even part of teaching reading? Do you find the counterarguments made by scientists convincing? If you're an educator, did you learn about the evidence supporting phonics instruction during your training? If you're a parent, do you think your child was taught to read through systematic phonics instruction or some other approach? Do you think it's possible that such instruction can "kill a child's interest in reading"? [p. 67] How might that be avoided?

20. The author says that despite the overwhelming evidence in favor of teaching phonics, "whole-language proponents dismissed the re-

search on the ground that it was conducted by cloistered academics who knew little of the realities of the classroom." [p. 70] How important are the realities of the classroom in figuring out the best way to teach? Do you understand teachers' skepticism about scientific findings on education? How can teachers' own experience help them determine what works, and how might it mislead them about what is working?

21. Why do you think the whole-language movement spread so quickly among teachers in the 1980s, and why do you think many teachers have continued to embrace its tenets in the face of scientific evidence to the contrary?

22. How does the scientific evidence on metacognitive reading comprehension strategies differ from the way it has been interpreted by educators? When might those strategies boost a reader's comprehension and when might they be useless—or even detrimental?

23. "Scripts themselves aren't the problem. . . . The real question is whether the script foregrounds skills and strategies at the expense of knowledge." [p. 94] Do you agree? If you're a teacher, do you see advantages to having a scripted curriculum, or do you feel it unnecessarily constrains a teacher's autonomy?

Covering Chapter 6: Billions for Education Reform,
but Barely a Cent for Knowledge

24. Do you agree with critics like Diane Ravitch who believe that philanthropists and other noneducators have had an outsize and detrimental influence on education? Or do you think that given longstanding deficiencies in the system, especially with regard to low-income students, education needed an injection of new ideas from the business world and elsewhere? Has your perspective changed as a result of reading this book?

25. Both the Gates Foundation and Doug Lemov—along with many others in the education reform movement—initially concluded that

teacher quality was the key to improving outcomes for low-income students. To what extent were they right? How and why have each of their perspectives shifted?

26. How is the lack of content in the elementary curriculum connected to other issues that education reformers have focused on, like teacher quality and school choice? How might it relate to newer initiatives such as personalized learning, social-emotional learning, and project-based learning?

PART TWO:
How We Got Here:
The History Behind the Content-Free Curriculum

Covering Chapter 7: Émile Meets the Common Core, and
Chapter 8: Politics and the Quest for Content

27. "A lack of familiarity with history and the world beyond one's experience might not have been such a terrible handicap for a young eighteenth-century aristocrat like Émile. But for a teenager today, it can represent a serious obstacle to success." [pp. 140–41] How have ideas and theories from the past influenced current approaches to education? How do these ideas match up to what we currently expect education to provide for children from a range of socioeconomic backgrounds?

28. Over the years, various arguments have been put forward to justify the "expanding environments" curriculum used in the early elementary grades, culminating in the idea that topics like history and science are developmentally inappropriate for young children. [pp. 134–35] In your experience, is it true that children in this age group are primarily interested in topics related to their own lives? Do you think social studies should focus on those kinds of topics in the early grades? What are the consequences of that approach for children from different socioeconomic backgrounds?

29. Do you see areas of possible agreement between progressive or constructivist educators and those who advocate for knowledge-building curriculum? How do you think each group can best approach the other in seeking to bring about change?

30. How has the work of E. D. Hirsch Jr. both helped and possibly held back the effort to build knowledge beginning in the elementary grades? Given the evidence that specificity about curriculum is crucial for equity—and that it's also likely to set off political controversy—can you think of a different and possibly more successful approach than creating something like "the List"? [p. 153]

31. Is education a "nonpartisan issue"? [p. 158] Do the controversies over Hirsch's *Cultural Literacy* and the national history standards show that efforts to provide a content-rich education inevitably become entangled in politics? Discuss the perspectives of Gary Nash and Lynne Cheney on how history should be taught to American students.

32. "Hirsch's goal was to provide disadvantaged students with access to references understood by the elite—whatever they might be—and knit the country together through a shared culture that could and should change over time. Cheney, on the other hand, was making a value judgment: American history and culture were superior." [p. 161] Do you agree with the author that this difference is important? Why or why not?

33. Many education reformers have pinned their hopes on national or state standards. What does the experience of Massachusetts suggest about the limits of standards-based reform? Are standards necessary or helpful, or would it make sense to focus reform efforts on curriculum instead? How much difference does it make if the standards specify content?

PART THREE:
How We Can Change:
Creating and Delivering Content-Focused Curriculum

Covering Chapter 9: The Common Core: New Life for Knowledge,
or Another Nail in Its Coffin?, and Chapter 10: No More Jackpot Standards

34. "Perhaps the most widespread misconception about the Common Core is that it requires specific content." [p. 179] Did you share this misconception? If so, what was it based on? Before reading this book, did you have a generally positive or negative view of the Common Core? Has your opinion changed?

35. On balance, do you think the Common Core has advanced efforts to inject content into the elementary curriculum—for example, by helping to spark the development of EngageNY? Or do you think the standards' call for more nonfiction, combined with the existing skills-focused approach to comprehension, has had the effect of making a bad situation worse?

36. "While close reading has gotten far more attention, [David] Coleman insists he has devoted just as much time and effort to spreading the message about knowledge." [p. 185] Why have so many educators and members of the general public nevertheless failed to see the connection between the Common Core and the need to build knowledge? Is there anything the authors of the standards could have done to make the message clearer, given that they wanted to avoid specifying content for political reasons? Was there any way to overcome what the author calls the Common Core's original sin of equating literacy and math skills? [p. 186]

37. Why did the teachers involved in Reno's Core Task Project begin with close reading of complex text rather than building knowledge? How did teachers benefit from beginning in that way? Is it better or worse for teachers to begin by building students' knowledge through a coherent curriculum, as at Center City, and only then asking them to grapple with complex text relating to the topics they've learned about?

38. The author quotes teacher Linnea Wolters as saying, "For an adult, reading is the most efficient way to gain new knowledge. For a child who is gaining the skills of literacy, it is a completely inefficient way for them to gain knowledge and vocabulary." [p. 208] Do you agree? How does this observation relate to the standard approach of teaching reading through comprehension skills and strategies and leveled texts? How does it relate to David Coleman's belief that close reading is a way of building knowledge?

39. "Westergard's experience suggests that adopting content-rich curriculum could address a long-standing and seemingly intractable problem: educational segregation." [p. 210] How might it do that? Is the author's argument undercut by the fact that Cannan, a low-income school with a content-rich curriculum, has failed to attract affluent families? On the other hand, even if an elementary school is socioeconomically diverse, are the benefits of integration at least partially undercut by a system of leveled reading that amounts to tracking?

Covering Chapter 11: Don't Forget to Write,
Chapter 12: Scaling Up: Can It Be Done?, and Epilogue

40. Is written English really "a second language"? [p. 218] If all educators adopted that perspective, how might it change their approach to teaching writing? If you're a teacher, how much training did you receive in how to teach writing? If you're a parent, do you feel your children are getting or have gotten effective writing instruction?

41. "Hochman discovered that writing, reading comprehension, and analytical ability were all connected—and that writing was the key to unlocking the other two." [p. 219] Do you agree? How can writing boost comprehension and lead students to make connections between bits of information? Is the knowledge gap exacerbated by a lack of writing instruction?

42. Judith Hochman and Lucy Calkins began with similar perceptions about what was missing from writing instruction but ended up

with very different approaches. What are the main differences between their methods? Why do you think their paths diverged? To what extent was each of them influenced by the students she was working with?

43. Do you see parallels between the standard approach to reading comprehension and the writers' workshop approach to writing instruction? Does the assumption that skills can be taught independently of content make more sense in one context than the other?

44. Should children be encouraged to write at length about their own experiences and develop their "voice" without worrying much about the conventions of written language? Or do you agree with Hochman that most students will learn to write only if instruction is grounded in the content of the curriculum and they're explicitly taught how to construct sentences and plan and revise paragraphs and essays?

45. How did New York's efforts to inject content into the elementary curriculum and change instruction differ from Louisiana's? Which approach do you see as more promising for large-scale change and why?

46. Discuss the effects of the internet and technology on curriculum and instruction. On balance, has the availability of free online resources—including both coherent knowledge-building curricula and isolated teacher-created activities and lesson plans—helped or hindered the effort to move away from a focus on comprehension "skills"? What are the potential advantages and pitfalls?

47. "One huge question is what to do about our system of high-stakes testing. That well-intentioned regime is not only narrowing the curriculum to reading and math . . . it's also contributing to the departure of gifted, dedicated teachers—like Ms. Masi and Ms. Townsell—from classrooms that need them." [p. 261] What do you think should be done about testing? Do you share the concern of some reformers that if test scores aren't factored into teacher evaluation, we'll "return to the days when the lower achievement of disadvantaged students was invisible"? [p. 253] Or do you think the focus on scores has unintentionally harmed those very students and deprived them of good teachers? Is there a way to reliably evaluate schools and teachers without either rendering vulnerable students invisible or limiting their access to knowledge?

48. Have your views changed as a result of reading the book? Did anything surprise you? Were you left with a sense of optimism, or do the obstacles to reorienting our decentralized education system seem insurmountable? Do you agree with the author that it's best to proceed gradually, or do you feel it's important to move more quickly, given the stakes involved?